Smoking, Drinking, and Drug Use in Young Adulthood

The Impacts of New Freedoms and New Responsibilities

Jerald G. Bachman
Katherine N. Wadsworth
Patrick M. O'Malley
Lloyd D. Johnston
John E. Schulenberg

Institute for Social Research
University of Michigan

LEA LAWRENCE ERLBAUM ASSOCIATES, PUBLISHERS
1997   Mahwah, New Jersey

Lawrence Erlbaum Associates, Inc., Publishers
10 Industrial Avenue
Mahwah, New Jersey 07430

Cover Design by Moneka Hewlett

Library of Congress Cataloging-in-Publication Data

Smoking, drinking, and drug use in young adulthood : the
impacts of new freedoms and new responsibilities / by Jerald
G. Bachman . . . [et al.].
    p. cm.
    Includes bibliographical references and index.
    ISBN 0-8058-2547-9 (c. : alk. paper) — 0-8058-2732-
3 (p. : alk. paper)
    1. Youth—substance use—United States. 2. Young
adults—Tobacco use—United States. 3. Young
adults—Alcohol use—United States. 4. Young
adults—Drug use—United States. I. Bachman, Jerald G.
    HV4999.Y68S65 1997
    362.29'12'0835—dc21   96–45203
                                                    CIP

Books published by Lawrence Erlbaum Associates are printed
on acid-free paper, and their bindings are chosen for strength
and durability.

Printed in the United States of America
10 9 8 7 6 5 4 3 2 1

Research Monographs in Adolescence
Nancy L. Galambos/Nancy A. Busch-Rossnagel, Editors

Côté • Adolescent Storm and Stress: An Evaluation
of the Mead–Freeman Controversy

Cohen/Cohen • Life Values and Adolescent Mental Health

Seiffge-Krenke • Stress, Coping, and Relationships in Adolescence

East/Felice • Adolescent Pregnancy and Parenting: Findings
From a Racially Diverse Sample

Bachman/Wadsworth/O'Malley/Johnston/Schulenberg • Smoking,
Drinking, and Drug Use in Young Adulthood: The Impacts
of New Freedoms and New Responsibilities

Contents

Preface

This book focuses on transitions into young adulthood—a critically important portion of the life cycle. Here we examine key roles and experiences of young adulthood—involving a wide range of new freedoms and new responsibilities—and how they are related to changes in drug use.

Our findings are based on the nationwide Monitoring the Future project, and represent the majority of individuals who entered young adulthood in the United States during the past two decades (i.e., the high-school classes of 1976 through 1994). We have tracked large samples of these young people from high school onward, surveying them throughout their twenties and into their thirties; more than 33,000 of them have contributed data for the present volume. We have asked our respondents about their schooling, employment, living arrangements, marriages, pregnancies, parenthood, and even their divorces. Each of these important aspects of adulthood has been examined for possible links with the use of two licit drugs, tobacco and alcohol, and two illicit drugs, marijuana and cocaine.

No survey research project, no matter how large or ambitious, could encompass all or even most of the "drug problem" in the United States. Any single study is necessarily limited in terms of the topics included, the survey methodology used, and the samples obtained. We mention limitations of the present study where relevant, and discuss them in some detail in chapter 3 and in the Appendix. We have tried to strike a balance in this book between providing too much and too little detail, but we recognize that some readers may have different preferences concerning what to analyze, what to emphasize, or both. We note, however, that some of the topics introduced in this book will be the subjects of further analyses and new reports; analysis of the Monitoring the Future data is an ongoing process.

HOW THIS BOOK IS LINKED WITH OUR
EARLIER RESEARCH

Several of the authors (Bachman, Johnston, O'Malley) gained their first longitudinal research experience while conducting the Youth in Transition project, which followed a single panel of young men from about age 16 (in

1966) to about age 24 (in 1974). That study, like the present one, was concerned with the twin themes of change and stability during late adolescence and early adulthood. It is fair to say that in many respects the Monitoring the Future study grew directly out of our experiences in the Youth in Transition study. We learned several general lessons from this early panel study, including (a) the utility of school-based sampling and initial data collections as a means for securing fairly large representative samples of youth; (b) the advantages gained from panel analyses tracking respondents over a long enough period to observe change; (c) the advantages of having nationally representative data, particularly when some of our findings were used as indicators of the scope of national problems; and (d) the limitations of focusing on a single cohort during periods of substantial social change, because we sometimes could not distinguish between age-related maturational changes on the one hand, and societal shifts or secular trends on the other.

Several additional lessons were learned from the Youth in Transition findings on drug use, first reported by L. Johnston (1973), and later reported over a greater longitudinal span by Bachman, O'Malley, and J. Johnston (1978). That research demonstrated the opportunities for examining drug use based on self-report survey data from nationally representative samples of young people; it also indicated that drug use among young people was sufficiently widespread that it should be monitored on an ongoing basis. The Youth in Transition findings, and the implications we drew from them, led directly to the initiation of the Monitoring the Future project.

Throughout the two decades Monitoring the Future has been in existence, it has generated a wide range of findings, which have been published in journal articles, chapters, research monographs, and press releases. It was not our purpose to incorporate all or most of our earlier findings in this book; but this book does build on our earlier work, and we have noted that work where relevant.

GUIDELINES FOR USING THIS BOOK

We recognize that users of research monographs are often selective, sometimes wanting only the "big picture," sometimes wanting full technical details, and sometimes wanting only one particular part of the picture—in the present book perhaps one particular drug, or one aspect of post-high-school freedoms or responsibilities. We have tried to organize this book to be responsive to all of those needs.

For the reader wanting the briefest sort of "executive summary," chapter 1 provides an introduction and overview, including an outline of the other chapters and a preview of key findings. The final chapter provides a much more extensive summary and integration of findings, so readers who want a fairly complete overview might wish to go directly from chapter 1 to chapter 8. Readers who want more background may wish to include the discussion of relevant literature in chapter 2 and the discussion of sample characteristics and analysis strategy provided in chapter 3. In addition, of course, readers wishing full details on the use of cigarettes, alcohol, marijuana, and cocaine can find them in chapters 4 through 7, respectively.

Another dimension along which readers are likely to vary is their need for technical detail. A great deal of analysis was carried out in the months and years leading up to the completion of this monograph—far more than would be possible to include in this book, and far more than most readers would wish to confront. Our task was to develop ways of presenting our main findings in a clear and straightforward manner, while still including the more complex multivariate findings that are an essential part of our overall analysis strategy. Acknowledging the trade-off between clarity and complexity, we concluded that we could not do justice to both in a single reporting format; instead, we chose to present our findings at two distinct levels within the book—text and Appendix. For those few readers desiring even more detail, there is also a supplementary technical report available from the authors.

In the text (especially chapters 4–8) we rely primarily on graphs rather than tables of numbers, because we ourselves find them much easier to use and interpret and we assume the same is true for most of our readers. These graphs provide a wealth of valuable descriptive detail, although they do not capture overlapping relationships that can be revealed by multivariate analyses. Such multivariate analyses are a key ingredient of this monograph and underlie all of our conclusions, so we refer to such results frequently in the text. Some readers may be content with our summaries of such findings; however, others will wish to see for themselves, and the Appendix is intended to meet their needs.

The findings from our regression analyses are not inherently difficult; indeed, we have selected a format (described in the Appendix) designed to make the results more readily interpretable than is often the case. Nevertheless, large numbers of variables were included in our regression analyses, and that necessarily produces large and complex tables of regression coefficients. We therefore opted to place these tables, along with guidelines for their interpretation, in the Appendix. (The Appendix also includes details of sampling and data collection procedures that will be of greater interest to some readers than to others.) Thus for readers interested in the regression details, and willing to invest a few minutes to review the guidelines for interpreting our tabular format, the information is all in the Appendix. However, for those readers who would rather "take our word for it"—either some of the time or all of the time—the book is organized in such a way that they can readily do so.

ACKNOWLEDGMENTS

Throughout the life of the Monitoring the Future project, the primary sponsor has been the National Institute on Drug Abuse (NIDA). We are indebted to the various NIDA directors, division directors, and project officers who provided their support and assistance during the past 22 years. The data collections and analyses reported here were carried out under NIDA Research Grant No. R01 DA 01411.

Our project has benefited from the efforts of many individuals in the Survey Research Center at the University of Michigan's Institute for Social Research. These include members of the Sampling, Field, Telephone, and Computing facilities and Field Interviewers throughout the nation. In addition, of course, past and present members of the Monitoring the Future staff contributed greatly to the success of the project.

We wish to thank three colleagues specifically for their contributions to this book in particular. Willard Rodgers collaborated with us in earlier research, and helped in developing some of the analysis techniques and strategies used here. Dawn Bare has been involved in panel analyses of Monitoring the Future data for many years, and was instrumental in conducting the present analyses. Jeannette Lim provided superb analytic, graphics, and editorial support.

We appreciate the contributions of our editor, Judi Amsel, and our series editors, Nancy Busch-Rossnagel and Nancy Galambos—especially the latter, whose early encouragement, prompt reading, and constructive suggestions have helped the authors and improved the book.

We are grateful to thousands of school principals and teachers, and to tens of thousands of high-school students whom we followed into young adulthood, for their willingness to participate in this research venture. They contributed generously to making this book and other products from the study possible. We are much in their debt.

Finally, we add a special word of thanks to those follow-up respondents who took the extra time to provide written comments on their questionnaires, offering suggestions, encouragement, and sometimes also a bit of humor. One of our first follow-up respondents, 20 years ago, included the following note to us:

> I am glad the University of Michigan is monitoring the future. Please let me know the results.

Well, here they are.

1

Introduction and Overview

Since the 1960s, few issues have captured more intense and enduring interest among so many different segments of our society than drug use among young people. From a public health perspective, anyone's use of licit or illicit drugs can be risky. However, when such use occurs among the nation's youth—the nation's future—concerns about potential health risks are joined with concerns about wasted potential, about significantly and negatively altered lives, about lifelong negative consequences, and even about lifelong drug abuse.

The ravages of youthful drug use have received much attention, as they should. It is clear that for some young people, illicit drug use does significantly and negatively alter their lives and those of their families and communities. Two facts remain, however. First, most young people who use illicit drugs do not use them to excess. Second, most who use illicit drugs eventually "mature out" of their drug use as they move into adulthood. Stating these facts is not an endorsement of a laissez-faire policy toward adolescent drug use—rather, it helps place adolescent drug use in a developmental context and underscores the need for continued scientific study about the natural history of drug use from adolescence through adulthood.

CHANGE AND STABILITY IN DRUG USE

Many aspects of personality and patterns of behavior are well developed by late adolescence. By the time young people graduate from high school and enter into young adult roles, many abilities and interests have been formed, along with patterns of interpersonal skills and relationships. These profoundly affect individuals throughout their adulthood.

Something else happens to most young people in the United States before they complete high school: they develop patterns of drug-using behavior. Among the nationally representative samples of high-school seniors we studied during the past two decades, (a) two-thirds or more had tried

1

cigarettes, and one in five was a daily smoker; (b) four-fifths or more had tried alcohol, and more than half had been drunk at least once during the past year; (c) half or more had tried at least one illicit drug, including one-quarter to one-half (depending on the year) who had used marijuana during the past year.

What happened to their drug-using behaviors after graduation? Did the patterns of drug use continue to be much the same as they were during the end of high school? Did the new freedoms that many experienced lead to increased substance use? Did their new responsibilities in marriage and parenthood lead to decreases in use? Each of these three questions implies a different pattern of change or stability; nevertheless, the answer to each is clearly "Yes."

First and foremost, drug use remains fairly stable in individuals over time. If we want to know whether an individual will use a given drug during young adulthood, by far the best predictor is the individual's use of that drug during the high-school years. In particular, cigarette use shows a great deal of consistency across time; most young adult users were regular daily users before they left high school. Although use of alcohol and use of illicit drugs does not reach the point of chemical dependency among the large majority of high-school users, these behaviors also show considerable constancy. This stability is hardly surprising; throughout high school young people develop and express appetites, attitudes about taking risks, patterns of recreational behavior, and friendships, all of which can influence drug use, and many of which do not change substantially on departure from high school.

However, many things do change after high school. New freedoms from the supervision of parents and teachers, as well as new "adult" legal status, provide greater opportunities for drug use than existed during high school. Conversely, new role responsibilities, such as becoming engaged, marrying, becoming pregnant, and having children, all have the potential to inhibit drug use.

In this book we focus less on stability and more on the changes in drug use that occur during young adulthood. Specifically, we examine drug use during the late teens, the twenties, and the early thirties, contrasting levels of use at those ages with the levels of use observed at the end of high school. Most importantly, we focus on just how those changes in drug use seem to be linked to changes in role experiences and responsibilities.

Here we concentrate on four widely used substances—two legally available (to adults), and two illegal. Cigarettes are used regularly by fewer than one-third of young adults, but the large majority of those are daily users who have formed a habit that is very difficult to break, a habit that is widely recognized to carry deadly risks. Alcohol is used by nearly all young adults;

although some use it only in moderation, substantial proportions at least occasionally use it to excess, which can involve serious risks to self and others. Marijuana is the most widely used of the illicit drugs; it can have serious consequences itself, and can also provide a "gateway" to the use of other illicit drugs. Cocaine is used by fewer young adults than is marijuana, but can be much more dangerous in its potential for generating acute adverse health effects, and for developing long-term dependency. We see here that there are some important parallels across several of these drugs in terms of their links with post-high-school roles and responsibilities, but we also see some interesting distinctions among the drugs.

DATA QUANTITY, QUALITY, AND BREADTH OF GENERALIZATION

Our findings are drawn from the Monitoring the Future project. For two decades we have been studying the drug use habits of young adults, surveying them first as high-school seniors and then resurveying them throughout their twenties and into their thirties. We have followed them every 2 years as they left their parents' homes and entered new living arrangements and new roles as college students, employees, spouses, and parents. More than 33,000 young adults surveyed in the high-school classes of 1976–1994, who also completed follow-up questionnaires from 1977 to 1995, contributed to the data presented in this book. Those from the earliest classes participated in seven follow-ups extending to 14 years beyond high school; those from later classes provided proportionately fewer follow-ups. The total number of questionnaires included in these analyses exceeds 139,000, representing more than 100,000 respondent hours.

Lest these samples seem extravagantly large, we should note that some of the drug-using behaviors routinely reported by the Monitoring the Future project are relatively rare and thus require large samples for reliable detection and meaningful examination (Johnston, O'Malley, & Bachman, 1997). Moreover, some of the post-high-school experiences that are the focus of the present analysis also involve fairly small proportions of the total population at any single point in time (e.g., military service, pregnancy, living in a dormitory). Thus a great advantage of the present sample, or compilation of samples, is our ability to focus not just on the most prevalent post-high-school experiences, but also on other experiences that may have substantial impacts on drug use.

In addition to being quite large and extending across two decades, our samples are nationally representative. Because of this broad coverage in

terms of both time and geography, the findings are more useful descrip-
tively and more broadly generalizable than is typically the case for panel
studies of drug use. Having said that, however, we must also caution that
our findings do not represent the entire age cohort. Our initial sampling
did not include the approximately 15% of young people who do not
graduate from high school, and it also underrepresents frequent absen-
tees (Johnston et al., 1997). Further, although the large majority of those
asked to participate in follow-ups did so, the loss of some respondents
further restricts our ability to generalize. Finally, for reasons noted later,
our present analyses omit the small proportion of respondents who, as
high-school seniors, were already married, living away from parents or
guardians, had children, or any combination thereof. (The samples and
survey methods are described in greater detail in the Appendix, and still
more information on sample characteristics is provided in a supplementary publication available from the authors; Bachman, O'Malley, et al.,
1996.)

   The quality of survey data depends, of course, on the ability and willingness of those surveyed to provide accurate responses. Accuracy is easy when
respondents are asked about their marital or parental status, but it can be
more difficult when they are asked about their use of various drugs. In the
case of cigarettes, young adults tend to use them on a regular daily basis, if
they use them at all, and thus can report such use with a good deal of
accuracy. However, alcohol use for many is less routine, and therefore more
subject to errors in recall. Furthermore, most who use marijuana or cocaine
do so infrequently, and the fact that such use is illegal might inhibit
reporting. Such problems in self-reports of drug use have been widely
discussed and studied, using many different data sets including our own. We
say more about these matters in the Appendix, and cite relevant studies.
For present purposes, it is important to stress our confidence that reporting
problems have not invalidated our findings. That said, we should add that,
to the extent that biases remain, we suspect they lie largely in the direction
of underreporting.

   In summary, these survey findings, like virtually all others, have inevitable
limitations in quality and generalizability. Nevertheless, we think the
strengths of this study design are substantial, and we believe that the findings
reported here provide important information about the early adult experiences of a large majority of high-school graduates during the past two
decades. Moreover, the consistency of our key findings across a number of
different analyses at different stages in time leaves us confident that many
of the basic relationships found for these samples are broadly generalizable
to the population of young adults in America.

STUDYING CAUSAL RELATIONSHIPS
IN NATURAL SETTINGS

The Monitoring the Future project, like many other social psychological studies, examines individuals (survey respondents) in "natural settings." This stands in sharp contrast to the experimental method, in which individuals (subjects) are placed in treatment groups by a process of random assignment intended to cancel out "extraneous" individual differences. A fundamental problem with survey studies of individuals in natural settings is that assignment to various social contexts is anything but random. The freedoms and responsibilities experienced in early adult roles (e.g., college, military service, civilian employment; living with parents, a spouse, others) differ from one individual to another largely as a result of the individuals' own backgrounds, prior behaviors, and preferences, as well as the (nonrandom) choices of many other people. Thus, even when the present analyses show that important differences in drug use are *correlated with* certain post-high-school experiences, we still have to make informed judgments about whether the changes in drug use were *caused by* those particular post-high-school experiences.

It is axiomatic that studies in natural settings can provide no certain demonstration of causation—the possibility always remains that other (perhaps unexamined) factors are more fundamental causes, and that our conclusions about causation are therefore spurious. Panel data, obtained by following the same survey respondents across a number of years, can be very helpful in ruling out some such alternative explanations and in demonstrating temporal sequences of events consistent with certain interpretations; however, panel data alone are not sufficient to establish causation with certainty.

It is also axiomatic that studies in natural settings can lead to erroneous conclusions if the analyses fail to include all important explanatory variables (i.e., if the implicit or explicit causal model is misspecified). One cannot argue with that assertion, at least in principle. In practice, however, the problem is how to figure out everything that might be relevant, measure it accurately, and then fit it all into an analysis model without overtaxing the capabilities of either the computer programs or the human interpreters. In the present monograph, our analysis strategy for dealing with this practical problem has three important features. First, we have focused on one broad area—post-high-school roles and experiences—in considerable detail, while attempting to provide adequate statistical controls for other relevant factors. Second, as outlined in chapter 3, we have streamlined our analyses in a number of important respects so as to make them more manageable and approachable. Third, we have chosen analysis methods that are in some respects intentionally neutral or agnostic about causal order, even though we ourselves are not so neutral and argue that some causal interpretations are more plausible than others.

CHAPTER OUTLINE AND PREVIEW OF KEY FINDINGS

Chapter 2 provides a review of relevant literature, summarizing previous findings and relevant theory that have inspired and informed the present work. We then turn to analysis of the Monitoring the Future panel data.

Chapter 3 describes our samples in terms of roles and experiences at each of seven follow-up points, with modal ages ranging from 19 to 32. We document also how some experiences in young adulthood seem to go hand in hand with others. In the first years after high school, for example, those who enter college are more likely than average to leave their parents' homes, but less likely than average to marry or have children.

Chapters 4 through 7 examine how usage patterns for four substances—cigarettes, alcohol, marijuana, and cocaine—change during young adulthood. We also examine how individuals' post-high-school drug use differs from their use during senior year, and we link those changes to their roles and experiences during young adulthood.

The final chapter summarizes and integrates our findings, and shows how they support our conclusions. Before leaving this introductory chapter, however, it may be helpful to preview several of the general conclusions that are illustrated again and again in the following chapters.

First, it bears repeating that use of any drug during the post-high-school years is predicted to a very considerable extent by the use of that drug during high school. This stability in drug using behaviors during late adolescence and early adulthood very likely reflects (a) relatively stable individual differences in personality (e.g., sensation seeking, willingness to take risks, nonconformity), as well as (b) relatively stable differences in social environments (e.g., friendships, behaviors and attitudes of friends, values and preferences of parents).

Second, we find that changes in drug use do occur between high school and young adulthood, and some of these changes are clearly linked to the roles and environments of young adulthood. Moreover, a central finding is that the *current* experiences are what seem to make the difference. Thus, for example, being married is linked with lower drug use, and it seems to make relatively little difference whether one has been married for nearly a decade or for only a year or two.

Third, the different post-high-school roles and experiences are complexly interrelated. Although our multivariate analyses provide some help in disentangling patterns of relationships, problems of overlapping effects remain and require some causal interpretations. Thus, for example, we observe greater than average increases in alcohol use among college students, and we attribute that to the marital status and living arrangements usually associated with college attendance.

Fourth, the impacts of most roles and environments in young adulthood seem widely generalizable. That is, the impacts are much the same whether measured in the first follow-up or two (i.e., late teens or early twenties), or in the sixth or seventh (late twenties or early thirties). Moreover, most of the impacts are very similar for men and women. One notable exception is that pregnancy has substantial impacts on the drug use of women, whereas among men the impacts of having a pregnant spouse are more limited.

Fifth, on average, the usage rates for most substances decline during the mid-twenties, and that seems largely attributable to the fact that increasing proportions of individuals during that period become married, and many take on the additional responsibilities of pregnancy and parenthood. In other words, these age-related changes are not simply "maturation" in general; rather, they reflect the impacts of specific new roles and living arrangements undertaken by increasing proportions of young adults as they move through their twenties.

Finally, we note that although there are many similarities across the four drugs in their relationships with post-high-school experiences, there also are clear differences. For example, patterns of cigarette use are more stable than those involving the other drugs, largely due to the high proportion of cigarette users who are nicotine dependent; another result of this high level of dependency is that cigarette consumption is less likely to be influenced by post-high-school experiences, compared with use of other drugs.

2

Reviewing the Influence of Social Roles on Drug Use During the Transition to Young Adulthood

This investigation is focused on how the new freedoms and new responsibilities in young adulthood affect drug use. In this chapter we review the empirical and theoretical literature concerning change during the transition to young adulthood. This chapter focuses on the influences of adult social roles on alcohol use, drug use, and other problem behaviors. We have attempted to highlight the central studies that inform this field of inquiry, and to incorporate disparate theoretical perspectives on these issues.

THE TRANSITION TO YOUNG ADULTHOOD

The critical developmental transition from adolescence to young adulthood is characterized by an increase in new and demanding social opportunities and expectations. Plans regarding education and occupation, financial independence, living arrangements, or intimate relationships may be made prior to leaving high school, but the actual experience of the transition may be very different from initial aspirations. Success or failure in each of these areas has important consequences throughout one's life course (Clausen, 1991; Jessor, Donovan, & Costa, 1991).

Along with roles that may continue across this period, as son or daughter, sibling, friend, and perhaps student, most adults must also choose and integrate the roles of full-time worker, spouse, or parent. In taking on these roles, new relationships and environments must be negotiated. Young adults face environments as varied as college campuses, dormitories, military bases, or the civilian workplace. The roles of spouse and parent bring the challenge of negotiating entirely new kinds of intimate relationships.

Such extensive change can be stressful and destabilizing. This may be especially true as the numbers of simultaneous role changes add up, reducing

8

the remaining *arenas of comfort*—major areas of life in which one can function easily and comfortably (Brooks-Gunn, 1987). Transitions in other periods of the life course—the transition from junior high to high school, for example—have been shown to have some severe disruptive influences on adjustment (Simmons, Burgeson, Carleton-Ford, & Blyth, 1987). The transition out of high school is potentially more disruptive than earlier school transitions because this period can simultaneously bring into question nearly every arena of meaningful human interaction. The tasks and experiences encountered as one moves from childhood to adolescence have a fair degree of continuity—family and school remain the primary contexts, and the environment is highly structured. The move from adolescence to young adulthood can be relatively discontinuous, however, with fewer familiar environments and tasks, and relatively little institutional structure (Hurrelmann, 1990; William T. Grant Foundation Commission on Work, Family, and Citizenship, 1988). Considering these demands, perhaps it is not surprising that young adulthood is also a period of major risk for the onset and increase in anxiety disorders, depression (Burke, Burke, Regier, & Rae, 1990), and drug and alcohol abuse (Chen & Kandel, 1995).

These stresses notwithstanding, this transition can also be seen as a period of exceptional opportunity. In support of such a view of the transition to young adulthood, Aseltine and Gore (1993) found that the transition out of high school is often a very positive one. Depression and delinquent behavior were found to be dramatically lower in the year following high-school graduation. These researchers also found that measures of mental health and problem behavior were less predictive of outcomes between senior year and postgraduation than between junior and senior years in high school. This suggests that the "shake up" created by high-school graduation provides an opportunity to escape unsatisfying situations or to break with past problems.

Relatively little is known about the transition to young adulthood compared to other portions of the life span (Jessor et al., 1991). A great deal has been learned in recent years about the prevalence of drug use during this period (e.g., Chen & Kandel, 1995; Johnston et al., 1997), but longitudinal studies of the causes of drug use that span the young adult transition period are rarer. One reason for this is that following adolescents into young adulthood is difficult from a practical standpoint, due in large part to the great geographic dispersal in the first few years following high-school graduation. Studies that concentrate exclusively on adolescence or that begin during college are more common. Such studies are certainly important, but they do not permit a direct examination of transitional experiences, and studies of young adults that focus exclusively on the college population also neglect the half of the young adult population who do not enter college (cf. William T. Grant Foundation Commission on Work, Family, and Citizenship, 1988). Additional difficulties are created when trying to study the influences of social roles during this period. Unlike the transition to adolescence, there is relatively little uniformity in the transition to young adulthood, as the social role options and activities available are extensive, and these roles and activities are undertaken at varying ages and rates. This creates great difficulty in acquiring a large enough sample to represent adequately the variety of life experiences that exist during this period of change (Schulenberg, O'Malley, Bachman, & Johnston, 1992).

There are longitudinal studies that have examined drug use in adolescence and into young adulthood (Brook, Whiteman, Cohen, & Shapiro, 1995; Brunswick, Messeri, & Titus, 1992; Chassin, Presson, Sherman, & Edwards, 1992; Chen & Kandel, 1995; Donovan, Jessor, & Jessor, 1983; Jessor et al., 1991; Johnson & Kaplan, 1991; Newcomb & Bentler, 1987, 1988; Pandina, Labouvie, & White, 1984), but only a few have been national in scope (e.g., Elliot, Huizinga, & Menard, 1989; O'Donnell, Voss, Clayton, Slatin, & Room, 1976; Robins, 1974), and fewer have directly examined the impact of adult roles. The research of Elliot and colleagues draws on a national probability sample (Elliot et al., 1989; Esbensen & Elliot, 1994), but the relatively small sample size limits the ability to capture a full representation of post-high-school experiences and environments. Each of these studies offered insights into processes of change in drug use, but most studies are hampered by limited population samples, age spans, and cohort representation, and thus cannot provide findings that generalize beyond a limited regional, ethnic, class, historical, or developmental period (Johnston, O'Malley, Bachman, & Schulenberg, 1992). The Monitoring the Future study has the advantage of national samples across a broad age span (18 to 32 years) and cohort representation (the high-school classes of 1976–1994 are included in the present monograph). Thus it can add to the limited but growing knowledge base regarding young adult development by addressing many of the frequently asked but still unanswered questions about the impacts of post-high-school social environments on drug use.

RELATING THE YOUNG ADULT TRANSITION TO CHANGES IN DRUG USE

Late adolescence and early adulthood are the most active periods of change in drug use in terms of both initiation and cessation. In a longitudinal study spanning the period from midadolescence to the early thirties, Chen and

Kandel (1995) found that the major risk periods for initiation of use reach their peak at age 16 for cigarettes, age 18 for alcohol and marijuana use, and between the ages of 21 and 24 for cocaine use; moreover, there was virtually no initiation of alcohol, cigarette, or illicit drug use after age 29. Thus, understanding the mechanisms that govern change in drug-use behavior during the late teens and early twenties is critical to preventing or intervening in the development of serious drug use problems (Baer, 1993; Zucker, 1979, 1987).

It is clear that drug use and alcohol use decline toward the end of young adulthood, but there are a variety of views about how or why this decline occurs. The fact that the decline occurs at the time when increasing proportions of young adults typically assume adult roles such as marriage, parenthood, and full-time employment suggests a causal relationship of some kind between the successful assumption of these roles and decline in drug use (e.g., Bachman, O'Malley, & Johnston, 1981, 1984; Donovan et al., 1983; Jessor et al., 1991; Kandel, 1984; O'Malley, Bachman, & Johnston, 1984, 1988a; Yamaguchi & Kandel, 1985a, 1985b, 1993; Zucker, 1979, 1987).

Theories developed to explain the initiation of drug and alcohol use in adolescence provide a number of plausible explanations for why the acquisition of adult roles would contribute to a decline of drug use. These explanations vary in the extent to which they focus on the influence of social structures, interpersonal social influences, or individual characteristics (Petraitis, Flay, & Miller, 1995). This range can be seen as representing a spectrum of distal (e.g., social structure) and proximal (e.g., attitudes toward drug use) causes of substance use, each with different implications for the effects of social roles. For example, social control theories (e.g., Hirschi, 1969; Shoemaker, 1990) addressing environmental or structural influences such as neighborhoods, family structure, cultural values, or the availability of drugs suggest that taking on conventional adult roles should be associated with strong commitments to conventional social institutions and behavior. The assumption of adult roles is hypothesized to lead to a greater investment in and commitment to conventional social institutions, and conformity to conventional expectations concerning drug use. Those who have particularly weak bonds to conventional society would presumably be less likely to undertake conventional adult roles. In contrast, social learning or social development theories (e.g., Akers, 1977; Bandura, 1982; Hawkins & Weis, 1985) are primarily concerned with the influence of the more proximal social environment of family and peer-group role models. These theories suggest that the most important influence of the structural changes associated with the assumption of adult roles is that (a) these structural changes lead to changes in proximal social influences, role models, learning opportunities, and reward structures; and (b) these new social influences more actively discourage drug use.

Other theorists have examined the association of a number of personality, temperamental, and affective dimensions with drug use, including sensation seeking, impulsivity, self-esteem, and depression. The implications of such theories of personal characteristics are broader and harder to define. New social roles have the potential to alter self-concept and affective states, but it is unclear whether these roles have strong or lasting impacts on personality or temperament factors associated with drug use. However, there is some evidence that social roles can influence some personal characteristics most proximal to drug use, including drug-use-specific cognitions, motivations, and values. Cognitive–affective theorists (e.g., Ajzen, 1985) view these factors as the final links in the causal chain through which more distal factors, discussed earlier, influence drug use.

The work of Jessor et al. (1991) integrates many aspects of the theories mentioned earlier, emphasizing the continuous interaction of individual and contextual risk factors for drug use over time. In their perspective, so-cial–structural factors and individual characteristics such as prior history of problem behavior may differentially predispose individuals toward certain social roles in adulthood, and the entrance into new roles will in turn influence individual characteristics and behavior. The acquisition of conventional adulthood social roles is thus hypothesized to have significant socializing or *conventionalizing* influences, altering the course of development and perhaps negating the adverse influences of problem behavior in adolescence. Jessor et al. (1991) found that many young adults became both more conventional and less prone to problem behavior as they made the transition. However, the influence of social role status on these outcomes was not directly tested.

As we suggested earlier, each of these perspectives has potential implications for understanding how changes in adult role status influence drug use, and need not necessarily be seen as competing theories of the causes of drug use. Rather, these concepts may outline a web of causation (Jessor, 1992), or links in a chain of causation (Petraitis et al., 1995). Each level of influence has the potential to reverberate throughout the web. For example, the structure of one's neighborhood can influence peer networks, which in turn may influence the structure of social learning environments and lead to change in drug-specific values and cognition. More specific to our current focus, the transition to adult roles clearly alters the physical and social settings in which individuals operate, which then alter the primary social interaction settings and opportunities for learning or modeling. These, in turn, may lead to a cognitive reassessment of drug use and a revaluation of the costs and benefits of drug use. In short, role changes are likely to be a pervasive influence on each of the major processes that drug use researchers have identified as important in the cause of drug use. Although it may not be possible to disentangle all of these effects in the current research, it is possible to examine evidence for change at each of these levels. The existence of anticipatory effects for major role changes—that is, changes in drug use occurring prior to the actual assumption of a new role—may also indicate the existence of internal or psychological processes in changing patterns of drug use.

Much of the research examining the interrelationships of drug use and adult roles has concentrated on role selection effects—that is, those factors such as drug use in adolescence that predispose individuals toward assuming or avoiding certain adult roles. Less work has been done to examine the influence of adult roles once they are adopted. There is certainly evidence to support the idea that adolescent drug use is related to the differential selection of adult roles. For example, Newcomb and Bentler (1985) found that adolescent drug users were more likely than nonusers to assume adult roles early in adulthood. Specifically, those individuals with high cigarette, alcohol, and illicit drug use in adolescence were less likely to be living with parents or in dormitories as young adults, and were less likely to have chosen college or military careers; they were more likely to be married or cohabiting, and more likely to be employed full time in a civilian job. Adolescent drug users were also more likely to be unemployed and not in school. These researchers hypothesized that early drug use is indicative of a general syndrome of precocious development; in this view, those who develop a sort of "pseudo maturity" in adolescence are more likely to emulate adults both by using drugs and by acquiring adult roles earlier, but they are not adequately prepared to succeed in these roles.

Kandel and colleagues also found evidence of the role selection process, but reported substantially different relationships. In one study (Kandel, 1984), adolescent marijuana users reported less participation in conventional adult roles such as marriage and parenthood, and greater instability in these roles. Continued involvement in a deviant subculture with nontraditional values was hypothesized to lead to the disruption of adult role acquisition. However, this explanation may be most appropriate for illicit drug use, and may not apply equally to licit drugs such as alcohol and cigarettes. Later results (Kandel, Davies, Karus, & Yamaguchi, 1986) testing the same model for other illicit drugs, alcohol, and cigarette use, found some important variation in the results depending on the kind of drug. Alcohol use had some negative effect on job stability, and cigarette use had some negative effect on marital stability; however, strong and consistent effects were limited to marijuana and other illicit drugs, which were related to lower participation and greater instability in each major adult role status. These results suggest that drug-using adolescents tend to avoid commitment to responsible adult roles, and that when they do assume these roles they may be unsuccessful in them.

The findings of Newcomb and Bentler (1985)—that drug use is associated with the earlier assumption of adult roles—would seem to be in direct conflict with those of Kandel and her colleagues that drug use is associated with avoidance and disruption of adult roles (Kandel, 1984; Kandel et al., 1986). Chassin et al. (1992) suggested that the role selection and precocious development theories can be reconciled by considering the role of college attendance as a mediating status. Because drug users in general are less likely to go to college, the college experience may represent a primary force of selective socialization—a funneling of adolescents into different streams of socialization in young adulthood based on prior characteristics. Noncollege youth are more likely to take on full-time employment, marry, and have children early in adulthood, not necessarily because of a precocious desire to do so, but because they are less likely to be engaged in educational pursuits. Meanwhile, the same processes or characteristics that made drug users less likely to pursue a college education may also reduce their likelihood of succeeding in other responsible roles. Thus, the interdependency of these primary roles would explain the seemingly contradictory selection effects found by these researchers. There is other evidence that the selection of some roles (e.g., college) and the exclusion of others (e.g., marriage) leads to differential socialization effects (Schulenberg, Bachman, O'Malley, & Johnston, 1994) such as living arrangements, social activities, and peer-group affiliation. Such results point to an interaction between role selection and role socialization leading to individual change.

It is also possible that selection effects are related more to overall levels of drug use, whereas socialization effects play a primary role in the process of change within groups. Thus, for example, adolescent drug users may be more prone to marry early in adulthood, and these adolescent drug users may then reduce their use due to the effects of the marriage role as compared to adolescent drug users who do not marry. Likewise, nonusers may be less likely to marry early on, but those who do marry may be less likely to begin using drugs.

A number of early sociological studies examined the power of behavioral constraints imposed by adult roles, such as changes in the organization of social life dictated by residence, occupation, and family obligations (Dickens & Perlman, 1981). For example, studies noted the decline in peer networks over the life cycle, with the major transitions of marriage and parenthood playing particularly important roles in constraining other relationships. Fischer and Phillips (1982) reported a high frequency of social contact with peers among single adults, intermediate social contact for childless married individuals, and the least peer contact among married parents. The contexts of friendship formation also change drastically from adolescence to adulthood, with new work and neighborhood contacts (Stueve & Gerson, 1977) and extended family relationships (Shulman, 1975) taking on new prominence in adulthood. This suggests that roles such as marriage and parenthood restructure social networks in important ways, and perhaps that the sheer time and energy involved in adult roles may prohibit excessive drug use, and the interpersonal relationships that promote such use.

Our own efforts seek to focus on these kinds of social role influences in this fairly neglected aspect of the causal chain, and to relate these effects specifically to patterns of change in drug use. Our emphasis on the importance of these influences is based on a life-span developmental perspective (e.g., Baltes, 1987; Baltes, Reese, & Lipsett, 1980; Featherman, 1983; Lerner, 1984, 1986; Pandina et al., 1984), a basic tenet of which is that people have the capacity for change throughout their entire life course (Brim & Kagan, 1980). Accordingly, our explanations for behavioral change in the transition to adulthood are located primarily in present circumstances rather than the past (Johnston et al., 1992). Clearly, each individual enters the transition with a certain history, having made certain choices that shape the experiences of the transition. However, the transition itself also exerts substantial influence by changing the environment, and thereby changing the individual. This stability and change is likely a function of both individual and contextual factors, and the interplay of the individual acting on, and reacting to, the environmental system in which he or she is embedded (Bronfenbrenner, 1979; Lerner, 1986).

EVIDENCE FOR THE INFLUENCE OF ADULT ROLES ON DRUG USE

The present research addresses the influences of marriage, engagement, nonmarital cohabitation, pregnancy, parenthood, living arrangements, student status, and employment on substance use in young adulthood. Because these roles also interrelate in complex ways, we consider a number of important overlapping role transitions simultaneously in our multivariate analyses. We also examine aspects of demographic background as important selection factors. The evidence for the relationship of adult role status to changes in substance use varies somewhat depending on the role under investigation, so we have organized the following sections according to specific roles to gain a clearer picture of what is known. The evidence is perhaps clearest for marriage and pregnancy, and somewhat more ambiguous for other adult roles.

Marriage

Marriage fundamentally alters the social environment of young adults. It usually involves a change in residence for at least one of the spouses, a substantial shift in geographic location that can prompt changes in friendship patterns and other social contacts, or both. Even when no change in neighborhood is involved, newly married partners generally commit more time to each other and to establishing their homes (Wallerstein, 1994), thereby leaving less time for "hanging out" with friends in settings conducive to drinking and other drug use.

In addition to changes in living arrangements and social interaction patterns, there may be other dramatic shifts in the social and emotional worlds of newly married couples (Dickens & Perlman, 1981). The personal commitment to a spouse may directly inhibit excessive drinking, illicit drug use, and other potentially damaging behaviors. Frequent close contact with a caring partner may be enough to tip the scales against such behaviors, as young adults become less concerned with their own identity and more concerned about intimacy with others (Erikson, 1968). Also, greater expectations of mature and responsible behavior may be held for married people—both personal expectations of self and spouse, and expectations expressed subtly or overtly by other family members, friends, and neighbors.

Marriage appears to protect people from many physical and psychological problems, including depression, suicide, victimization, injuries, overall mortality, and alcohol abuse (as summarized by Miller-Tutzauer, Leonard, & Windle, 1991). Cross-sectional studies have long suggested that being married is negatively related to alcohol and illicit drug use (Brown, Glaser, Waxer, & Geis, 1974; Kandel & Davies, 1991; Robbins, 1991). The specific influence of marriage on drug use has also been documented in several prospective studies. For example, Donovan et al. (1983) found declines in problem drinking among women and men after marriage, and Miller-Tutzauer et al. (1991) also found that married people moderated their alcohol use after marriage and that this effect stabilized within a year after marriage. In a recent study of role socialization influences on cocaine use among men (Burton, Johnson, Ritter, & Clayton, 1996), researchers found that the marital role was the only adult role that had a significant impact on the initiation of cocaine use. Several other studies have shown marriage effects for women, but not for men: Horwitz and White (1991) found declines in alcohol use among newly married women; Yamaguchi and Kandel (1985b) reported declines in women's marijuana use after marriage; Newcomb and Bentler (1987) reported that marriage was significantly linked to decreases in women's use of alcohol, marijuana, and cocaine; and Brunswick et al. (1992) reported changes in women's heavy drug use (including both marijuana and cocaine) after marriage. Thus, there is evidence for an influence of marital status on drug and alcohol use for both men and women, but the evidence is perhaps stronger in the case of women. Stronger, more consistent results for women in these studies may reflect effects of pregnancy and the assumption of a primary caregiving role.

Because marriage may often be undertaken with the expectation that parenthood will soon follow, some of the personal and social transformations observed to coincide with marriage actually may be better understood as anticipatory to parenthood. Indeed, many couples who already live together or are sexually intimate choose to marry precisely because they feel ready to have children and prefer to do so as a married couple. Some anticipatory reductions in drug use may occur prior to pregnancy or parenthood, as young adults planning for parenthood become more sensitized to health practices in general, and particularly to those practices (such as smoking, alcohol use, and use of illicit drugs) that could adversely affect their ability to conceive or affect the health of their child before and after birth (Serdula, Williamson, Kendrick, Anda, & Byers, 1991).

Engagement

Getting engaged, as an anticipation of marriage and perhaps parenthood as well, is an act of commitment to future roles. As such it may be expected to contribute significantly to the process of socialization for conventional adult roles, although it is less likely to alter fundamentally the physical setting or social environment. Surprisingly little is known about how people's relationships and social lives change as they move from acquaintance to courtship and marriage, and less about how engagement is related to drug use.

Some work has shown that the social environment of young adults is altered to some extent by becoming engaged. Surra (1985) found increased contact with one's romantic partner and reduced contact with other peers as couples moved from a dating relationship toward marriage. For example, both men and women increased the amount of leisure time they spent alone with their partners from about 35% while dating and identified as a couple, to 40–45% once they were certain of marriage (engaged), and to about 50% of leisure time spent with one's spouse alone after marriage.

Although there is wide variation in the length of time spent in these different relationship stages, some research indicates that typical engagement periods vary from about 7 months to a year and a half (Cate, Huston, & Nesselroade, 1986). Interestingly, this time span roughly corresponds to some evidence of reduced drug use prior to marriage. Yamaguchi and Kandel (1985b) found declines in marijuana use among both men and women in the year preceding marriage. This suggests an anticipatory effect for the marital role, that is, changes that occur after commitment to marriage but before the wedding. These changes may be environmental, personal, or both; however, the fact that drastic changes in residence and lifestyle often do not occur until after marriage suggests that a purposive psychological commitment to the new role as intimate partner has at least some impact. The wedding day itself may be only the final consolidation of this gradual merging of two life plans.

There are also intriguing implications from the consistent evidence suggesting that people tend to marry those similar to themselves in many ways, including age, race, education, religious commitment, expectations for the marital relationship and parenting (Buss, 1984; Coombs & Fernandez, 1978; Mare, 1991), and in the frequency and type of substance use (Yamaguchi & Kandel, 1993). This homophily in drug use between marital partners suggests that the marital relationship itself need not impose constraints on drug use, and might in fact be expected to promote stability in use. In fact, the findings of Yamaguchi and Kandel show that the drug-use behaviors or attitudes of one spouse do not substantially influence a marital partner's drug-use behaviors over time. So perhaps it is not primarily the specific behaviors or expectations of the marital couple that alter drug use, but rather some larger shared influences that shape the marriage partners in tandem.

Cohabitation

Nonmarital cohabitation might be viewed as anticipatory to marriage in the same way that engagement is; it might involve many of the emotional and practical constraints involved in marriage, and thus might be expected to have some of the same effects on drug use as marriage.[1] However, nonmarital cohabitation has been linked to increases in overall levels of drug use

---

[1]Data are only available concerning cohabitation with partners of the opposite sex, so we are not able to investigate cohabitation with same-sex partners.

(Bachman et al., 1984), especially among men (Newcomb, 1987). This may be due in part to lower traditionalism and higher deviance among people who choose to cohabit outside of marriage (Newcomb, 1987; Thornton, Axinn, & Hill, 1992; Yamaguchi & Kandel, 1985a).

Previous research has suggested that those with nontraditional beliefs and behaviors are drawn to nonmarital cohabitation as a lifestyle (DeMaris & MacDonald, 1993; DeMaris & Rao, 1992; Nock, 1995), and some longitudinal work has suggested that cohabitation itself increases nontraditional attitudes and values (Axinn & Thornton, 1992). Previous results from the Monitoring the Future project (Bachman et al., 1984) showed (a) that young adults (modal ages 19–21) who cohabited with an unmarried partner were more likely to have used drugs before cohabiting, and (b) that increases in substance use were associated with the transition into nonmarital cohabitation.

Pregnancy

In recent years there has been a considerable increase in the scientific evidence that drug use by pregnant women can have substantial effects on their infants. For some time it has been known that heavy alcohol use by pregnant women is associated with fetal alcohol syndrome, but more recent evidence points to possible effects even from usage levels previously thought to be moderate (Wyngaarden, 1988). Cigarette, marijuana, and cocaine use have also recently been demonstrated to be harmful to the developing fetus (Armstrong, McDonald, & Sloan, 1992; Chasnoff, 1991; Fried, Watkinson, & Willan, 1984; Hatch & Bracken, 1986). In light of this evidence, it is not surprising to find that more young women are taking this information seriously, and are consequently reducing their drug use during pregnancy. Yamaguchi and Kandel (1985b) reported evidence indicating a clear decline in the use of marijuana among pregnant women, and some decline also among the spouses of pregnant women. Fried, Barnes, and Drake (1985) found declines in cigarette and alcohol use during pregnancy, particularly a reduction in heavy use. Ihlen, Amundsen, Sande, and Daae (1990) also reported significant reductions in the use of alcohol, cigarettes, and illegal drugs during pregnancy. However, these studies have generally been based on small samples, often clinical and often nonrepresentative, so it is not clear whether these effects would be found in national samples.

In previous analyses, we found reductions in drug use during pregnancy (Bachman, O'Malley, Johnston, Rodgers, & Schulenberg, 1992; Bachman, Wadsworth, O'Malley, Schulenberg, & Johnston, 1997), and although these are most pronounced among women, reductions in some behaviors (such as heavy drinking) also occurred among husbands with pregnant spouses. Some portions of such pregnancy effects seem to be transitory, but to the extent that there are any lasting effects of drug reduction during pregnancy, lower levels of use would be expected among parents.

Parenthood

In contrast to marriage, researchers have identified the transition to parenthood as a period of extreme psychosocial stress, often leading to negative feelings about self and spouse (Ruble, Fleming, Hackel, & Stangor, 1988), marital dissatisfaction (Belsky & Pensky, 1988), and depression (Fedele, Golding, Grossman, & Pollack, 1988). In fact, first-time parents may suffer personal and marital distress for several years after the arrival of the first child (Cowan & Cowan, 1988; Cowan, Cowan, Heming, & Miller, 1991). These findings are likely linked to the numerous profound demands on the individual that are unique to parenthood. New parents experience a sudden and intense introduction to their new role as nurturer, new skills are needed and must be learned on the spot, and there are enormous consequences for failure. This sudden introduction of 24-hour responsibility, severe time constraints, and strong emotional responses that may be surprising and unsettling often overwhelms new parents for a time (Antonucci & Mikus, 1988).

Some evidence has been found for a negative relationship between parenting and drug use. For example, Yamaguchi and Kandel (1985b) found that individuals who entered into parenthood were significantly less likely to initiate or continue marijuana use. However, other studies have shown no effects of parenting beyond the influence of the marital status (Bachman et al., 1997; Burton et al., 1996).

Reduced opportunities for socializing may also result from the burdens of parenthood (Antonucci & Mikus, 1988), as parents who are busy caring for their young children simply have less time available for "hanging out" or partying with friends, thereby reducing their opportunities for drug use. However, the demands of parenthood may also transform social interactions and social networks in other ways, as parents are forced to reassess their needs for social support and advice versus leisure time and fun. Thus, some relationships may increase in their importance and intensity (notably extended family members and other parents) and others may decrease (those with nonparent friends; Gottlieb & Pancer, 1988).

Parenthood is clearly an emotionally and physically stressful undertaking, but it is also one of the most highly valued adult social roles (Fawcett, 1978;

Hoffman, 1978), one which becomes a central aspect of the self-concept and a key component of life satisfaction for many people (Chilman, 1980; Cowan & Cowan, 1988; Hoffman & Manis, 1978). Thus, becoming a parent can drastically affect one's psychological landscape, greatly altering priorities and values (Galinsky, 1981; Heath, 1978; Mikus, 1981). Drug use is likely to be especially incompatible with the new priorities and values associated with parenthood. Finally, the fact that young children quickly become astute observers of parents' behaviors may strongly impinge on substance use, as the need to set a good example leads to greater parental discretion in drug-use behavior with each passing year.

Single Parenthood

Single parenthood may operate very differently from the processes we have just described. Single fathers rarely reside with their children, and thus would not experience many of the practical restraints or psychological ramifications of parenthood. Single mothers usually do reside with their children, but may be less likely than married mothers to receive social approval for their role as a parent or clear norms for their parental behavior. This may be especially true for young never-married mothers, who constitute a growing proportion of the single-parent population (Weintraub & Gringlas, 1995). Young unwed mothers face other particular burdens. They are less likely to go on to postsecondary education, to have stable employment, or to enter a stable marital relationship, and are much more likely to endure long-term financial hardship (Brooks-Gunn & Chase-Lansdale, 1995).

However, most single-parent families are created through divorce or separation (Weintraub & Gringlas, 1995), and divorced parents face their own particular burdens resulting from marital disruption. They may experience greater disruption of extended family relationships and other social networks (Tschann, Johnston, & Wallerstein, 1989), and may be at greater risk of depression and other psychological disorders (Aseltine & Kessler, 1993; Booth & Amato, 1991). Overall, it is clear that single parents generally have more limited social support networks (Gunnarsson & Cochran, 1990), substantial economic hardship (Duncan, 1991), and significant psychological distress (McLoyd & Wilson, 1991), all of which may place single parents at greater risk for substance abuse. They may use drugs as a way of escaping or reducing stress, and there are fewer interpersonal constraints on drug use behavior.

Education

Research on how educational success and college attendance influence drug use has produced a somewhat paradoxical picture. Early adolescent drug use has been linked to early educational failure (e.g., Dishion, Patterson, Stoolmiller, & Skinner, 1991), and educational commitment and success are clearly negatively related to drug use and other problem behavior during high school (Bachman, O'Malley, & Johnston, 1986; Bailey & Hubbard, 1990; Kandel, 1980; Newcomb & Bentler, 1986; Schulenberg et al., 1994). However, in spite of the fact that educational success is generally associated with less involvement in drug use, some substance use and problems with use are clearly more prevalent among college students than among their noncollege peers.

College attendance involves a great deal of personal freedom in contrast to the other adult roles discussed, and thus may have a very different socialization role in regard to drug use. Problem alcohol use—particularly binge drinking or heavy party drinking—tends to be higher among college students (Johnston et al., 1997; Wechsler, Dowdall, Davenport, & Castillo, 1995). Social aspects of dormitory living and fraternity/sorority living in particular have been cited as promoting frequent and intense use of alcohol (Brennan, Walfish, & AuBuchon, 1986; Wechsler, Dowdall, Davenport, & Castillo, 1995). Other drugs show varying relationships to college attendance. As mentioned previously, those who smoke cigarettes are less likely to be in college, primarily due to selection effects related to social class and college aspirations (Chassin et al., 1992). College plans and college attendance have also been found to be negatively related to post-high-school cigarette use (Schulenberg et al., 1994), but had no effect on illicit drug use in young adulthood.

Living Arrangements

Many of the roles already discussed impinge heavily on decisions regarding living arrangements, but there are other important living contexts that may bear important relationships to substance use. Living with one's parents, in a dormitory, with roommates, or living alone offer varying levels of constraint or opportunity with regard to substance use. Newcomb and Bentler (1985) found significant covariation between substance use and living arrangements, although their work emphasized the selection interpretation of these results. Those living with their parents as young adults reported the lowest levels of alcohol and marijuana use of any group in adolescence. Those living with roommates, alone, or in "other" arrangements did not evidence distinct patterns of substance use.

Employment

The relationships of employment to drug use are complex, and varying results have been found depending on what aspect of employment is under consideration. The costs and benefits of employment in adolescence have been the subject of some controversy. Work intensity in adolescence is related to such negative outcomes as substance use, delinquency, and poor school performance (Bachman, Bare, & Frankie, 1986; Bachman & Schulenberg, 1993; Greenberger & Steinberg, 1986; Steinberg & Dornbusch, 1991). There is evidence that suggests, however, that employment is not a direct cause of those poor outcomes. Rather, greater investment in work roles during high school and greater problem behavior may be correlated outcomes of preexisting individual differences in the level of investment in schooling and prior history of problem behavior (Bachman & Schulenberg, 1993).

These relationships might be expected to differ in adulthood, as work roles become more central to self-concepts and more vital for financial survival. Drug use has been found to be a risk factor for job instability in young adulthood (Kandel & Yamaguchi, 1987; Yamaguchi & Kandel, 1985b). Newcomb and Bentler (1985) reported differential acquisition of certain occupational roles for adolescent drug users, indicating that adolescents with high alcohol use were more likely than others to report no life pursuit (i.e., not married, working, or going to school) or to be in military service.

An often-overlooked work role is that of military service. There have been mixed findings regarding the influence of military service on drug use, and the results suggest that the effects vary a great deal across cohorts. In reviewing several large-scale surveys some years ago, Segal (1977) concluded that illicit drug use was clearly higher among those in military service. Data from Johnston (1973) were consistent with that conclusion, and Robins (1974) also reported very high levels of marijuana and heroin usage among young men returning from Vietnam. In an analysis of a more recent cohort (i.e., senior-year cohort of 1976), Johnson and Kaplan (1991) found little difference in marijuana use as a function of military status. In recent years the military services have undertaken extensive, and apparently successful, efforts to reduce the levels of illicit drug use among their personnel, which may have further reduced differences between the military and civilian labor forces. The most recent surveys show steady declines in cigarette, alcohol, and other drug use from 1980 to 1992, but military personnel were still found to be more likely than their civilian counterparts to use alcohol and smoke cigarettes, although less likely to use other drugs (Bray, Marsden, Peterson, 1991; Kroutil, Bray, & Marsden, 1994).

THE INFLUENCE OF DEMOGRAPHIC/
BACKGROUND FACTORS ON DRUG USE

There are a number of important demographic or background factors that are influential for both substance use and social roles in adulthood. These include gender, ethnicity, parent education, region, population density, cohort, and age effects. Many of these factors have their primary influence in the selection of roles and on relative mean levels of drug use, and less influence on the relationships between adult roles and change in drug use over time (Bachman et al., 1992). Our earlier findings and the studies discussed in this chapter suggest that the roles and experiences encountered in young adulthood are at least as influential as background factors, and possibly more so. In order to examine this assertion directly, we include these background factors jointly with measures of adult roles and experiences as potentially important predictors and control variables.

Some direct influences on changes in drug use may also exist, particularly in the case of gender. Higher proportions of men than of women are users of most substances, and these differences increase with age and at higher levels of use (Johnston et al., 1997; Kandel, 1991). There are also gender differences with regard to adult role occupancy, with women likely to be married at earlier ages than men, and men more likely to be employed than women (Chassin et al., 1992; Schulenberg & Ebata, 1994). Pregnancy and parenthood are likely to have differential impacts on men and women, as suggested in other work (e.g., Bachman et al., 1997; Horwitz & White, 1991; Yamaguchi & Kandel, 1985b).

There are important age, period, and cohort influences on the use of most of the drugs under investigation here (O'Malley, Bachman, & Johnston, 1988a, 1988b). These effects are potentially important for the kinds of relationships we are examining. However, our analyses indicate that cohort and secular trend effects are primarily related to mean levels of use, and do not substantially influence the analyses of change in use, or substantially alter relationships between adult role status and drug use.

CONCLUSIONS

Our own research (e.g., Bachman et al., 1984; Schulenberg et al., 1994), as well as the work of many others (e.g., Kandel, 1984, 1995), shows that drug use increases throughout adolescence and early adulthood, and declines thereafter. Evidence suggests that the notable declines in drug use among young adults during their midtwenties can be attributed in large part to transitions in role responsibilities such as marriage, pregnancy, parenthood, and career establishment. The concomitant influence of the many overlapping social roles we described makes the task of sorting out these effects very difficult. However, this is a reflection of the complexity of the social world of early adulthood, so the overlapping and differential influences of these roles are of great interest to us. The promise of this research is to consider a number of these influences simultaneously, retaining much of the complexity encountered in the real world.

A central question throughout this monograph is to what extent the typical age-related changes in drug use during young adulthood can be explained in terms of the important role transitions that occur during this period. As we investigate the influence of a number of dimensions of post-high-school experience on drug use, we focus our inquiry on whether these factors, taken in combination, can explain the totality of the changes in drug use that occur as young adults move out of their teens and through their twenties. Our panel data are well suited to exploring such questions, and our analysis methods have been designed to do so, as is discussed in the next chapter.

The importance we place on adult experience, and the support we find for such an approach, offers an essentially hopeful perspective. It suggests that potentials for change and improvement during the transition to adulthood are as important as the detrimental effects of problem behavior in adolescence.

3

Examining Roles and Experiences During the Post-High-School Years—Sample Characteristics and Analysis Strategy

Dramatic role changes occur during the years after high-school graduation. In all cases, the role of high-school student comes to an end, and is replaced by other roles such as college student, civilian employee, member of the armed forces, or various combinations of these and other roles. There also are changes in living arrangements for the majority of young adults; they leave their parents' homes to begin married life, to live in a dormitory or apartment while attending college, to live with friends, or simply to be on their own. Within the first few years of high-school graduation, substantial numbers have earned college degrees, and substantial numbers also have taken on the responsibilities of parenthood.

Each of these experiences has shown impacts on drug use during the post-high-school years, and in subsequent chapters we examine these impacts. Before doing so, it is useful to consider the timing of these experiences during young adulthood, and how they are interrelated. The first half of this chapter describes our samples in terms of their patterns of role experiences during the first 14 years after high school. With that as background, the second half of the chapter provides an overview of our analysis strategy.

The present descriptions of role experiences, based on large and nationally representative samples, may be of some interest in their own right, above and beyond the analyses in later chapters linking post-high-school role experiences with drug use. However, it is important to keep in mind that our obtained samples are limited in several respects, as we outline next.

SAMPLE CHARACTERISTICS AND REPRESENTATIVENESS

As noted in chapter 1, our analyses make use of Monitoring the Future panel data from the high-school classes of 1976–1994 and follow-up surveys conducted from 1977 through 1995. (Descriptions of sampling and survey methods are provided in the Appendix.) Our decision to use all of the available panels means that we have complete (i.e., 13–14 year) follow-up data on only the early cohorts, whereas the later cohorts have aged less and thus contribute data only for the earlier follow-ups. This can be seen clearly in Fig. 3.1, which summarizes the panel data used in these analyses. Note that follow-up surveys were conducted during even years for one random half of each cohort, and during odd years for the other half.

Age and cohort are somewhat confounded in these analyses; data from the oldest age brackets (modal ages 31–32) are necessarily limited to those who graduated in the classes of 1976 through 1982, whereas the youngest age bracket (modal ages 19–20) includes data from 19 graduating classes from 1976 through 1994. This presents a few complications in the analyses; however, our techniques for studying impacts on drug use are able to manage such problems to a large extent. In any case, it is important to recognize that because the cohorts differ in some important respects, any analysis that seeks to reach general conclusions applicable across cohorts must take such differences into account.

Our obtained samples are limited in several other respects. Most notably, our panels of respondents begin with high-school seniors, thus omitting those who dropped out before reaching the end of 12th grade. Additionally, panel attrition further reduces representativeness (e.g., men and non-Whites showed lower than average rates of follow-up participation—see Bachman, O'Malley, et al., 1996, Table 2.1 for details).[1] Finally, for reasons discussed later in this chapter, our present analyses exclude the small proportions of respondents who by the end of 12th grade were married, had children, were not living with parents, or any combination thereof.

These limitations notwithstanding, our general conclusion is that the obtained samples were in most respects quite similar to the target samples, and thus reasonably representative of the large majority of young adults in the United States during the past two decades (see Bachman, O'Malley, et al., 1996, Table 2.1 for details). Moreover, it should be kept in mind that our primary purpose in this monograph is to examine the potential impacts of different post-high-school roles and experiences, rather than to provide

---

[1]In other analyses and publications, we carefully adjusted for panel attrition in order to provide more accurate estimates of trends in drug use during young adulthood (e.g., Johnston et al., 1997; O'Malley, et al., 1984, 1988a, 1988b). Such adjustments provide small but useful corrections to our data on overall trends. However, a similar attempt at adjustment would be complex and cumbersome if applied throughout the present analyses, and would not have any appreciable impact on our main findings concerning differential changes in drug use associated with different post-high-school experiences.

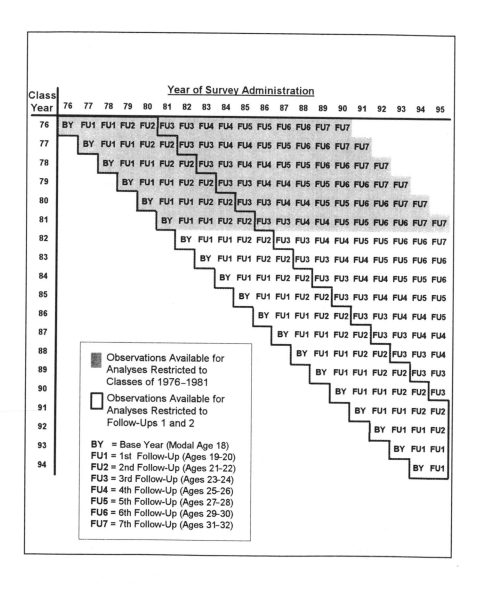

FIG. 3.1. Observations available for analyses. Full sample analyses were based on observations collected from all the survey administrations represented in this figure. Restricted analyses were based on subgroups shown.

precise estimates of the proportions of young adults who fall into each of our analysis categories. Our obtained samples are very well suited to that purpose.

PATTERNS OF POST-HIGH-SCHOOL EDUCATION AND EMPLOYMENT

The primary occupation of most high-school seniors is being a student. Many work part time, but for the great majority the chief role and corresponding identity remains that of being a student. On graduation from high school, most young people embark on one of two new paths, each with its distinct role characteristics; some become full-time college students, others become full-time employees.

Just as is the case during high school, in young adulthood the student and employee roles are not mutually exclusive. Some full-time college students also work part time, and some who enter full-time employment after high school also take college or other postsecondary courses. In most such cases, one of the two roles is clearly predominant; during the first 4 years after high school, only a few (2–3%) of our panel respondents were classified as part-time students and also part-time employees, whereas slightly more (5–6%) were classified as full time in both roles.

A small portion of the young adults in our samples were neither students nor employed, many of whom were women who described themselves as full-time homemakers. There remained only a few (roughly 5% of both men and women) who were defined as belonging to none of the aforementioned categories—neither student, nor employed, nor a full-time homemaker.

Student Experiences

The majority of our respondents entered some form of higher education during their first years after high school. Figure 3.2, based on the classes of 1976–1981, shows that more than half were full-time students at the time of the first follow-up (modal ages 19–20), and another 7% were part-time students. The percentages of full-time students dropped somewhat by the time of the second follow-up (modal ages 21–22), dropped much more sharply by the third follow-up, and continued to decline thereafter. Proportions who were part-time students increased slightly during the first few years after high school, and then decreased slightly.

Many of our respondents completed a bachelor's degree during their twenties, as shown in Fig. 3.3. Just over one quarter had done so by the fifth

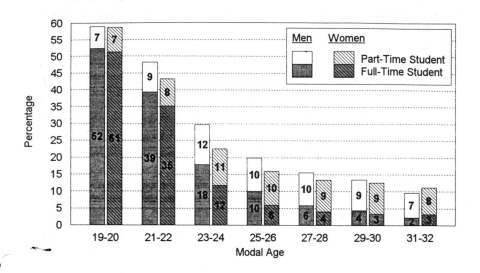

FIG. 3.2. Proportions of panel respondents in post-high-school education, by gender. Percentages are based on data from classes of 1976–1981, only.

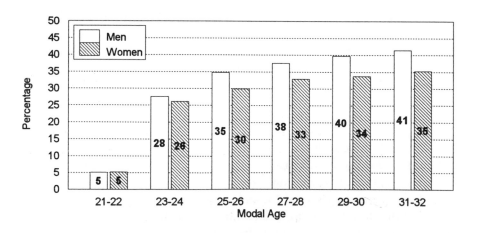

FIG. 3.3. Proportions of panel respondents who reported completing a bachelor's degree, by gender. Percentages are based on data from classes of 1976–1981, only. Follow-up surveys are conducted during the spring, when many respondents are on the verge of graduating, but have not yet graduated.

or sixth year after high school and the proportions continued to rise thereafter. Figures 3.2 and 3.3 are based on only those classes that contributed fully to all seven follow-ups (specifically, the classes of 1976 through 1981), in order that developmental trends not be confused with cohort differences in college attendance. Specifically, during the past two decades there was an increase in the proportions of young people, especially young women, who entered and graduated from college. When the histories of the younger cohorts are traced throughout their twenties and into their thirties, we expect that they will be similar to those in Fig. 3.3 except that the male–female differences will be diminished.

Employment Experiences

The path of full-time civilian employment was followed by about 30% of our respondents in the first 2 years after high school, and rose to about 43% in the next 2 years, as shown in Table 3.1. Then, corresponding closely to the decline in proportions of full-time students, the proportions in full-time employment increased substantially to about 63% by the third follow-up (modal ages 23–24). Thereafter (i.e., during the later twenties), the proportions in full-time civilian employment continued to rise among men, whereas among women a more substantial rise occurred in the proportions describing themselves as full-time homemakers with no outside job.

Part-time employment dropped off sharply after the first two follow-ups, again corresponding to the decline in the number of students. Among men, the rates of part-time employment continued to drop thereafter. Among women, however, the drop-off was more limited, and from the midtwenties onward the proportions in part-time employment remained steady as increasing numbers of women took on additional responsibilities associated with homemaking and child care, the time demands of which still generally fall more heavily on wives than on husbands.

Rates of full-time military employment peaked early at just over 6% for men and slightly under 1% for women. Although military service involved only small numbers of our follow-up respondents, we see later that it showed some important relationships with drug use. A few of those in military service also described themselves as full-time or part-time students, but about four out of five were nonstudents (see Table 2.3, Bachman, O'Malley, et al., 1996).

Another dimension of "employment experience" is actually the absence of employment; at each follow-up point, roughly 4–5% of respondents, both men and women, were neither students, nor employed, nor full-time home-

TABLE 3.1

Proportions of Panel Respondents in Various Employment Statuses

	Women							
	FU1	FU2	FU3	FU4	FU5	FU6	FU7	Total observations
Modal age:	19-20	21-22	23-24	25-26	27-28	29-30	31-32	19-32
Class years included:	76-94	76-92	76-90	76-88	76-86	76-84	76-82	76-94
Number of cases (Wtd.):	14,127	11,913	9,974	8,204	6,595	5,174	3,859	59,845
Employment Status:								
Full-time civilian	28.7	42.8	62.0	67.7	67.1	65.1	62.4	52.0
Full-time military	0.7	0.8	0.8	0.7	0.5	0.4	0.3	0.7
Part-time job	33.5	28.1	16.2	11.6	11.4	12.1	14.0	21.0
Full-time homemaker	3.0	4.9	7.5	9.1	11.4	12.3	13.8	7.4
Not employed & not student	4.5	4.9	5.3	5.0	5.0	5.4	5.5	5.0

	Men							
	FU1	FU2	FU3	FU4	FU5	FU6	FU7	Total observations
Modal age:	19-20	21-22	23-24	25-26	27-28	29-30	31-32	19-32
Class years included:	76-94	76-92	76-90	76-88	76-86	76-84	76-82	76-94
Number of cases (Wtd.):	11,696	9,890	8,241	6,691	5,443	4,285	3,223	49,469
Employment Status:								
Full-time civilian	31.9	43.7	64.1	76.4	82.0	84.8	85.7	59.2
Full-time military	5.3	6.3	5.3	4.7	4.1	3.4	3.1	5.0
Part-time job	27.7	22.7	13.8	7.8	5.3	3.7	2.9	15.5
Full-time homemaker	0.4	0.3	0.2	0.2	0.3	0.3	0.5	0.3
Not employed & not student	4.4	4.5	5.7	4.5	4.1	3.8	4.3	4.5

Note: Employment status percentages for each follow-up add to less than 100.0 percent because full- and part-time students who were not in any of the above employment statuses are omitted.

makers. Some of these individuals were actively seeking employment and thus would be considered unemployed members of the workforce.

Previous analyses (Bachman, O'Malley, et al., 1992, 1996) examined several other aspects of employment experience. At each follow-up, respondents reported the number of weeks that they were unemployed and looking for work during the past calendar year. The mean was about 5 weeks of unemployment during the first year or two after high school, but that dropped to only about 2 weeks by modal ages 27–28 and thereafter. Levels of income rose considerably, and job status levels also rose—changes that were heavily influenced by the increased proportions of respondents who graduated from college and assumed new roles as full-time employees.

It should be noted that preliminary analyses using measures of weeks of unemployment, annual income, and job status all showed little or no relationship with changes in drug use; accordingly, these predictors were not included in the multiple regression analyses reported in subsequent chapters.

MARITAL STATUS AND LIVING ARRANGEMENTS

In general, individuals' living arrangements strongly affect their day-to-day interpersonal contacts, an issue of particular interest in this monograph. Marriage is foremost among living arrangements that seem to have potential for influencing drug use. Thus, for analysis purposes we combined marital status with other living arrangements, setting up a single nonoverlapping scale with each respondent placed in the *first* applicable category:

1. Married.
2. Living with a partner of the opposite sex.
3. Living with parents.
4. Living in a dormitory.
5. Living alone.
6. All other living arrangements.

Marital Status

More than half of the young adults in our sample were married within 10 years of graduation from high school, and by 14 years after high school (modal ages 31–32) two-thirds were married, as can be seen in Fig. 3.4. The

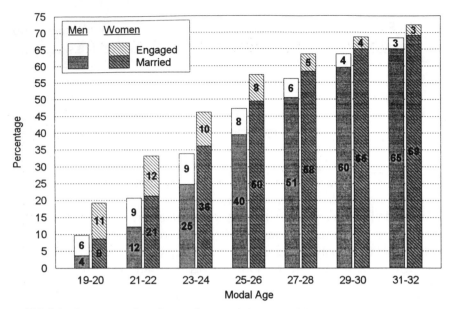

FIG. 3.4. Percentages of panel respondents married or engaged, by gender.

figure also shows that marriage rates for men lagged behind those for women by almost 2 years; for example, 65% of female respondents were married by age 29–30, whereas male respondents reached 65% married by age 31–32. Also shown in Fig. 3.4 are the proportions at each follow-up point who reported that they were engaged to be married.

Other Living Arrangements

Table 3.2 shows the percentages of high-school graduates in each of the six categories of living arrangements listed earlier. We have already described the rise in proportions married; now we look briefly at changes in each of the other five categories.

Although living with a partner of the opposite sex has some obvious parallels to being married, there are usually important differences in strength and length of commitment. Some instances of cohabitation are preludes to marriage; other cohabitation arrangements, however, are rather tenuous, involving little in the way of mutual commitment. At the time of the first follow-up, about 3% of men and nearly 6% of women were cohabiting. Proportions cohabiting increased during the early twenties, but at a much slower rate than marriage. Still, at any point during their midtwenties we found that about 8% of male respondents and 9 or 10% of female respon-

TABLE 3.2

Proportions of Panel Respondents in Various Living Arrangements

	Women							
	FU1	FU2	FU3	FU4	FU5	FU6	FU7	Total observations
Modal age:	19-20	21-22	23-24	25-26	27-28	29-30	31-32	19-32
Class years included:	76-94	76-92	76-90	76-88	76-86	76-84	76-82	76-94
Number of cases (Wtd.):	14,127	11,913	9,974	8,204	6,595	5,174	3,859	59,845
Current Living Arrangements								
Married	8.7	21.4	36.2	49.5	58.3	65.0	69.1	35.6
Partner of opposite sex	5.8	8.5	10.1	9.5	8.5	6.8	6.2	8.0
Parents	48.7	33.9	26.1	16.4	10.6	7.5	5.5	27.0
Dormitory	23.9	9.9	1.5	0.4	0.3	0.0	0.0	7.9
Alone	1.6	4.4	8.4	9.1	9.9	9.1	8.9	6.4
All other arrangements	11.3	21.9	17.7	15.1	12.4	11.5	10.2	15.1

	Men							
	FU1	FU2	FU3	FU4	FU5	FU6	FU7	Total observations
Modal age:	19-20	21-22	23-24	25-26	27-28	29-30	31-32	19-32
Class years included:	76-94	76-92	76-90	76-88	76-86	76-84	76-82	76-94
Number of cases (Wtd.):	11,696	9,890	8,241	6,691	5,443	4,285	3,223	49,469
Current Living Arrangements								
Married	3.7	12.2	24.8	39.5	50.5	59.5	65.1	27.7
Partner of opposite sex	3.0	6.4	7.7	8.6	8.2	7.2	6.2	6.4
Parents	51.6	38.0	31.4	20.0	13.3	8.6	6.8	30.4
Dormitory	22.3	9.9	2.4	0.9	0.3	0.2	0.1	7.8
Alone	2.7	5.8	10.6	12.8	13.4	14.0	13.5	8.9
All other arrangements	16.7	27.8	23.1	18.3	14.3	10.5	8.3	18.8

dents reported cohabiting with a partner of the opposite sex.[2] Of course, the percentages shown in Table 3.2 are estimates of cohabitation at any one point in time; many instances of relatively brief cohabitation (including many that occurred directly ahead of marriage) are unobserved in our data, simply because they happened to take place at "in-between" points in our 2-year cycle of follow-up surveys.

Living with parents was the most typical arrangement for recent high-school graduates (see Table 3.2), especially those who did not go to college.[3] By 5 or 6 years after high school, about one in three men and one in four women continued to live with one or both parents. To put it another way, among those not married or cohabiting by age 23 or 24, nearly half were living with their parents.

For many high-school graduates, entrance into college provided the occasion for leaving the parental home. Among those who were full-time students, about 41% at first follow-up continued to live with parents, but that dropped to 28% by the second follow-up. About 41% of full-time students lived in dormitories during the first follow-up, and that dropped to 23% by the second follow-up 2 years later. The single most popular living arrangement among full-time students at the second follow-up, reported by about 36%, was the "all other" category, which consisted largely of shared apartments or houses.[4]

Living alone was relatively rare during the first few years after high school, but Table 3.2 shows that the proportions who chose this living arrangement grew steadily throughout the early twenties. From age 25 onward, rates of living alone leveled off at about 13–14% for men and 9% for women.

PREGNANCY AND PARENTHOOD

Pregnancy

About 3% of the female respondents in the first year or two after high school reported being pregnant at the time of the survey, and this proportion rose gradually to about 7% for women in their later twenties. Among men,

---

[2]Our measures omitted cohabitation with partners of the same sex—a step we considered necessary because making distinctions between same-sex lovers and those who were simply roommates or housemates would have required more extensive and complex items than we were willing to include in the questionnaires.

[3]This cross-tabulation is documented in Bachman, O'Malley, et al. (1996) along with other cross-tabulations among student status, employment status, and living arrangements (see Tables 2.3–2.5 of that report).

[4]The percentages reported in this paragraph were derived from Table 2.4 in Bachman, O'Malley, et al. (1996).

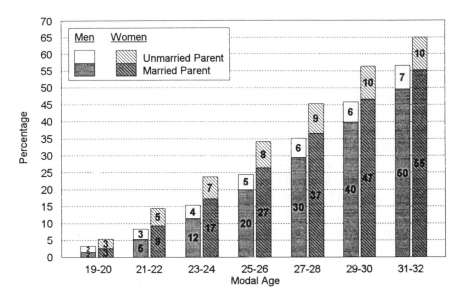

FIG. 3.5.   Percentages of panel respondents who were married or unmarried parents, by gender.

proportions reporting a pregnant spouse were slightly lower, although by age 29–30 the rate reached 7%. The somewhat later ages of marriage for men explain much of the gender difference here, although an additional factor is that the question for men referred to a pregnant spouse, whereas for women the question did not require that they be married.[5]

Parenthood

By the first or second year after high school, only a few of our panel respondents reported being parents—about half of them married and the other half unmarried. Then with each succeeding follow-up the proportion of parents rose, as can be seen in Fig. 3.5. By age 31–32, nearly two-thirds of all women were parents, as were more than half of all men, and most of these parents were married. Indeed, a comparison of Figs. 3.4 and 3.5 shows that by age 31–32 four out of five married women, and almost as many married men, were parents.

[5]See Bachman, O'Malley, et al. (1996), Table 2.2 for specific percentages at each of the seven follow-ups. It should be noted that because questions on pregnancy were not included in our earliest follow-up surveys, our estimates are based on data obtained from 1984 onward. The questionnaire item asked, "Are you (or is your spouse) currently pregnant?"

___.j shows that by age 31–32 about 7% of men and 10% of women were parents but were not married (some, of course, had been married but then divorced). Thus, we found that single parenthood occurred often enough to be examined in our analyses. And, because marriage and parenthood both can have impacts on drug use, and because the roles of spouse and parent can overlap in complex ways, our regression analyses maintained the distinction between married and single parents, thereby avoiding possible confounding that we would not otherwise be able to detect.

SUMMARY AND IMPLICATIONS
FOR ANALYSES OF DRUG USE

Among the most fundamental choices facing young people as they leave high school is whether or not to devote the next several years to further education. During the first year or two after high school, more than half of those in our follow-up samples did become full-time students in college (or some other post-high-school educational institution). Compared with their age-mates, these college students were less likely to marry, more likely to leave the parental home, and thus more likely to live in housing (dormitories and student rentals) with large numbers of people their own age and relatively few children or older adults. Many full-time college students (especially those living in dorms) were nonemployed, and most of the rest were employed only part time.

In contrast, high-school graduates who did not go on to college were more likely to remain living with their parents for a while, and more likely to marry within the first few years. Full-time employment was clearly the norm for those who did not go on to college. From their midtwenties onward, substantial numbers of women reported being full-time homemakers; many other women reported part-time employment, and no doubt many of these had heavy responsibilities as homemakers.

How do the lives of college students and their noncollege age-mates compare in terms of new freedoms and responsibilities? On the one hand, college students confront new responsibilities for managing their time and dealing with the pressures of exams and other course requirements. On the other hand, most college students experience more flexibility in their schedules, their housing arrangements, and their lives in general, compared with their age-mates who did not go to college. As we see in the following chapters, these and other differences in living arrangements and role responsibilities have important implications for drug use during young adulthood.

Two observations concerning the timing of various post-high-school roles and experiences are worth keeping in mind as we move on to our examination of impacts on drug use. The first observation, well illustrated in this chapter, is that the proportions of young adults in various roles and living arrangements shift substantially with increasing age. In particular, the role of full-time student is prominent in the late teens and early twenties, whereas the proportion of respondents in the roles of spouse and parent increased steadily during the first decade after high school. The second observation is that such shifts in roles and living arrangements may be sufficient to explain much of the age-related change we observe in drug use. For example, if marriage tends to lower drug use, and if increasing proportions of young adults marry as they go from their early twenties to their late twenties, then on those grounds alone we should expect that average levels of drug use would decline during the twenties. Thus one of the central questions addressed in subsequent chapters is whether overall age-related changes in young adult drug use are mostly, or perhaps entirely, explainable in terms of shifting roles and experiences.

ANALYSIS ISSUES AND STRATEGIES

There are many ways in which survey panel data can be analyzed, and previous analyses of Monitoring the Future data employed a variety of such methods. One set of panel analyses examined the cross-time correlations for self-reports of drug use, and then decomposed these into estimates of stability and reliability (Bachman, Johnston, & O'Malley, 1981; O'Malley, Bachman, & Johnston, 1983). Another set of analyses used panel data to distinguish among age, period, and cohort effects (O'Malley et al., 1984, 1988a, 1988b). Our annual descriptive reports of drug use among college students and other young adults also make use of panel analyses to correct for the effects of differential sample attrition on drug use estimates (e.g., Johnston et al., 1997). One early analysis reported "before and after" percentages of drug users for subgroups defined in terms of various post-high-school experiences (a technique also used in the present monograph), and also reported regression analyses in which the "before" (i.e., senior-year) measure of drug use was included among the predictors of the "after" (i.e., post-high-school) measure of drug use (Bachman, O'Malley, et al., 1981; Bachman et al., 1984). Other analyses used LISREL to estimate more complex structural equation causal models (Bachman, Schulenberg, O'Malley, & Johnston, 1990; Osgood, Johnston, O'Malley, & Bachman, 1988; Schulenberg et al., 1994), and some recent analyses have taken a pattern-centered approach to examining change over time (Schulenberg, O'Malley,

Bachman, Wadsworth, & Johnston, 1996; Schulenberg, Wadsworth, O'Malley, Bachman, & Johnston, 1996).

Each of the aforementioned methods has advantages and disadvantages, and each has been useful in extending our understanding of changes in drug use during the post-high-school years. We have used these multiple methods in part because our purposes have varied from one analysis to another. However, another motivation for using multiple analysis methods is that we do not consider any single approach to be free of risks and potential blind spots; we have greater confidence in findings that replicate across analysis methods. The findings reported here have met that criterion.

The Complexity of Panel Data and the Need to Simplify

We offer a hypothetical example to illustrate the rich complexity of the Monitoring the Future panel data—and also the need to simplify. Imagine that John Jones, a Monitoring the Future respondent from the high-school class of 1979, was included in the follow-up sample and that he participated as requested in 1981, 1983, 1985, 1987, 1989, 1991, and 1993. In high school, John Jones had gotten good grades and planned to attend college. In 1981, 2 years after graduating from high school, he was a full-time college student, also working part time in a dining hall, living in a dormitory, unmarried, and with no children. In 1983 he was still a full-time student, still working part time, still unmarried and childless, but living off campus in a rented house with other students. In 1985 he was a college graduate, working full time, and cohabiting with a woman to whom he also was engaged. In 1987 his life was different in two important ways: he was now married, and his wife was pregnant. In the 1989 survey he reported being a father, and his wife was again pregnant. In the 1991 survey he was unemployed. In the 1993 survey he reported being employed, being the father of two children, and being divorced.

This brief history of the hypothetical John Jones scarcely begins to illustrate the rich level of detail that is potentially available for our panel analyses. Moreover, most of the aforementioned aspects of Jones' life have been found—in our research and in the research of others—to be related to substance use. It would be possible—theoretically, at least—for us to map out a fairly detailed case study for John Jones, including not only all of the information mentioned earlier, but also his use of cigarettes, alcohol, marijuana, and cocaine, as of 1979, 1981, 1983 . . . 1993. We could also map out literally thousands of other equally detailed case studies, as well as thousands more with similarly rich detail over shorter spans of time (i.e., those who began their participation in the mid-1980s and later).

But how is one to analyze tens of thousands of case studies and discover underlying patterns that can be considered generally applicable—i.e., how can we generalize from this rich mass of detailed data? Clearly, we have to simplify along either or both of two dimensions. One approach is to restrict drastically the range of current role experiences we examine; another approach is to limit the number and complexity of time points we examine. We have had experience with both approaches, and these are worth illustrating.

As one example, we have analyzed various "trajectories" from single to married, covering five points in time, and thus four time intervals (from the senior year of high school up to 8 years later), in analyses originally reported in 1987 (Bachman, 1987) and later updated showing the same results with much more extensive data (Bachman, Johnston, O'Malley, & Schulenberg, 1996). Specifically, we distinguished five different groups—those who remained single throughout, and those who made a transition from single to married in the first interval, the second, the third, or the fourth. A sample of the results from these analyses is shown in Fig. 3.6. These analyses showed clearly that marriage was associated with a decline in the proportion of marijuana users, and that the decline was much the same whether the marriage occurred in the late teens, early twenties, or midtwenties. In order to keep things manageable across five time points, however, we needed to omit those who followed less typical trajectories, such as moving from single to married to divorced to married again, and so forth. Additionally, we did not control statistically for a variety of other potentially relevant factors such as pregnancy and parenthood (because other analyses had led us to conclude that the impacts of marriage were of primary importance).

Another example shows a different trade-off between the number of time points and the complexity of material considered at any one point. In this approach we wished to examine more complex transitions into and out of marriage, so we considered many—but certainly not all—of the possible transition patterns involving four categories of marital status—single, engaged, married, or divorced; however, the transition patterns were based on just three points in time (Bachman et al., 1997). A sample of the results is shown in Fig. 3.7. Nine different transition patterns are shown; among the points they illustrate is that the transition *into* marriage was linked to a decline in likelihood of heavy drinking, whereas the transition *out of* marriage was linked to an increase of roughly comparable size. Figure 3.7 also illustrates the complexity of discriminating among nine distinct trajectories—even when the main patterns of results are strong and clear.

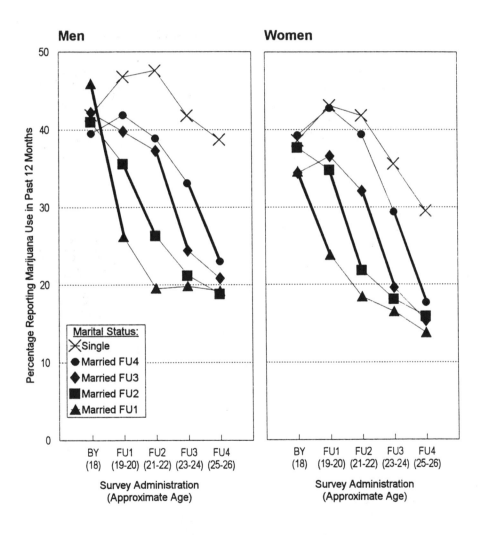

FIG. 3.6. Annual marijuana use related to marital status across five points in time. Bold line indicates the time interval during which marriage occurred.

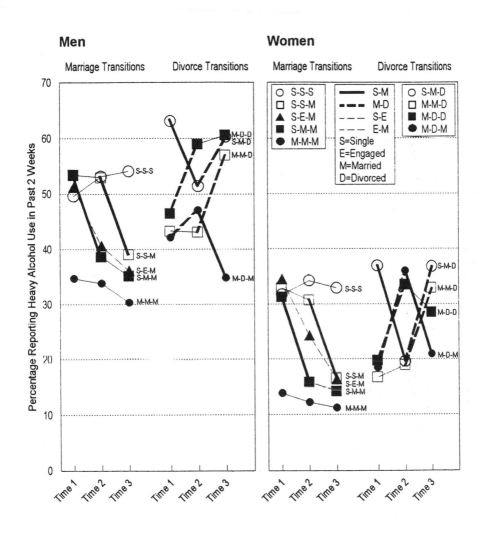

FIG. 3.7. Heavy alcohol use in the past 2 weeks related to transitions in marital status. Bold lines indicate intervals during which marriage (solid line) or divorce (broken line) occurred.

Distinctions in terms of marital status are relatively simple, compared with the more complex dimension of living arrangements, where one could be living with parents, a spouse, a cohabitant, dormitory mates, other nonrelatives, or alone. Those six categories of living arrangements, considered at multiple points in time, immediately generate an unmanageably large set of possible transition patterns. If one considered just three follow-up points, the number of possible patterns is six to the third power, or 216. Even if most of these patterns were excluded, the remainder would overwhelm the unfortunate analyst!

Studying Change Across Just Two Points in Time

Our solution to this problem required a great deal of preliminary work, followed by some drastic streamlining for the final analyses. Our first major streamlining decision was to restrict many, but not all, of our panel analyses to just two time points—an initial "before" measure, plus one follow-up "after" measure.

Treating Senior Year as the Starting Point

The second major streamlining decision was that the "before" measure for nearly all analyses would be the base-year survey, which occurred when our respondents were seniors in high school. This had the effect of giving everyone much the same starting point in terms of primary role responsibilities. The primary occupation of high-school seniors was considered to be student. Additionally, nearly all seniors surveyed were single, living with their parents, and did not have children of their own; the fewer than 7% who did not meet those three criteria as seniors were excluded from the present analyses. By thus streamlining the before point in our before–after analyses, we are able to deal with a complex set of post-high-school experiences examined at the after point. This is so because each of the after conditions reflects not only the situation at that point in time, but also a change (or nonchange) from the before conditions. For example, an individual living in a dormitory at the time of follow-up has made a major transition in living arrangements, whereas someone (still) living with parents has not.

Pooling Data Across Multiple Follow-Ups

Most of our panel respondents have participated in several follow-up surveys, and many have participated in seven. As our hypothetical John Jones illustrates, our respondents are not necessarily in the same circumstances from one follow-up to another. Although some transitions (e.g., from single to married) typically occur only once in young adulthood, there are many exceptions; moreover, other transitions (e.g., changes in living arrangements or student status) tend to occur several times and thus are less permanent. Accordingly, we found it useful to consider each new follow-up survey completed by a panel respondent as providing a new set of findings, both in terms of drug-use measures and also in terms of then-current post-high-school role experiences and responsibilities. Each of these follow-up surveys, when coupled with the senior-year surveys (i.e., the "before" measures), provided a different set of drug use change scores, as well as a different set of "predictor" measures.

In exploratory analyses conducted some years earlier, we compared findings across four base-year to follow-up intervals: spans of 1 or 2 years, 3 or 4 years, 5 or 6 years, and 7 or 8 years. These unpublished analyses yielded two important lessons. First, conducting analyses separately for each of four follow-up intervals generated a nearly overwhelming amount of detail. Second, such detail proved to be unnecessary, because the general patterns of findings for those relationships were quite similar no matter which of the four intervals was considered. Indeed, the findings shown in Fig. 3.6 provide one such example: the effects of marriage on marijuana use are much the same whether the transition from single to married occurs in the late teens or during the twenties.

Based on these preliminary findings, plus additional confirming analyses, we decided to combine findings across all base-year (before) to follow-up (after) intervals. Thus, an individual such as John Jones who participated in seven follow-ups would generate seven different "cases" for inclusion in these analyses; each case would correspond to his circumstances and behaviors at one of the seven follow-ups, and in each instance his senior year (or before) behaviors would provide a comparison point.[6]

One exception to this generalization is worth noting. When examining the correlates of college attendance, it is most useful to concentrate on the first 4 years after high school in order to compare students with their age-mates who did not go on to college. If later follow-ups are included, the

---

[6]In effect, this approach takes account of the fact that John Jones is not exactly the same person at each follow-up point, and it does so by treating him as seven different cases. It may be useful to think of these cases as "John Jones #1" (corresponding to the first follow-up), "John Jones #2" (corresponding to the second follow-up), and so on up to "John Jones #7." The seven cases generated by John Jones would not, of course, be independent of each other, because they share a common before measure. Accordingly, it might be inappropriate for us to base tests of statistical significance on the total numbers of cases or observations, as shown in Table A.1 in the Appendix. Instead, we have taken the very conservative approach of basing such tests on the numbers of individuals involved. Accordingly, John Jones would add only 1.0, rather than 7.0, to the total N used in tests of statistical significance.

result is to compare college students not only with their age-mates who did not go to college, but also with older adults who may have attended college years earlier. Accordingly, we repeated many of our analyses with only the first and second follow-ups included. The contrast between the full set of panel data and the first two follow-ups can be seen in Fig. 3.1; the first two follow-ups, outlined in gray, form a diagonal area from the left of the figure to the lower right.

Pooling Data Across Multiple Cohorts

Just as it would have been overwhelming to sort through detailed analysis data for seven different follow-up intervals, it also would have been unwieldy to examine and interpret analyses separately for each of the different cohorts of high-school seniors. Instead, we have generally combined results across all of the cohorts. One exception is that when we describe overall patterns of change over time in use of a drug, we focus on the earliest cohorts (graduates of the classes of 1976–1981), represented by the six shaded rows in Fig. 3.1. This approach allows us to give a complete "natural history" of age-related changes in drug use from the teens through the early thirties.

Multiple Regression Analyses Predicting to Change Scores

Although we make use of several descriptive analytic approaches in this monograph, at the core of the effort is the use of multiple regression analyses in which a variety of post-high-school roles and environments are examined simultaneously, with several key background factors also taken into account, and with all of these factors treated as "predictors" of *changes* in drug use between senior year and follow-up. This approach enables us to take account of a considerable number of factors simultaneously; further, by looking at various subsets of these factors separately, we are able to sort out some of the ways in which post-high-school experiences may have overlapping effects. The Appendix provides considerable detail on our multiple regression analysis approach, including tables of regression coefficients and guidelines for interpreting the tables. In the following paragraphs we discuss our regression analysis strategy at a more general conceptual level.

An important feature of these regression analyses is the use of change scores, calculated in a straightforward manner; specifically, the before measure of drug use (derived from the senior-year survey) is subtracted from the after measure of drug use (from the follow-up survey). Positive change scores thus indicate an increase over time, whereas negative change scores indicate a decrease. There has been much discussion of the advantages and disadvantages of change scores in panel analyses. Our own views, along with a good deal of supporting argument, have been spelled out by Rodgers and Bachman (1988).[7] For additional discussions see Cronbach and Furby (1969), Kessler and Greenberg (1981), Liker, Augustyniak, and Duncan (1985), and Rodgers (1989). In summary, we judged the advantages of change scores to far outweigh the disadvantages for our present purposes; moreover, as noted earlier, the present findings correspond quite closely with our earlier findings based on a variety of other methods.

Comparison Among Overlapping Predictor Sets

In our regression analysis we entered predictor variables in three groups. The first includes background and control variables, the second includes work and student status, and the third includes living arrangements (including marriage), engagement, pregnancy, and parenthood. This allows us to draw inferences about the extent and nature of overlap in their impacts on changes in drug use.

Many of the background and control variables are of considerable and substantive interest in their own right. However, in terms of our primary focus here, all of the control variables are viewed as *background* in the sense that we consider them primarily as a set of control measures used to ensure that we do not give misleading readings of the relationship of post-high-school roles and experiences to drug use.

The first regression analysis, predicting change in each of the drugs, uses only the background and control variables as predictors. The second regression analysis treats work and student status (along with the background and control variables) as predictors. The third regression analysis uses living arrangements, engagement, pregnancy, and parenthood (along with background and control variables) as predictors. The fourth and final set includes all predictors.

This sequence of regression analyses reflects our view that for most high-school seniors a key decision is whether or not to attend college, and then a variety of other decisions—at least as to the timing of other role experiences—flow from that decision. College and work often compete for

[7]Change scores provide a single meaningful measure of the dependent variable that controls for earlier use, and offers a clear advantage over the use of static scores by reducing measurement error. Although conventional wisdom suggests that the use of change scores should be avoided because the standard errors of estimates based on change scores are greater than those based on static scores, such is not always the case. For reasonably large sample sizes, the ratio of sampling errors for estimates based on change scores to those based on static scores is not excessively large. See Rodgers and Bachman (1988) for further discussion.

the finite number of hours young adults have to use, and these roles overlap in the complex ways we have described, so we include these as a single predictor group so as not to assign priority to one over another. We are also especially interested in patterns of prediction when this second group is considered jointly with the third group, which includes living arrangements, engagement, pregnancy, and parenthood. By entering these predictors in separate blocks we can assess shared (i.e., overlapping) and unique (i.e., nonoverlapping) contributions of each.

We do not commit to one interpretation of the relationship between the work and student status on the one hand, and living arrangements on the other. On the contrary, the strategy was designed to be neutral as to which is causally prior, while dealing with the obvious interrelationships between the two groups.

Overview of Analyses Used in the Following Chapters

In each of the following chapters we present central findings from several types of analysis (with complete documentation provided in Bachman, O'Malley, et al., 1996). Although basic findings are largely parallel for men and women, there are also some important differences. Accordingly, we report results separately for men and for women. Findings for the drug-use categories of cigarette smoking, alcohol use, marijuana use, and cocaine use are presented separately in chapters 4 through 7. Findings common to all of these drugs, as well as important differences among drugs, will also be discussed in chapter 8.

The following types of data are presented for each drug:

1. Percentages of users of each drug at each follow-up (based only on the classes of 1976–1981, so that cohort differences are not confounded with age-related differences). These data illustrate the basic changes that occur across the full age span, providing a complete "natural history" of role changes in this sample.

2. Percentages of users, at both base year and follow-up, engaged in each of a variety of post-high-school roles and experiences. These data indicate the overall relationship of each of the adult role statuses to mean levels of drug use. This provides a clear look at starting and ending points as a point of reference, before we move on to examining change directly.

3. Multiple regression analyses of drug use change scores controlling for key background experiences and using several groups of post-high-school roles and experiences as predictors. These provide the core inferential statistics that allow us to examine specific patterns of change in drug use in relation to specific role transitions.

4. A summary of mean drug use change scores by modal age, shown both unadjusted and after controls for other predictors in the multiple regression analyses. These results illustrate the extent to which role changes associated with age account for age-related changes in drug use.

As indicated earlier, these analyses by no means exhaust the possible approaches to analyzing such panel data on drug use. However, taken together they provide what we consider to be strong and consistent evidence of the ways in which certain experiences during young adulthood lead to important changes in the use of cigarettes, alcohol, marijuana, and cocaine.

4

Changes in Cigarette Use

Since the Surgeon General's landmark report it has been widely known that cigarette smoking is associated with a number of serious long-term health consequences, including cancer, heart disease, and stroke (Public Health Service, 1964). Cigarette smoking is also closely associated with the use of alcohol and illicit drugs, and is often described as a "gateway" drug that helps initiate young people into the culture of substance use (Kandel & Yamaguchi, 1993; Kandel, Yamaguchi, & Chen, 1992; Yamaguchi & Kandel, 1984). At the risk of stating what is obvious to everyone (with the possible exception of some tobacco company executives), tobacco is the only drug on the market that, when used as directed, may kill, and it is only the historical accident of the prior existence of large populations of addicts and moneyed interests in the tobacco industry that keep this substance on the market today.

The dangers of cigarette smoking are particularly insidious; most of the health consequences are slow, gradual, and cumulative. The immediate impact that the use of other substances may have, like drunk driving, drug overdose, or incarceration, may help persuade young people not to take such risks. The long-term consequences of cigarette use may be easier for many young people to ignore because they feel inherently invulnerable to these far-off risks (Gerber & Newman, 1989), and many young smokers believe they can quit smoking before the long-term health "bill" comes due for their smoking behavior. However, the evidence suggests that most people who begin smoking regularly in adolescence will continue to do so, regardless of their intentions to quit. For example, of those who smoked a half-pack a day or more in high school, over one-third said that they expected not to be smoking in 5 years. However, 5–6 years later, nearly 80% of those who intended to quit were still smoking a half-pack or more a day (USDHHS, 1994).

Early analyses of Monitoring the Future data pointed to the distinctiveness of cigarette use among drug-using behaviors:

Certainly, it is by far the most widespread addictive behavior among young people, which helps to explain some of our longitudinal findings. For example, we found cigarette smoking to be the most stable of the drug using behaviors analyzed here . . . and it shows no clear differential effects of post-high-school experiences. (Bachman et al., 1984, p. 644)

Those analyses dealt with changes during only the first 3 years after high school, and did not include some of the measures incorporated in the present analyses. Thus we see in this chapter that some important changes occur in cigarette use as a result of the new freedoms and responsibilities in young adulthood. However, it also remains true that cigarette use is by far the most stable of the drug-using behaviors examined in this book.

Cigarette use in the first years after high school is highly predictable from senior-year smoking patterns. After adjusting for measurement error, we estimate annual stability to be about .90 during the first year after high school and even higher (rising from about .94 to about .98) during subsequent years. Others have found similarly high stability in smoking during the transition into young adulthood (e.g., Chassin et al., 1992; Jessor et al., 1991; Newcomb & Bentler, 1988). These high stability coefficients mean that individuals who smoke during high school are very likely to continue smoking after high school, and that nonsmokers are likely to continue to be nonsmokers. However, high stability does not necessarily mean that the average *quantity* of cigarettes used remains unchanged. On the contrary, we find that the number of cigarettes smoked tends to increase during the first few years after young adults leave the constraints of high school.

Although leaving the high-school environment seems to reduce constraints on smoking, our early analyses (Bachman et al., 1984) did not provide any clear indication that some post-high-school environments are more likely than others to cause a rise in smoking rates. We did find substantial differences in rates of smoking between those who went to college and those who did not, but those patterns were firmly established before the end of high school. We thus concluded that the different rates of smoking did not result from post-high-school educational experiences; rather, we suggested that earlier educational failures may play an important role in the initiation into smoking (see Bachman, Schulenberg, et al., 1990; Schulenberg et al., 1994, for further discussion and supporting data).

Our prior findings of high stability and lack of differential change are fully consistent with the growing tendency to view cigarette use as a form of drug dependence. Based on such findings, we had little reason to expect that further exploration would reveal important shifts linked to post-high-school experiences. Although the recent analyses replicated the finding of stability, they also revealed that certain post-high-school roles and experiences do contribute to changes in smoking.

We begin this chapter with a fairly detailed look at changes in cigarette smoking during the first decade after high school. Then we examine how such changes are linked to key roles and experiences during young adulthood.

PATTERNS OF CHANGE IN CIGARETTE USE

In other publications we have reported how overall shifts in cigarette use can be linked to age, historical period (secular trends), and cohort differences (O'Malley et al., 1984, 1988a, 1988b). In addition to the age-linked rise in cigarette consumption associated with leaving high school, we found stable cohort differences; specifically, smoking rates among high-school seniors were at peak levels with the graduating classes of 1976 and 1977, then for the next several years each succeeding class had a smaller proportion of regular smokers—both as seniors and during the early years after high school. We now find that the differences between these graduating classes remain evident years later. However, this distinct downward trend extended only through the class of 1980. Throughout the 1980s and into the early 1990s the rate of smoking from one senior class to another showed only small and irregular declines (see Johnston et al., 1997), and since 1992, rates of use among high-school students have increased substantially.

These cohort differences in smoking are of considerable interest, but are not a primary focus of our present analysis effort. In this volume, we focus on individual-level change, and possible differential effects of post-high-school experiences. Some of these experiences are relatively infrequent, and thus affect only a few cases from any one senior-class follow-up sample. Accordingly, as we indicated in chapter 3, we generally pool data across multiple cohorts for analysis. The cohort differences in cigarette use noted earlier complicate the analyses of pooled data to some extent; however, the gains in accuracy and simplicity more than offset the small complications.

Rates of Daily Smoking

Figure 4.1 shows proportions of daily and half-pack or more a day smokers among graduates of the high-school classes of 1976–1981[1]—those who began the study early enough to participate for the full 13–14 year follow-up interval.[2]

---

[1]The measure of cigarette use was the following question: "How frequently have you smoked cigarettes during the past 30 days?" The response scale is included in Table A.2 in the Appendix.

[2]We limited Fig. 4.1 to the earliest cohorts to show how smoking rates shifted throughout the twenties and into the early thirties. Similar figures for later cohorts would, of course, not extend into the thirties, but would show similar rises in the first few years after high school. However, overall rates of smoking for later cohorts were somewhat lower at all ages, and such cohort differences would have distorted the change patterns shown in Fig. 4.1. Most other analyses (such as those for Fig. 4.2) include controls for cohort differences, and in such instances our practice is to include all cohorts.

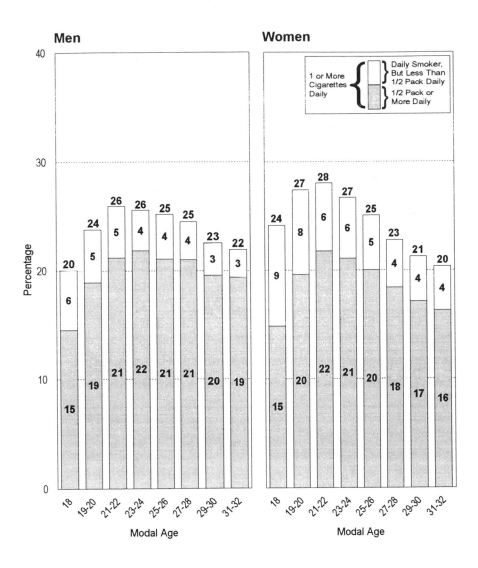

FIG. 4.1.   Percentages of panel respondents who smoked cigarettes daily. Percentages are based on base year (high-school senior) data, plus follow-ups 1–7, from classes of 1976–1981, only. In this figure, one person could contribute up to seven follow-up observations (see Analysis Issues and Strategy section in chapter 3). Approximate numbers of observations for men: 22,500, for women: 26,900. Any apparent inconsistency between data labels in the bars and cumulative percent noted is due to rounding.

Rates of smoking increased in the first few years after high school, then quickly reached the point where more than one in four young adults smoked daily and most of them smoked a half-pack or more per day. Figure 4.1 also shows that by the time they reached their late twenties and early thirties, there was some decline in proportions of smokers, especially among females. We see later in this chapter that several factors contributed to the declines in smoking rates among women in their later twenties.

Among those who had been daily smokers from their senior year onward, there still were significant increases in the quantities of cigarettes consumed after leaving high school. The average consumption for these consistent smokers had been a little more than a half-pack daily when they were seniors, but by their midtwenties their average consumption rose to a full pack among men and nearly as much among women (derived from Bachman et al., 1992).

Stability and Transitions in Daily Smoking

The largest and most stable category, with respect to daily smoking, consisted of the more than 70% who were *not* daily smokers at either senior year or follow-up; the great majority of those individuals did not smoke at all. The next largest category, comprising about 14% of the sample, consisted of those who were daily smokers at *both* senior year and follow-up. The remainder were those who made transitions into, or out of, the ranks of daily smokers.

After graduation the rate of cigarette consumption increased for many smokers. Roughly one-third of those who were daily smokers as adults had not smoked daily during their senior year. More than one-third of those who smoked a half-pack or more daily as adults had smoked less than a half-pack a day during senior year (Bachman, O'Malley, et al., 1996).

Perhaps the most interesting category of smoking transition, as well as the smallest, consists of those who ceased daily smoking sometime after high school. This group is interesting because most of them quit smoking entirely—a task that many people find very difficult. The group is also interesting because in our early analyses of change during the first years after high school, we were unable to isolate any aspect of post-high-school experience or environment that clearly contributed to quitting (Bachman et al., 1984). It is noteworthy that although only 3% of men and 4% of women in the total sample ceased daily smoking by the time of the first follow-up (1 or 2 years after high school), these percentages increased with each time interval, so that by the seventh follow-up 7% of the men and 10%

of the women had stopped daily smoking. These figures are more impressive when expressed as the proportion of those who had been daily smokers as seniors: about 20% of such daily smokers had ceased daily smoking by the first follow-up, and by the seventh follow-up the proportions had risen to 35% of the men and 43% of the women (derived from Bachman, O'Malley, et al., 1996, Table 3.1).

A similar perspective on reducing or quitting smoking is provided in Fig. 4.2, which focuses on the roughly 12% of the total sample who had reached the half-pack or more level of daily smoking before graduating from high school. The first observation prompted by Fig. 4.2 is that half-pack or more smoking did show a great deal of stability; in the first 2 years after high school about 80% of the young men and women who had been half-pack-a-day smokers in high school continued to smoke at the half-pack or more level, and fewer than 10% had quit smoking altogether. However, the second observation is that over longer time intervals the rates of quitting increased among these former half-pack-a-day smokers; by 13 or 14 years after high school, 26% of the men and 31% of the women had quit daily smoking altogether. Understandably, these quitting rates for those who smoked most heavily as seniors were somewhat lower than the rates reported in the preceding paragraph for all seniors who had been daily smokers, but it is important to note that some change did occur among even the heavier smokers. Perhaps a balanced commentary on the data in Fig. 4.2 is that the news is mostly discouraging, given that two-thirds of the women and three-fourths of the men who had been fairly heavy smokers in high school were still smokers 13–14 years later; however, some encouragement can be drawn from the fact that significant proportions of young adults apparently were able to quit entirely.[3]

ANALYSES LINKING CIGARETTE USE WITH POST-HIGH-SCHOOL EXPERIENCES

In this section we examine *before* and *after* proportions of smokers for subgroups defined in terms of post-high-school roles and living arrangements. In our preliminary analyses we looked at two different measures, or thresholds, of smoking—all those who smoke on a daily basis, and the large subset of daily smokers who consume a half-pack or more each day. The findings are closely consistent for the two measures, so we have selected the

---

[3]We must note, of course, that some individuals who quit resume smoking at a later time, so not all quitting should be viewed as permanent; nevertheless, we suggest that most of the early quitters remained nonsmokers, and Fig. 4.2 suggests that they were joined by others during succeeding years.

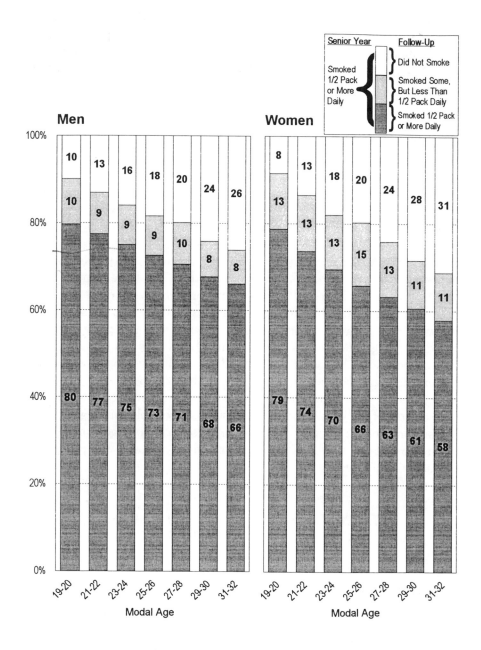

FIG. 4.2. Continuation of cigarette smoking among those who smoked a half-pack or more daily during senior year of high school. Percentages are based on follow-ups 1–7 from classes of 1976–1994, and are limited to those who as seniors smoked a half-pack or more. In this figure, one person could contribute up to seven follow-up observations (see Analysis Issues and Strategy section in chapter 3). Approximate numbers of observations for men: 5,700, for women: 7,300.

more serious half-pack or more threshold as the focus of our commentary, and for display in Figs. 4.3–4.8. In our reporting in this section we also take into account the bivariate and multivariate change scores for total amount of cigarette use, as shown in Table A.5 in the Appendix. With respect to smoking, these several forms of analysis generally lead to similar conclusions; however, the multivariate results substantially expand our ability to offer causal interpretations.

Student Status Related to Cigarette Use

Half-pack or more smoking rates were far lower among college students compared with their age-mates (modal ages 19–22) who did not go on to college, as can be seen in Fig. 4.3. The figure also shows that this pattern of differences was clearly in evidence before the end of high school. It is worth adding that our ongoing studies of 12th graders, as well as our more recent studies of 8th and 10th graders, consistently show daily smoking rates about two to three times higher among those who do not expect to complete 4 years of college compared with those who do; the differences are even larger with respect to smoking at the rate of a half-pack or more daily (Johnston et al., 1997).

High-school grades, educational aspirations, college attendance, and other factors related to educational success are related to cigarette use; these relationships have been examined extensively in other reports based on Monitoring the Future panel data (Bachman, Schulenberg, et al., 1990; Schulenberg et al., 1994). That earlier work led us to conclude that the link between actual college attendance and low smoking rates is primarily indirect, reflecting three relationships that are more fundamental: (a) most individuals who attend college were academically successful in high school, (b) such individuals are unlikely to be regular smokers during high school, and (c) nonsmokers are unlikely to take up the habit after high-school graduation.

Employment Status Related to Cigarette Use

Figure 4.4 shows half-pack smoking rates, both during high school and afterward, for various employment categories using the full set of panel responses (i.e., all seven follow-ups are included).

Full-Time Civilian Employment.   Although those employed full-time in civilian jobs showed some increase in proportion of half-pack smokers

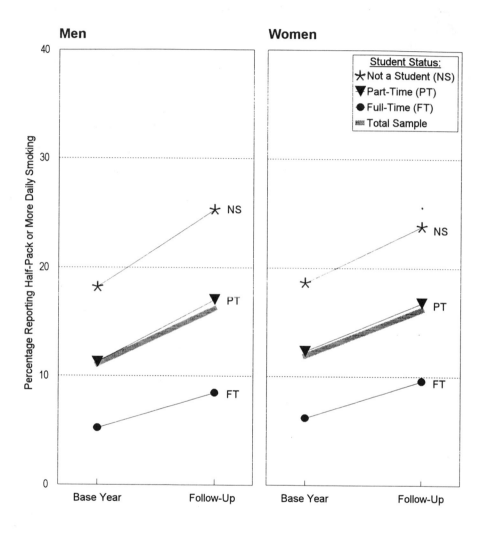

Men   **Women**

Student Status:
✳ Not a Student (NS)
▼ Part-Time (PT)
● Full-Time (FT)
▨ Total Sample

FIG. 4.3. Half-pack or more daily smoking related to student status at time of follow-up. Percentages based on follow-ups 1 and 2.(modal ages 19–22, only), from classes of 1976–1994. In this figure, one person could contribute up to two follow-up observations (see Analysis Issues and Strategy section in chapter 3). Approximate numbers of observations for men: 20,600, for women: 25,100.

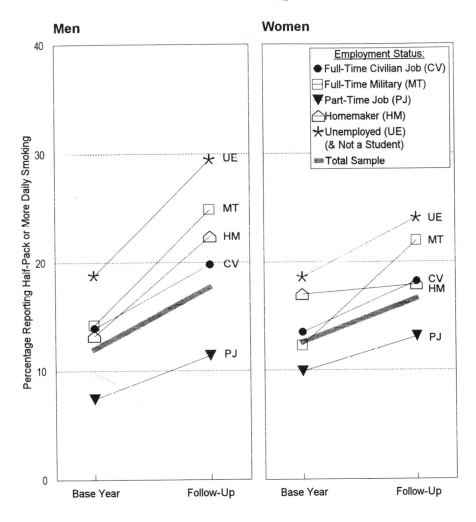

FIG. 4.4. Half-pack or more daily smoking related to employment status at time of follow-up. Percentages based on follow-ups 1–7, from classes of 1976–1994. In this figure, one person could contribute up to seven follow-up observations (see Analysis Issues and Strategy section in chapter 3). Approximate numbers of observations for men: 47,400, for women: 57,900.

compared with high school use, Fig. 4.4 shows that the increases were only about 5 or 6 percentage points. Larger increases occurred for several other categories of post-high-school experience.

Part-Time Employment. Part-time employment occurred most frequently during the first two follow-ups, as shown earlier in Table 3.1, and most of those reporting part-time employment were also full-time college students. Thus, we can expect the data for part-time employees to look a good deal like the data for full-time students, and a comparison between Figs. 4.3 and 4.4 reveals that is the case. Those in part-time employment were less likely to be smokers both before and after leaving high school. The trend lines are not quite as low as those for full-time students, but this is consistent with the fact that not all of the part-time employees were also full-time students.

Military Service. Those who entered military service were more likely than the college-bound to have been smokers before they left high school; moreover, being in the service was linked with greater than average increases in proportion of half-pack smokers (see Fig. 4.4). The bivariate and multivariate regression analyses shown in Appendix Table A.5 revealed much the same pattern; men in the military had smoking increases almost twice as large as the total male sample, and women in the military had increases more than three times those for the total female sample. Multivariate controls for background, marital status, parenthood, and other aspects of living arrangements produced virtually no change in these relationships between military service and smoking; therefore, it seems highly likely that being in the service played some fairly direct role in these greater than average increases in smoking rates.

Homemakers. Figure 4.4 shows that young women who identified themselves as full-time homemakers were less likely than other nonstudents to increase smoking rates. Based on all of our regression analyses, including those reported in Appendix Table A.5, the most parsimonious interpretation is that this finding occurred not because there is something special about the role of homemaker per se which inhibits smoking, but rather because these women were in most cases married and often also parents, pregnant, or both.

Interestingly, Fig. 4.4 shows that for the very small number of *men* who identified themselves as homemakers, proportions of half-pack smokers increased fairly markedly. These individuals are highly atypical, representing only about 0.3% of all male respondents; accordingly, we are very cautious about drawing any conclusions about this category of male post-high-school experience.

Unemployment. Figure 4.4 shows that those unemployed at the time of follow-up were more likely than average to have been half-pack smokers before they left high school. Despite their presumably restricted income, the unemployed men also showed slightly larger than average increases in rates of half-pack smoking, although in multivariate analyses that modest relationship was reduced by controls for background, living arrangements, and so forth (see Table A.5 in the Appendix), and was not large enough to be statistically significant.

Living Arrangements and Marital Status Related to Cigarette Use

We chose to combine marital status with the other five categories of living arrangements because our primary interest is with the interpersonal aspects of living arrangements. Among all six categories, being married (and thus living with a spouse) is likely to be the most permanent. It is also arguably the most important in terms of the depth and breadth of interpersonal relationship involved.

Being Married. Marital status is an important correlate of changes in alcohol and illicit drug use—behaviors that for most young adults are heavily influenced by social situations. But how does marital status relate to changes in cigarette smoking, a behavior that, by young adulthood, generally reflects dependence more than the impacts of social situations? Figure 4.5 shows that married men were slightly less likely than average to have become initiated into half-pack smoking after high school, and married women were also less likely. Moreover, the average numbers of cigarettes consumed by married men in our samples were only very slightly higher than their average consumption when they had been high-school seniors, and among married women the average numbers consumed were actually slightly lower than when they had been seniors (based on data in Table A.5 in the Appendix).

The multivariate regression analyses reveal that controlling background and other factors left the "marriage effect" on smoking virtually unchanged among women, and actually enhanced it among men (see Table A.5). It thus seems likely that some aspects of being married led to modest reductions in smoking rates among both women and men—in addition to any impacts of pregnancy noted later.

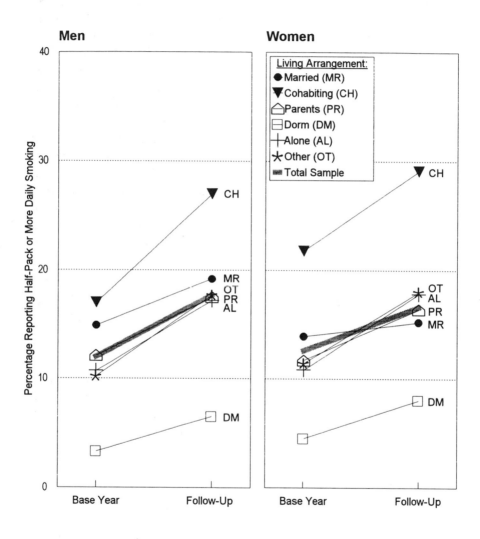

FIG. 4.5. Half-pack or more daily smoking related to living arrangement at time of follow-up. Percentages based on follow-ups 1–7, from classes of 1976–1994. In this figure, one person could contribute up to seven follow-up observations (see Analysis Issues and Strategy section in chapter 3). Approximate numbers of observations for men: 47,400, for women: 57,900.

Cohabiting.   Individuals who indicated in the follow-up questionnaire that they were living with a partner of the opposite sex were the group most likely to have been half-pack or more smokers before they left high school, as can be seen in Fig. 4.5. Among those who did not smoke at that level when they were seniors, cohabitation was associated with an increased likelihood of initiating half-pack smoking (Bachman, O'Malley, et al., 1996).

Contrasting these findings with those for marriage, Fig. 4.5 shows, especially for women, that cohabitants tended to be somewhat different individuals before leaving high school (i.e., more likely to be smokers), and that they were also more likely to increase their smoking after high school. The multivariate regression analyses controlling background and other factors (Table A.5) left the "cohabitation effect" on smoking virtually unchanged among both men and women. It thus appears, at least with respect to smoking, that cohabitation and marriage are not closely parallel living arrangements. These findings support a selection theory for cohabitation consistent with previous research suggesting that those with nontraditional beliefs and behavior (including drug use) are more likely to cohabit outside of legal marriage as young adults.

Living With Parents.   Those living with parents at the time of follow-up showed essentially average levels of change in cigarette use, as can be seen in Fig. 4.5 and Table A.5.

Living in a Dormitory.   Figure 4.5 shows what could be anticipated based on the findings already shown for full-time students—those living in dormitories were very unlikely to have been half-pack smokers (or any kind of smokers, for that matter) while in high school. Moreover, the figure shows that among dormitory residents there were relatively few recruits into the ranks of half-pack-a-day smokers.

Living Alone and Other Living Arrangements.   Among those not in one of the previous four living arrangements, we further distinguished between those living alone and those in all other living arrangements. The latter typically were living in apartments or houses shared with several others, but the category also includes most of those in military service (i.e., those living in barracks, shared off-base housing, etc.). With respect to changes in cigarette smoking, the two categories were quite similar, as shown in Fig. 4.5 and Table A.5; they were a bit more likely than average to increase their smoking after high school.

Pregnancy and Parenthood Related to Cigarette Use

The Monitoring the Future follow-up questionnaires include measures of both pregnancy and parenthood. Obviously, these two life experiences are closely related. For example, if a woman was motivated to quit smoking because of pregnancy or impending pregnancy, that could be considered a "pregnancy effect." But if she continued as a nonsmoker after giving birth, thus making her a nonsmoking parent, should that be considered a "parenthood effect"? Well, that depends. In fact, many women in that situation may not themselves be able to assess accurately the extent to which the continued nonsmoking was due to (a) the new role and responsibilities of parent, or (b) the desire to maintain nonsmoking once the added motivation of pregnancy made it possible to quit (with the latter perhaps characterized as a "longer term pregnancy effect"). We harbor no illusions that survey research, even with long-term panel data such as ours, can be counted on to disentangle such complexities. Often we must acknowledge that several causal patterns remain inextricably confounded.

Pregnancy.   Among all factors we have studied, pregnancy stands out most clearly and consistently as likely to cause a decline in smoking. Proportions of smokers in every subgroup in Figs. 4.3–4.5 either increased or remained essentially unchanged, but the proportion of smokers among pregnant women actually decreased. Figure 4.6 shows a modest drop in proportion of half-pack smokers among pregnant women; the proportion of all daily smokers dropped more substantially—from 22% to 14%. Analyses of transition patterns reveal that pregnant women were much more likely than average to stop smoking, or at least to reduce to less than daily smoking or less than a half-pack daily (Bachman, O'Malley, et al., 1996). For men, on the other hand, Fig. 4.6 suggests no impact of their spouse's pregnancy on their own smoking behavior.

We noted earlier that pregnancy effects might be confounded with parenthood effects. It also should be noted that most pregnant women surveyed were married, thus opening up the possibility of a further confounding with the modest marriage effect described previously. The multivariate analyses reported in Appendix Table A.5 do show that when marriage and parenthood, as well as background factors, are included in the equation, the pregnancy effects are reduced—but only slightly. It remains true that pregnancy is linked with a reduction in women's smoking fully twice as large as the reduction associated with being married (see Table A.5). It also remains true that having a pregnant spouse shows no impact on men's smoking.

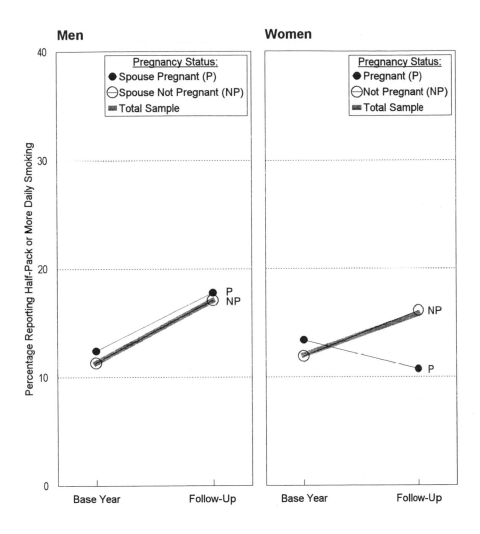

FIG. 4.6. Half-pack or more daily smoking related to pregnancy status at time of follow-up. Percentages based on follow-ups 1–7, from classes of 1976–1994. The pregnancy item was not added to the follow-up questionnaire until 1984. In this figure, one person could contribute up to six follow-up observations (see Analysis Issues and Strategy section in chapter 3). Approximate numbers of observations for men: 39,300, for women: 48,400.

Summarizing our findings regarding pregnancy (including those reported in Bachman, O'Malley, et al., 1996), we can say that (a) many of the pregnant women who had been regular smokers during high school were able to stop, or at least substantially reduce, their use of cigarettes; (b) this effect seems entirely independent of student and employment status, and largely independent of background and marital status; and (c) this reduction in cigarette use is quite specific, holding for pregnant women but not their husbands. These findings strongly suggest a primary influence of individual health-related choices, rather than general contextual influences of living arrangements.

In recent years it has been widely publicized that cigarette use by pregnant women can have adverse consequences for their fetuses, and this concern for unborn children appears to have provided the motivation for large numbers of young women to do something that is very difficult for most smokers. For many of these women, the reduction or cessation of smoking is only temporary, and the habit is resumed after pregnancy. However, as we see next, motherhood also is associated with reduced smoking, and it seems likely that at least a portion of any "motherhood effect" is actually a longer term effect of reduced smoking during pregnancy. In contrast to these effects among women, it is somewhat disappointing to note the lack of change among men with pregnant wives, despite widespread media coverage of the threats posed by secondhand smoke.

Parenthood.   Most parents in our sample were married, but a significant minority were not. We consider the social environments of married and unmarried parents to be considerably different, especially in the case of unmarried fathers who often do not live with their children. Accordingly, our regression analyses involving parenthood employed three categories: married parent, unmarried parent, and nonparent.

Our bivariate regression analyses (see Table A.5) showed that being a married mother was associated with some decline in smoking, and the multivariate regression analyses indicated that most but not all of this was attributable to being married. Being a married father was not, however, associated with any significant differential change in smoking. Mothers who were unmarried at the time of the follow-up showed greater than average increases in smoking rates, and the same was true to a greater extent among unmarried fathers.

A separate analysis of Monitoring the Future data, which focused specifically on 2-year change intervals in which respondents made the transition from nonparent to parent, also showed that *prior* rates of smoking were distinctly higher than average among those who became unmarried mothers, and the same was true for those who became unmarried fathers. That analysis also showed no differential changes among men in smoking during the 2-year interval in which they went from nonparent to parent, and the only differential decline among women occurred in those who went from single to married during the same 2-year interval (Bachman et al., 1997).

It is of interest that the findings for unmarried parents are similar to the patterns we noted earlier for unmarried cohabitants. Within both categories, high-school smoking rates had been distinctly higher than average. The fact that these groups had more smokers to begin with may be one of the factors underlying their large increases in change scores, because increases occur primarily among those who had smoked—at least to some extent—during high school. Of course, both categories also tend to include individuals who feel less constrained by social strictures against sex outside of marriage; perhaps this reflects general tendencies to disregard social constraints and to take risks, which may also be a factor in cigarette smoking. Because smoking behavior is initiated at an earlier (younger) developmental stage, it becomes to some extent a predictor of such events as cohabitation and single parenthood. (Smoking is also a predictor of divorce, as we note later, and this no doubt accounts for some of the association between smoking and single parenthood.)

Further Findings on Marital Status and Cigarette Use

Earlier separate analyses of Monitoring the Future panel data, which focused on 4-year patterns of change in marital status, enabled us to examine the marriage effect noted earlier in greater detail (Bachman et al., 1997). Those analyses revealed small declines in proportions of cigarette users occurring during the specific 2-year interval (between follow-up measurements) in which respondents changed from being single to being married. Those findings, although quite modest, lend further support to our interpretation that some aspect(s) of marriage can cause at least a few smokers to reduce or cease their use of cigarettes.

Engagement. Additional findings from the 4-year pattern analyses strengthen and extend the notion of a marriage effect. One such finding emerged when we examined transitions from single to engaged (2 years later) to married (2 years after that). We found small declines in proportions of smokers that roughly paralleled those involved in transitions from single to married, except that the declines were spread roughly equally across the 4-year interval (Bachman et al., 1997, Fig. 2). Those results for smoking, along with parallel results for use of alcohol (see Fig. 3.7 in the previous chapter) and use of other drugs, prompted us to include engagement status as a variable in our regression analyses. The results for cigarette use, included in Table A.5, suggest a modest "engagement effect" on smoking, with other factors controlled, in the same direction as the marriage effect. Among women the effect was slightly smaller than the marriage effect, whereas among men the engagement effect was less than half as large as the marriage effect and fell short of statistical significance.[4]

The relationships involving engagement are quite different from those for cohabitation—cohabitation was associated with greater than average increases in smoking, whereas the opposite was true for engagement. Because engaged couples often cohabit at some point prior to marriage, it is of interest to consider the effects of these two experiences jointly—especially given the fact that our regression analysis approach treats the two factors as additive (i.e., noninteractive). Figure 4.7 displays smoking data for the four possible combinations of cohabitation and engagement, along with data for married respondents—a very important comparison group. Focusing first on cohabitants, we can see that engaged cohabitants were slightly less likely than nonengaged cohabitants to have been half-pack or more smokers as high-school seniors, and they were slightly less likely to have become so at the time of follow-up. Among noncohabitants, the figure shows that among women, engagement is associated with a lowered likelihood of becoming (or remaining) a half-pack smoker. These findings in Fig. 4.7 thus confirm and extend our notions of a small engagement effect on smoking. They also show little in the way of interactions that would complicate interpretation of our regression analyses.

Divorce. The analyses of 4-year change patterns (Bachman et al., 1997) also included the first use of Monitoring the Future data to examine possible impacts of divorce on drug use. Several findings emerged linking cigarette use and divorce. First, proportions of smokers rose during the 2-year interval

---

[4]The reader who examines the data for engagement in Table A.5 will note that the *bivariate* coefficient is virtually zero for women, and for men it is actually in the opposite direction from the multivariate coefficient. An "unmasking" occurs when other factors are included in the multivariate equations, because at that point the distinction between those who are married and those who are not married is taken into account. In other words, when engaged individuals are compared with *all* others (about half of whom are married, and half of whom are not), there is little overall difference in smoking change data. However, in the multivariate analyses the engaged individuals are contrasted with other *single* individuals who are not engaged, and that accounts for the unmasking.

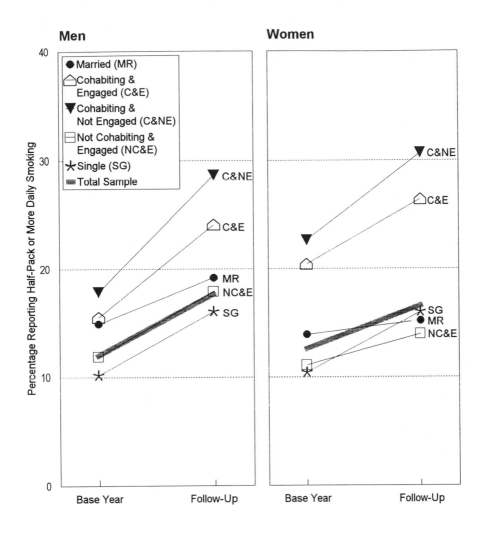

Men

Women

FIG. 4.7. Half-pack or more daily smoking related to engagement, cohabitation, and marriage at time of follow-up. Percentages based on follow-ups 1–7, from classes of 1976–1994. In this figure, one person could contribute up to seven follow-up observations (see Analysis Issues and Strategy section in chapter 3). Approximate numbers of observations for men: 47,400, for women: 57,900.

in which respondents went from married to divorced, and among women the increases generally equaled or exceeded the declines associated with going from single to married. In other words, the "divorce effect" rather neatly canceled the marriage effect among women. Incidentally, this canceling out is also why we chose not to include divorce in the multivariate analyses of change scores; change in opposite directions with marriage and then divorce leads to essentially zero change when divorce is considered as a separate variable.

In order to examine the impacts of divorce in the present analyses, we carried out additional tabulations that are reported in Fig. 4.8 (and comparable figures in later chapters). The key distinction between this figure and Figs. 4.2–4.7 is that Fig. 4.8 takes a different starting point and measures change over a 2-year interval. For analyses of divorce, it would be of little value to show transitions between senior year of high school and the follow-up, because we could not highlight the particular 2-year interval in which divorce occurred; moreover, we could not examine the transition from divorced to (re)married. Thus, in Fig. 4.8 we focus on 2-year intervals (from any of the first six follow-ups to the next follow-up). The figure shows transitions into and out of divorce, as well as those who were divorced at both points. (Figure 4.8 also displays the other transitions in marital status, now shown in terms of 2-year intervals; consistent with the findings in previous figures, we see marriage and engagement effects that are small for women and very small for men.)

Figure 4.8 clearly shows that, among both men and women, becoming divorced is associated with an increased likelihood of becoming a half-pack or more daily smoker, and becoming remarried is associated with a corresponding decrease. Moreover, remaining divorced at both times is associated with a consistently high rate of half-pack smoking (about 39% among the men, and about 35% among the women). The figure also shows that smoking rates were far above average among those men and women who would later divorce; thus, smoking is a predictor of divorce. This evidence is not adequate to demonstrate that smoking actually increases the likelihood of divorce, although some such causal impact is not altogether implausible. Rather, we think that the bulk of the relationship between smoking and divorce reflects patterns of behavior with much earlier origins. We have already noted here and elsewhere (Schulenberg et al., 1994) that smoking is often part of a long-standing syndrome of behavior which includes poor grades in high school and low likelihood of attending college. It seems plausible that individuals with such characteristics may also be more prone to divorce.

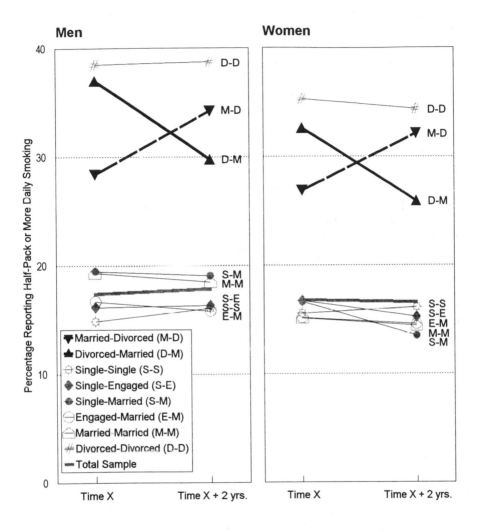

FIG. 4.8. Half-pack or more daily smoking related to transitions in marital status. Percentages based on follow-ups 1–7, from classes of 1976–1994. Observations are drawn from two consecutive follow-ups, providing measures at two points in time that cover an interval of 2 years. That is, observations are based on individuals' data from follow-ups 1 and 2, follow-ups 2 and 3, follow-ups 3 and 4, and so forth. Note that an individual who participated in all seven follow-ups would contribute six observations. Approximate numbers of observations for men: 32,400, for women: 41,200.

CONCLUSIONS FROM MULTIVARIATE ANALYSES LINKING CIGARETTE USE WITH POST-HIGH-SCHOOL EXPERIENCES

The multivariate analyses linking smoking and post-high-school experiences are detailed in the Appendix, Table A.5, and some key findings have already been noted in the descriptive analyses reported earlier. In this section we summarize those findings, and consider the extent to which relationships appear to be unique or overlapping.

In later chapters we find it useful to present charts illustrating in some detail the ways in which multivariate relationships involving alcohol use or marijuana use differ from the corresponding bivariate relationships. In the present chapter, however, there are relatively few such differences, and those that we consider important have already been noted. Accordingly, we can limit this section to a summary of key multivariate findings.

The most general multivariate finding has just been mentioned: Most of the effects discussed in this chapter were nonoverlapping, or nearly so. One interesting, albeit rather obvious, exception involves women who reported their work status as "full-time homemaker." Female homemakers constitute the only category of employment experience that did not show some overall increase in smoking rates after high school. However, the multivariate analyses showed no such "homemaker effect" remaining once other factors such as marital status, pregnancy, and parenthood were included as predictors in multivariate regression analyses (Table A.5). The multivariate analyses also revealed that much of any "married mother" effect is attributable to other factors, such as marriage, rather than motherhood.

Explained Variance

Table A.5, as well as the other tables in the Appendix, includes summary R-squared values indicating the amounts of variance explained. We use these primarily to examine the overall impacts of different sets of predictors. In the case of cigarette use, the values in Table A.5 indicate also that our measures of post-high-school experience explain very little of the variance in the cigarette use change scores. The limited amount of explained variance is not surprising when we recall the very high degree of stability in cigarette use. Most individuals who were regular smokers in high school remained smokers; although there was a widespread increase in numbers of cigarettes consumed after leaving the constraints of high school, those who had smoked most heavily in high school generally continued to do so in subsequent years, those who smoked at intermediate levels continued to do so, and so on. Moreover, we must keep in mind that some of the "change" in our change scores actually reflects only random measurement error. We estimate that the measurement errors for reports of cigarette use are lower than the errors for reports of other drug use (O'Malley et al., 1983); nevertheless, against the backdrop of relatively little real change, these errors may make up a relatively large proportion of the overall variance in change scores.

Table A.5 shows that all of the background measures taken together capture less than half of one percent of the variance in our change scores for smoking. That is, in fact, reassuring, because a primary purpose of using change scores in these analyses is to make each individual his or her own control. In other words, the use of change scores should cancel out consistent effects of background factors—and our analyses suggest that they do, at least with respect to cigarette use. Incidentally, our descriptive findings reported earlier in this chapter, as well as other analyses of the Monitoring the Future data (e.g., Bachman, O'Malley, et al., 1996; Schulenberg et al., 1994) show that if we focus not on change scores but on levels of smoking in high school (or afterward), we see substantial relationships involving such background factors as grades and college plans. That is, background factors were powerful predictors of differences in mean levels of smoking, but did not predict change.

The measures of student and work status add very little in the way of explained variance in the change scores for smoking—only about 0.2% of variance above and beyond the small amount explainable by background factors. That is not surprising in light of the lack of relationships reported earlier. The one rather substantial relationship had to do with military service, but this involved a small proportion of men and a far smaller proportion of women, and thus could not be expected to make much contribution to total variance explained.

The measures of marital status, living arrangements, pregnancy, and parenthood explained an additional half percent of the variance in cigarette use among men, but nearly three times that much among women. We can note two factors that contribute to the male–female differences. First, we found substantial declines in smoking among pregnant women, but no such declines for men with a pregnant spouse. Second, more women than men were married at any given follow-up, so (other things being equal) the overall impact of the marriage effect on explained variance should be a bit larger for women.

· Accounting for Age-Related Changes in Cigarette Use

Figure 4.1 showed that rates of daily smoking and half-pack or more daily smoking increased somewhat among both men and women during the first several years after high school, and thereafter continued largely unchanged among men, but eventually declined somewhat among women. Figure 4.9 presents a different look at changes across time in cigarette use, this time plotting mean changes in cigarette consumption rather than proportions of daily smokers. More importantly, the figure presents the mean change scores both unadjusted and adjusted for all of the factors included in our multi-variate regression analyses in Table A.5.

Why do rates of smoking increase after young people leave high school? Are there things about most post-high-school experiences that tend to encourage increased amounts of cigarette consumption? An alternative question may be more to the point: Is there something about the typical high-school environment that constrains young smokers from consuming as many cigarettes as they might wish? Clearly there is. Virtually all high schools have rules not only against students smoking in school but also against stepping out of school buildings for a smoke between classes. An increasing proportion of colleges, universities, and workplaces also have "smoke-free" buildings; however, individuals in these settings are generally free to step outside from time to time to take a cigarette break. In other words, it is likely that many high-school smokers would prefer to consume more cigarettes per day than they do, and the rather abrupt increase in consumption after graduation reflects the reduction or removal of situational constraints. One implication of this line of thinking is that if the trend toward smoke-free workplaces continues, the progression to higher levels of consumption after high school may be reduced to at least some extent.

Other factors that might contribute to an increase in the amount of smoking after high school include more time spent away from the parental home (some parents probably inhibit their minor children's smoking in their presence or in their home), and an increased amount of funds being available for purchasing cigarettes. However, we found little indication that changes in living arrangements made a substantial difference in smoking rates, nor that becoming employed full time (presumably increasing available funds) made a substantial difference.

Turning now to the age-related decline among women during their late twenties and early thirties, Fig. 4.9 shows that much of it is removed when other factors are held constant. In other words, much of those declines can be attributed to factors such as marriage, pregnancy, and parenthood, which involve increasing proportions of women during those later years. For men, by way of contrast, the age-related declines were smaller, and adjustments for other factors had virtually no impact.

Finally, however, we note that Fig. 4.9 does show some declines among men at the end of their twenties and into their thirties; it also shows some

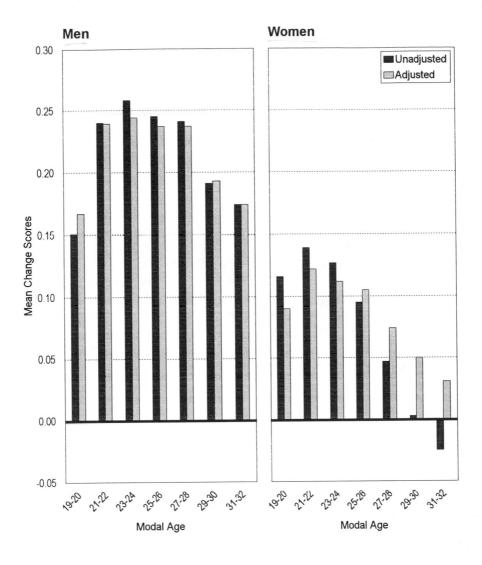

FIG. 4.9. Mean change scores in 30-day cigarette use, unadjusted and adjusted, related to modal age. The mean change score is the predicted amount of change in 30-day cigarette use between base year and modal age indicated. The unadjusted mean change score controls only the follow-up survey interval (or, modal age). The adjusted mean change score controls all the predictor variables. Positive change scores indicate an increase in use over time, and negative scores indicate a decrease. Calculation of change scores is discussed in detail in the Appendix.

declines among women that are not attributable to marriage, pregnancy, and parenthood. How might these declines be explained? Several factors are probably involved. One is that as time passes, more and more smokers are successful at quitting permanently. (Most smokers indicate that they would like to quit.) Another factor is that there may be increased motivation to quit, due to (a) manifest health problems such as "smoker's" cough or shortness of breath, (b) a recognition that continuing to smoke raises the odds of eventual health consequences, and (c) the high costs of the habit.

5

Changes in Alcohol Use

Among all of the drugs examined in the Monitoring the Future study, alcohol is by far the most widely used. Nearly all high-school seniors and young adults have tried alcohol at least once. Although the proportions declined during the 1980s and early 1990s, nearly two-thirds of all seniors in the classes of 1976–1994 (the classes included in these analyses) were "current" users—that is, they had used alcohol at least once during the month prior to the survey (Johnston et al., 1997). The proportions of young people who reported *any* use during the past month increased during the first years after high school; moreover, the *frequency* of use (i.e., number of occasions in the past month), especially among men, also rose during the post-high-school years.

It is hardly surprising to find alcohol use increasing during young adulthood. After all, the purchase of alcohol becomes legal during the first few years after high school. Also, as we see in this chapter, changes in living arrangements during the early adult years can contribute to increased use. Nevertheless, most young adult drinkers in our surveys reported drinking only once or twice per week. If this frequency of use involved only one or two drinks per occasion, there would be little reason for concern. In fact, however, many of the occasions involved five or more drinks, and such instances of heavier use are worrisome. One reason for concern is long-term consequences; as we have recently shown, some individuals continue or increase heavy use during the transition to young adulthood, and this carries risks of serious health problems (Schulenberg, O'Malley, et al., 1996; Schulenberg, Wadsworth, et al., 1996). Another more immediate reason for concern is that heavy use, however often it occurs, is likely to produce at least short-term impairment and thus dramatically increase the likelihood of a variety of undesirable outcomes—accidental injuries, vandalism and other criminal behavior, violent behavior, risky sexual behavior, rape, drowning, fires, and of course, automobile-related deaths and injuries.

Post-high-school usage rates for alcohol, including frequency of heavy use, are fairly predictable from senior-year drinking patterns. Taking account

77

of measurement reliability, we estimate annual stability to be about .85–.89 during the first year after high school, and then it rises gradually from about .90 to .95 during subsequent years. These estimates are impressively high, suggesting that much of post-high-school drinking behavior is influenced by factors present before the end of senior year, many of which continue to exert influence through young adulthood. Nevertheless, a good deal of room for change remains, especially over spans of several years or more.[1] Compared with cigarette consumption, for example, nearly twice as much variance in alcohol use is *not* interpretable in terms of senior-year use and related factors.

What kinds of experiences in the post-high-school years are likely to affect alcohol consumption? Our earlier analyses of Monitoring the Future data, based on follow-up questionnaires collected 1 to 3 years after graduation, revealed some important impacts of marital status and other aspects of living arrangements (Bachman et al., 1984). Our present analyses permit us to explore such relationships over a much longer period, and also to examine a number of additional factors. Before looking at the impacts of these post-high-school experiences, however, it will be useful to review overall changes in alcohol use during young adulthood.

PATTERNS OF CHANGE IN ALCOHOL USE

Extensive analyses using the full Monitoring the Future cohort-sequential design for the years 1976 through 1986 revealed no *cohort differences* in alcohol use, very small *period effects* (secular trends), and somewhat larger *age effects* (O'Malley et al., 1988a, 1988b). In those analyses, the period effects consisted of declines in monthly use of alcohol, and in instances of heavy drinking, beginning about 1980. More recent reports have documented continuing and somewhat steeper declines during the later 1980s and the beginning of the 1990s, with the largest declines evident among the youngest age strata—ages 18–22 (Johnston et al., 1997); some, but not all, of these changes were due to the fact that many states increased the minimum drinking age to 21 (O'Malley & Wagenaar, 1991).

The age-related differences in alcohol use are of particular interest for our present analysis effort. We describe them in detail in the next section, then later we consider to what extent these changes are related to other post-high-school experiences.

---

[1]For example, we estimate 10-year stabilities for both alcohol measures, from modal age 18 (senior year of high school) to modal age 28, as roughly .50.

Rates of Alcohol Use and Heavy Drinking

Figure 5.1 shows that the majority of young adults continued to be at least occasional drinkers.[2] The proportions shown in Fig. 5.1 are based on the graduates of the high-school classes of 1976–1981—those who were able to participate for the full 13–14 year follow-up period.[3] Among men, the proportions who reported any use of alcohol in the past month were 81% among those at the first follow-up (modal ages 19–20), then rose to 85% at ages 21–22, and remained much the same for several years until declining modestly to 76% by ages 31–32. Among women the rates were slightly lower than among men initially—74% at ages 19–20, rising to 76% at ages 21–22; then proportions of current users dropped fairly steadily, reaching 64% at ages 31–32.

The data in Fig. 5.1 include proportions who reported that on one or more occasions during the preceding 2 weeks they had consumed five or more drinks in a row (with a drink defined as a glass of wine, or a shot of liquor, or a bottle of beer), and it can be seen that among men roughly half or more of all who reported any use in the past month also reported at least one instance of heavy use during the past 2 weeks.[4] Thus, although most of these young men were only occasional drinkers, many of them were occasional *heavy* drinkers. Rates were somewhat lower among women, although we must observe that the five-drink criterion represents a somewhat heavier level of drinking for the average woman than the average man, given average male–female differences in body weight and metabolism of alcohol.[5]

Figure 5.1 shows that instances of heavy drinking dropped off among both men and women throughout their twenties. Among men, proportions declined from more than half (55% at ages 21–22) to just over one-third (36% at ages 31–32). The drop was even more pronounced among women,

---

[2]The measure of current (monthly) alcohol use was the following question: "On how many occasions have you had alcoholic beverages to drink during the last 30 days?" The response scale is included in Table A.2 in the Appendix.

[3]When we focus on the earliest cohorts and track them across time, we capture not only age-related differences but also the moderate secular trend noted earlier. The results, however, are only slightly different from what we observe for the total sample (as documented in Bachman, O'Malley, et al., 1996).

[4]The measure of heavy drinking was based on the following question: "Think back over the last 2 weeks. How many times have you had five or more drinks in a row? (A 'drink' is a glass of wine, a bottle of beer, a shot glass of liquor, or a mixed drink.)" The response scale is included in Table A.2 in the Appendix.

[5]If detailed data on amounts of alcohol consumed were combined with measures of body weight, and if other sex differences in metabolism of alcohol were taken into account, one could develop a more refined and less biased sex comparison for heavy drinking (e.g., see Wechsler, Dowdall, Davenport, & Rimm, 1995). Such refinement is not fully feasible with the available data; fortunately, this does not represent a serious problem, because our primary emphasis is on *changes* in drug use—including heavy drinking.

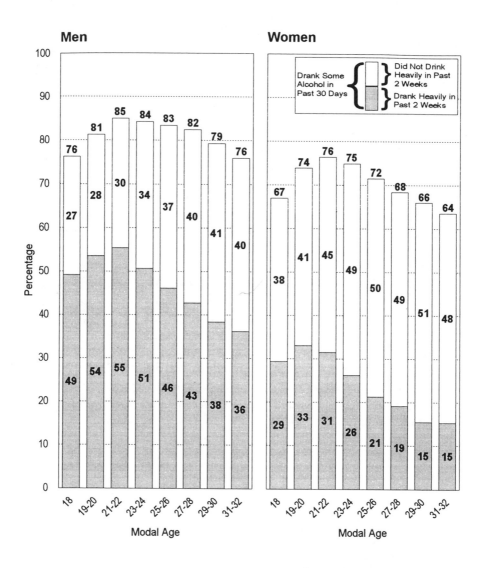

FIG. 5.1. Percentages of panel respondents who used alcohol in the past 30 days. "Heavy" alcohol use is defined as having five or more drinks in a row. Percentages are based on base-year (high-school senior) data, plus follow-ups 1–7, from classes of 1976–1981, only. In this figure, one person could contribute up to seven follow-up observations (see Analysis Issues and Strategy section in chapter 3). Approximate numbers of observations for men: 21,500, for women: 25,600. Any apparent inconsistency between data labels in the bars and cumulative percent noted is due to rounding.

from one-third (33% at ages 19–20) to less than half that many (15% at ages 31–32). These age-related declines during young adulthood are of considerable interest, because this "heavy use" measure, in contrast to the "current use" measure, is a less ambiguous indicator of problem behavior—behavior that can involve significant risks and that is fairly widely disapproved.[6] Nevertheless, as we recently have shown, there are identifiable groups of young people who maintained or increased their frequency of heavy drinking from adolescence through young adulthood. For example, between the ages of 18 and 24, 12% of the men and 3% of the women engaged in heavy drinking at a constant rate of about twice a week (i.e., 3–5 times per 2-week period), and 14% of the men and 7% of the women increased their rate from almost none at age 18 to nearly twice a week at ages 23–24 (Schulenberg, O'Malley, et al., 1996). In contrast to those who engage in heavy drinking intermittently or even consistently for only a year or two, these chronic and increasing heavy drinkers are likely to be dependent on alcohol and may well be on the path to alcoholism.

ANALYSES LINKING CURRENT AND HEAVY ALCOHOL USE WITH POST-HIGH-SCHOOL EXPERIENCES

We next examine "before" and "after" proportions of drinkers for various categories of post-high-school experience, looking both at proportions of current drinkers (those who reported any use in the past month) and at proportions who reported any "heavy" use (one or more instances of five or more drinks in a row during the past 2 weeks).

Student Status Related to Alcohol Use

We have reported elsewhere that college students show greater than average increases in alcohol use in general, and also in instances of heavy drinking (Johnston et al., 1997; Schulenberg et al., 1994; Schulenberg, O'Malley, et al., 1996). This can be seen to a slight extent in Fig. 5.2, and to a greater extent in Fig. 5.3, both of which compare college students with their age-mates (modal ages 19–22).

---

[6]Establishing concepts such as "heavy drinking" or "problem drinking" in any comprehensive fashion would be complex, almost surely controversial, and in any case outside the scope of the present monograph. We do, however, see our measure of five or more drinks in a row as a useful *indicator* of such behavior patterns, and we have chosen as a matter of convenience to refer to it as a measure of heavy drinking—or as a measure of *instances* of heavy drinking. In some of our previous analyses (Schulenberg, O'Malley, et al., 1996; Schulenberg, Wadsworth, et al., 1996), we labeled this *binge drinking*, a term used by others in the literature (e.g., Kusserow, 1991; Wechsler & Isaac, 1992).

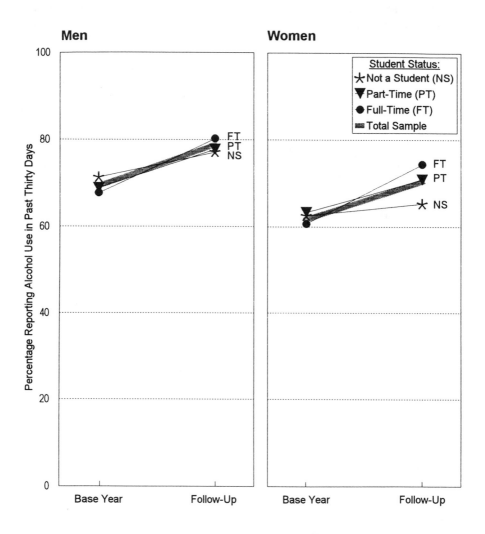

FIG. 5.2. Alcohol use in the past 30 days related to student status at time of follow-up. Percentages based on follow-ups 1 and 2 (modal ages 19–22, only), from classes of 1976–1994. In this figure, one person could contribute up to two follow-up observations (see Analysis Issues and Strategy section in chapter 3). Approximate numbers of observations for men: 19,200, for women: 23,200.

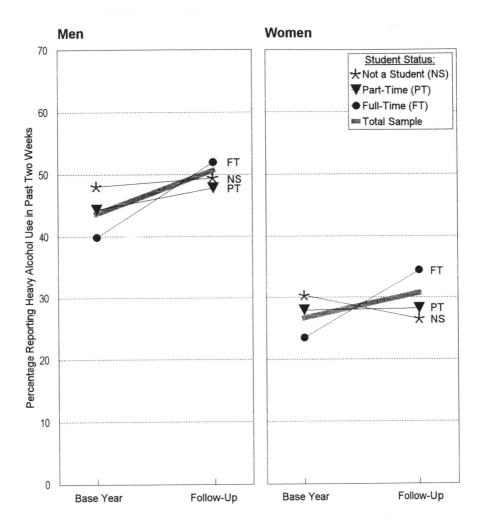

Men   **Women**

Percentage Reporting Heavy Alcohol Use in Past Two Weeks

Student Status:
⚹ Not a Student (NS)
▼ Part-Time (PT)
● Full-Time (FT)
▬ Total Sample

FT
NS
PT

FT
PT
NS

Base Year   Follow-Up   Base Year   Follow-Up

FIG. 5.3. Heavy alcohol use in the past 2 weeks related to student status at time of follow-up. "Heavy alcohol use" is defined as having five or more drinks in a row. Percentages based on follow-ups 1 and 2 (modal ages 19–22, only), from classes of 1976–1994. In this figure, one person could contribute up to two follow-up observations (see Analysis Issues and Strategy section in chapter 3). Approximate numbers of observations for men: 19,900, for women: 24,400.

83

Figure 5.2 shows that most full-time college students were current drinkers; among men the proportion increased from 68% in high school to 80% (compared with an increase from 71% to 77% among nonstudents), and among women the proportion increased from 61% to 74% (compared with a slight rise from 63% to 65% among nonstudents). The *frequency* of monthly alcohol use also showed greater than average increases among full-time college students (as can be seen in the bivariate coefficients in Table A.6 in the Appendix).

Figure 5.3 shows more pronounced differences between students and nonstudents with respect to heavy drinking. Those who would become full-time college students were less likely than average to have reported heavy drinking in the senior year of high school, but they were more likely than average to have done so in college (see also Bachman, Schulenberg, et al., 1990; Schulenberg et al., 1994). Compared with high school, the proportions of full-time college students who reported any heavy drinking during the past 2 weeks rose by 12% among men and 11% among women; among those not attending college the changes during the same time interval were minimal—an increase of 1% among men and a drop of 4% among women.

There are a number of possible interpretations of the relationship between college attendance and alcohol use. First it must be emphasized that when the college-bound students were still in high school they were *below* average in alcohol use; thus, to some extent their behavior might be viewed as merely "catching up" with their age-mates who had tended to start drinking earlier (when it was less likely to be legal). However, the college students did more than simply catch up; their levels of drinking, especially instances of heavy drinking, surpassed those of their age-mates who did not go on to college. The likely explanation lies in the living arrangements of college students, as we shall see later in this chapter.

Employment Status Related to Alcohol Use

Figure 5.4 shows proportions of current drinkers, and Fig. 5.5 shows the proportions who drank heavily at least once in the past 2 weeks, both during high school and at the time of follow-up, for various employment categories using the full set of panel responses (all seven follow-ups are included).

Full-Time Civilian Employment.   Those in full-time civilian employment at the time of follow-up showed slight increases in proportions of current drinkers, and slight decreases in proportions reporting any heavy drinking

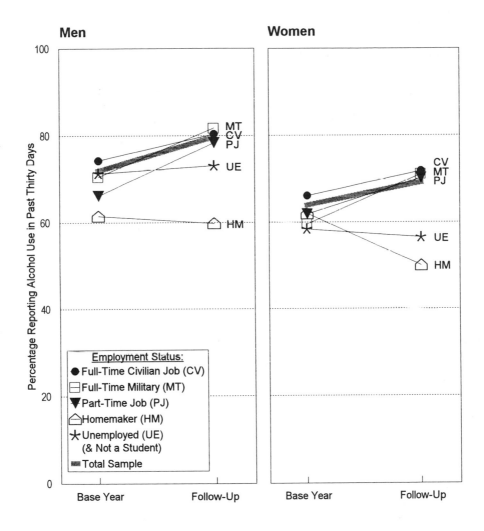

Men **Women**

FIG. 5.4. Alcohol use in the past 30 days related to employment status at time of follow-up. Percentages based on follow-ups 1–7, from classes of 1976–1994. In this figure, one person could contribute up to seven follow-up observations (see Analysis Issues and Strategy section in chapter 3). Approximate numbers of observations for men: 44,300, for women: 53,700.

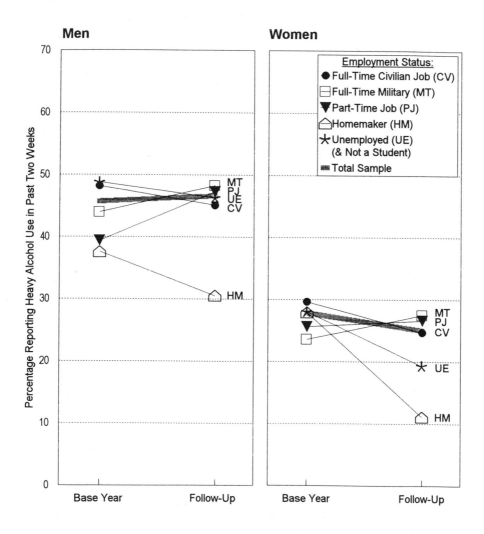

FIG. 5.5. Heavy alcohol use in the past 2 weeks related to employment status at time of follow-up. "Heavy alcohol use" is defined as having five or more drinks in a row. Percentages based on follow-ups 1–7, from classes of 1976–1994. In this figure, one person could contribute up to seven follow-up observations (see Analysis Issues and Strategy section in chapter 3). Approximate numbers of observations for men: 45,800, for women: 56,200.

during the past 2 weeks. Neither of these patterns of change was an important departure from the overall average of changes.

Part-Time Employment.   Recalling that most part-time employees were also full-time students, it is not surprising to see that their alcohol-use patterns, especially heavy drinking shown in Fig. 5.5, were similar to those for full-time students (especially the men) shown in Fig. 5.3. Here again, our interpretation of these findings is that they reflect primarily the impacts of the living arrangements associated with attending college.

Military Experience.   Those in military service showed slightly greater than average increases in proportion of current drinkers, and also showed some increase in proportions who reported any heavy drinking (whereas most other groups showed some decline). Here, as in the case of smoking, multivariate controls did not appreciably reduce the relationship, suggesting that some aspect of the military experience itself contributed to increases in use of alcohol.

This is not to say that the increased drinking resulted from specific work roles associated with the military, or even any more general problems or tensions associated with service in the armed forces. A more likely explanation, in our view, would focus on the "after-hours" aspects of the lifestyle of young adults in military service. The important point to note is that for this relationship, unlike our findings for student status, the explanation does not seem to lie simply in different proportions married, living with parents, or both. Presumably, there were factors more specifically linked to the military lifestyle that contributed to the increased use of alcohol.

The military leadership in recent years has become aware of problems of alcohol use and abuse among service members, and has taken steps to try to reduce these problems. In this connection it is worth noting that the present findings concerning alcohol use by those in military service are somewhat weaker than those observed in earlier analyses (Bachman et al., 1992). The most important difference between the two sets of analyses is that the present ones include an additional six cohorts (classes of 1989–94) and an additional 6 years of follow-ups (1990–1995). This suggests that during recent years there has been a lessened tendency for military experience to heighten the use of alcohol, perhaps indicating that the military's effort to reduce alcohol abuse is succeeding—a topic we hope to examine in future analyses.

Homemakers.   Figure 5.4 shows that proportions of current drinkers declined somewhat among women who identified themselves as full-time homemakers; more importantly, Fig. 5.5 shows that proportions who reported any heavy drinking dropped by more than half, compared with their rates as high-school seniors.

Our regression analyses reveal substantial declines in *frequency* of current alcohol consumption among women who were homemakers, and controlling for background and student status reduced the relationship only slightly (see Table A.6 in the Appendix). On the other hand, controlling for marital status, pregnancy, and parenthood reduced the relationship to only about one-sixth of its original size. A similar reduction occurred in the relationship involving instances of heavy drinking (see Table A.7 in the Appendix). It thus appears that it is not so much the role of homemaker itself which leads to reduced alcohol use, but rather that most of these women were also married, many had children, and some were pregnant.

Figures 5.4 and 5.5 show lower than average alcohol use among the handful of men who identified themselves as full-time homemakers. Given the small numbers of cases involved, the relationships are not statistically significant; thus we remain cautious about drawing conclusions.

Unemployment.   Figure 5.4 shows that among the unemployed the proportions of current drinkers were lower at the time of follow-up than any other employment-status category except full-time homemakers. Further, the regression analyses (Table A.6) show that *frequency* of current drinking increased rather little among men in the nonstudent, not-employed category, and it actually decreased among women in that category. In the case of women, the departure from average disappeared when other factors were controlled. Among men, however, a significant negative effect of unemployment on drinking remained after all other factors were controlled.

Figure 5.5 shows that instances of heavy drinking among unemployed men matched exactly those of men employed in full-time civilian jobs, whereas among women those unemployed showed a slightly greater drop in proportion reporting any heavy drinking. The regression analyses for instances of heavy drinking (Table A.7) were similar to those for current drinking, although none of the relationships reached statistical significance.

One other point to be noted in Figs. 5.4 and 5.5 is that those who would be unemployed at follow-up were, as high-school seniors, no more likely than average to have been current drinkers, or to have reported heavy drinking. In summary, these data provide no evidence either of alcohol use leading to unemployment, or of unemployment leading to alcohol use in this population.

Living Arrangements and Marital Status Related to Alcohol Use

We saw in chapter 4 that changes in cigarette use were only modestly linked with marital status and other living arrangements, perhaps because the smoking habit seems to be so strongly formed before young people leave high school. In contrast, most alcohol use during high school and young adulthood does not reflect nearly as great a degree of habituation, thus leaving it more susceptible to changes in role responsibilities and social environments. Alcohol is also more closely associated with social situations and is generally used with others, whereas tobacco is primarily a drug of individual use. Its essentially social nature may make alcohol use more responsive to changes in the organization of social life and subject to greater social controls, particularly use to the point of intoxication. We have already seen that alcohol use increased more substantially among college students than among their age-mates. Now we examine factors that seem to explain that finding.

Being Married.   As noted in earlier chapters, being married is generally the most permanent of the several living arrangements delineated here, as well as the most important in terms of depth and breadth of interpersonal relationships. Married people are more likely than those not married to experience pregnancy and parenthood, with all of the changes and additional responsibilities such roles involve. Even setting those important factors aside (which we are able to do to a considerable extent in our regression analyses), there remain a number of factors about marriage that might be expected to have an impact on overall alcohol use and especially on instances of heavy drinking. In particular, the mutual caring and commitments associated with marriage, as well as the closeness and frequency of contact, may operate to reduce the likelihood of dangerous behaviors such as instances of heavy drinking. Additionally, young married people may tend to associate with other marrieds rather than with singles, and these new and more "adult" associates may have less time and inclination to use alcohol—especially heavily. For these reasons, as well as the prior research findings summarized in chapter 2, we expected to find that overall frequency of alcohol use would be less likely to rise among marrieds than among singles, and that instances of heavy drinking would be more likely to decline among the marrieds.

Differences in proportions who drink in these different living arrangements, shown in Figs. 5.6 and 5.7, as well as regression analyses presented

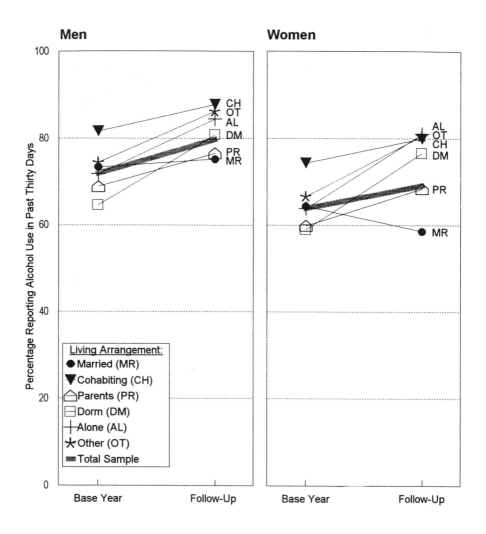

FIG. 5.6. Alcohol use in the past 30 days related to living arrangement at time of follow-up. Percentages based on follow-ups 1–7, from classes of 1976–1994. In this figure, one person could contribute up to seven follow-up observations (see Analysis Issues and Strategy section in chapter 3). Approximate numbers of observations for men: 44,300, for women: 53,700.

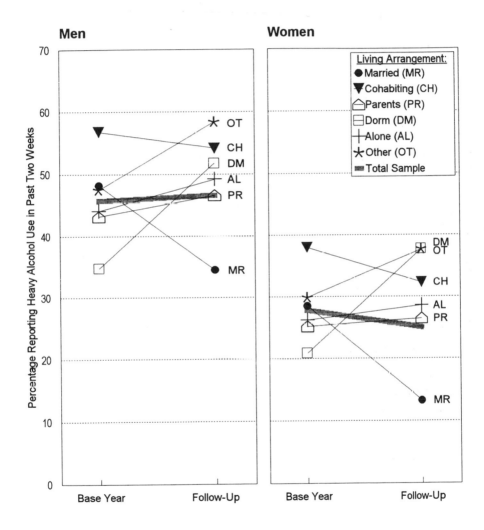

FIG. 5.7. Heavy alcohol use in the past 2 weeks related to living arrangement at time of follow-up. "Heavy alcohol use" is defined as having five or more drinks in a row. Percentages based on follow-ups 1–7, from classes of 1976–1994. In this figure, one person could contribute up to seven follow-up observations (see Analysis Issues and Strategy section in chapter 3). Approximate numbers of observations for men: 45,800, for women: 56,200.

in Appendix Tables A.6 and A.7, all are consistent with these expectations. Among married women, the frequency of alcohol use declined appreciably, and that remained true to a considerable extent even after controls for other relevant factors such as pregnancy and parenthood (see Table A.6). Among married men, the average frequency of alcohol use was no higher than when they were seniors in high school; even after controls for other factors there was only a slight increase in their use. Men in all other categories of living arrangements showed increases in alcohol use several times larger than those for married men (see Table A.6).

The results for instances of heavy drinking are more dramatic, as can be seen in Fig. 5.7 and Table A.7. Among married men and women, proportions who reported any heavy drinking were distinctly lower than when the same individuals were high-school seniors, and they were also clearly lower than proportions for any other living arrangement. Here again multivariate controls reduced the overall size of effects only slightly (see Table A.7).

In summary, these findings clearly indicate that distinctive changes in alcohol use *are associated with* marriage, even with a large number of other relevant factors included in the regression equations (i.e., controlled statistically). But does that mean that marriage *caused* those changes? The answer is complicated, because some of the causal process seems to be anticipatory. The data shown in Figs. 5.6 and 5.7 indicate that those who were married at time of follow-up were not much different from their classmates, on average, with respect to alcohol use during high school; in other words, there is no evidence that those with different levels of alcohol use *during high school* were differentially predisposed toward marriage. Moreover, other analyses (including those illustrated by Fig. 3.7 in chapter 3) strongly indicate that most of the marriage effect on alcohol use occurred fairly close to the time when marriage took place—that is, within a year or two. But that is not to say that all of the changes in alcohol use occurred *after* marriage; on the contrary, findings concerning engagement, as illustrated in Fig. 3.7 and detailed later in this chapter, indicate that some of the effects associated with being married may anticipate the formal status of marriage, but take place after making a mutual commitment—sometimes in the form of engagement.

Cohabiting.   Figures 5.6 and 5.7 show that those who at follow-up were living with a partner of the opposite sex were somewhat more likely than average to have been drinkers, and occasional heavy drinkers, while they were still in high school. These figures, as well as the regression analyses (Tables A.6 and A.7), also indicate that the rates of change associated with cohabitation differed little from the average rates of change for the samples as a whole. Perhaps a more useful way of looking at those "mostly average" rates of change is to note that drinking did not decline among cohabitants to the extent that it did among those who married, but neither did it rise as much as it did among unmarried respondents in other living arrangements. However, the initial and continuing high rates of heavy drinking in this group are cause for concern.

Living With Parents. Those who were living with parents at follow-up showed slightly lower than average rates of current alcohol use and heavy use when they were in high school. They showed roughly average levels of increase in proportions of users, as can be seen in Figs. 5.6 and 5.7. A more refined examination of changes is provided in Tables A.6 and A.7. Specifically, the regression analyses involving all seven follow-ups show slightly larger than average alcohol use increases among those living with parents (except for the current use measure for men); however, the regression analyses focusing on only the first two follow-ups (which would seem the more appropriate basis for comparison) show slightly (but statistically significantly) smaller than average increases in alcohol use among those living with parents.

Living in a Dormitory. Among both men and women, those who went to college and lived in a dormitory were least likely to have been current or occasional heavy drinkers while in high school, but they were most likely to have taken up such practices while living in a dorm (Figs. 5.6 and 5.7). In addition, Tables A.6 and A.7 show that the increases in *frequency* of such behaviors were larger than for most other living arrangements, and the regression analysis results show also that this "dormitory effect" is largely independent of other aspects of living arrangements. Moreover, the regression analyses show that additional controls for student status do not diminish the coefficients for dorm living at all, thus indicating that dormitory life rather than the student role in general contributed to the rise in drinking.

Living Alone. Among the relatively small numbers of young adults who reported living alone (and not in a dormitory), the proportions of current alcohol users (Fig. 5.6) and frequency of use (Table A.6) increased more than average, although not as much as among those who lived in dormitories. Instances of heavy drinking were roughly average among those living alone (Fig. 5.7 and Table A.7).

Other Living Arrangements. The living arrangements in this residual category often included a social life similar to that in a dormitory. As can be seen in Fig. 5.6 and Table A.6, the changes in current alcohol use were closely similar between the two. Much the same can be said for instances of heavy drinking (see Fig. 5.7 and Table A.7).

Pregnancy and Parenthood Related to Alcohol Use

Pregnancy. In recent years, pregnant women have been strongly urged to quit smoking and to suspend their use of alcohol. In chapter 4 we saw that being pregnant stood out clearly as the factor most likely to cause women to stop or decrease their smoking. If pronounced changes can occur in the face of the strong levels of habituation (and often dependency) typically involved in cigarette use, then we can expect also to observe substantial changes in alcohol consumption—a behavior that has seldom reached the point of habituation or dependency among women who become pregnant.

In earlier analyses (Bachman et al., 1992) we found that pregnancy was more strongly linked with current (30-day) alcohol use than with annual alcohol use, and we attributed that to the fact that the 12-month reporting period included a number of months prior to pregnancy. Thus, our focus here on 30-day use and heavy drinking in the past 2 weeks should have a good sensitivity to the influence of pregnancy.

Indeed, our present analyses show that current alcohol use dropped dramatically among pregnant women; only 21% reported any use in the past month (Fig. 5.8), and *frequency* of use also was greatly lowered (Table A.6). The decline in instances of heavy drinking associated with pregnancy was even more dramatic, dropping almost to zero (Fig. 5.9).

When faced with figures this low, it is important to recall that our samples cannot represent the total population of young adults. The initial sampling limited to high-school seniors, plus the effects of panel attrition, mean that those women most likely to be pregnant and abusing alcohol are underrepresented in these panel analyses. That said, it is also worth recalling that these surveys do represent the substantial majority of young adults, and the data they have provided show an impressive restraint in alcohol use during pregnancy.

To what extent were the declines in alcohol use during pregnancy actually due to pregnancy rather than to other correlated factors such as marriage? The regression analyses in Tables A.6 and A.7 show that the very large bivariate relationships were reduced only moderately when controls for marriage, parenthood, and other living arrangements were added to the equations; the bivariate relationships were completely unaffected by con-

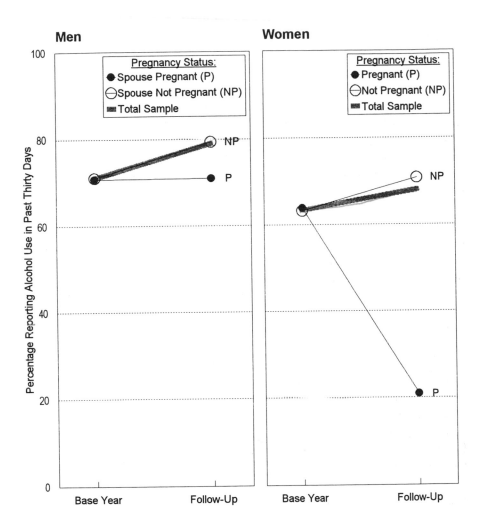

FIG. 5.8. Alcohol use in the past 30 days related to pregnancy status at time of follow-up. Percentages based on follow-ups 1–7, from classes of 1976–1994. The pregnancy item was not added to the follow-up questionnaire until 1984. In this figure, one person could contribute up to six follow-up observations (see Analysis Issues and Strategy section in chapter 3). Approximate numbers of observations for men: 36,400, for women: 44,600.

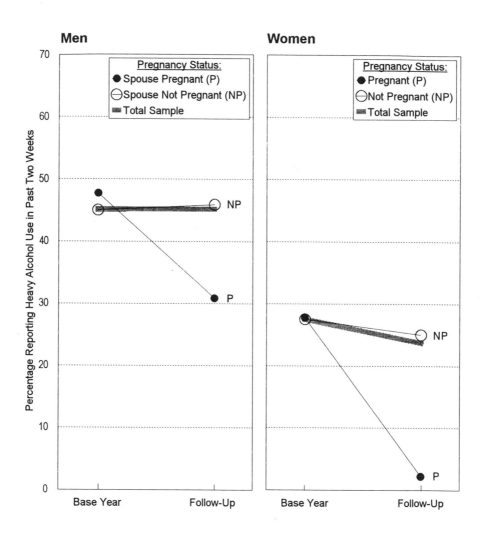

FIG. 5.9. Heavy alcohol use in the past 2 weeks related to pregnancy status at time of follow-up. "Heavy alcohol use" is defined as having five or more drinks in a row. Percentages based on follow-ups 1–7, from classes of 1976–1994. The pregnancy item was not added to the follow-up questionnaire until 1984. In this figure, one person could contribute up to six follow-up observations (see Analysis Issues and Strategy section in chapter 3). Approximate numbers of observations for men: 38,000, for women: 47,000.

trols for student and employment status. The most simple and straightforward interpretation of these relationships, in our view, is that pregnancy—*including the intention or anticipation of becoming pregnant*—did cause women to cut down and in most cases eliminate their use of alcohol. Moreover, we assume that much of this reduction in drinking was prompted specifically by concern for the possible effects of alcohol on the fetus.

Any responsible prenatal care now includes strong cautions against alcohol use, alcohol containers now include a message warning against use by pregnant women, and additional coverage of the issue has been widespread in the media. It is of interest in this connection to note that analyses reported elsewhere (Bachman, Johnston, & O'Malley, 1991) have shown that even during the short interval from 1984 through 1988, corresponding to dramatic increases in media coverage of this issue, the avoidance of alcohol by pregnant women in our surveys became more pronounced. We see this as evidence that the messages about fetal alcohol syndrome and related risks came through more clearly with each successive year.

Does having a pregnant spouse cause men to reduce their use of alcohol? We saw in chapter 4 that having a pregnant spouse had no important impact on men's smoking behavior. With respect to alcohol use, however, there did seem to be some changes. Proportions of current drinkers were modestly lower among men with pregnant spouses (see Fig. 5.8); however, the pattern was not appreciably different from that for all married men (see Fig. 5.6), and the regression results showed that most of the relationship disappeared once marital status was included in the equation (see Table A.6). Much the same may be said for instances of heavy drinking (see Figs. 5.7 and 5.9, and Table A.7).

In summary, whereas most pregnant women eliminated their use of alcohol, most of their husbands did not. Some reduction among men, especially in heavy drinking, did correspond with having a pregnant spouse; however, it appears that the reduction was due *primarily* to the general condition of being married rather than the specific situation of having a pregnant (and probably nondrinking) spouse.

Parenthood. Among both married men and married women, being a parent was associated with declines in frequency of alcohol use. Just over half of the bivariate relationship was attributable to other factors in the multivariate analysis, most notably the marriage effect. Nevertheless, the remaining multivariate coefficients for married parents remained significant and nearly as large as the multivariate coefficients for being married (see Table A.6). With respect to instances of heavy drinking, there was also a substantial bivariate relationship showing lower instances among married parents; however, in the multivariate analyses the relationship was largely eliminated, indicating that for heavy drinking the marriage effect was more dominant than any effect of parenthood (see Table A.7).

Among single mothers, the multivariate coefficients for frequency of alcohol use were virtually identical to those for married mothers, suggesting that the effects of children present in the home may inhibit alcohol use, on average, in much the same way whether the mothers are married or single (see Table A.6). A significant multivariate coefficient indicated that among single women—who, of course, experienced no marriage effect—parenthood had the effect of reducing heavy drinking (see Table A.7).

Among single fathers, there was no appreciable parenthood effect on their frequency of alcohol use (Table A.6) or on instances of heavy drinking (Table A.7). This is not altogether surprising; most unmarried fathers would not be subject to inhibitions due to children in the home, because most do not have custody of their children.

Further Findings on Marital Status and Alcohol Use

Two earlier analyses of Monitoring the Future data, first introduced in chapter 3, provide additional perspectives on the impacts of marital status on alcohol use. The first of these analyses showed that major changes in drinking behavior occurred within the 2-year interval in which respondents made the transition from single to married. The transition in drinking behavior may have been somewhat gradual (i.e., extending over a number of months); however, the findings did not suggest that the change process extended over a number of years (see Bachman, Johnston, O'Malley, & Schulenberg, 1996).

The second of the earlier analyses focused on 4-year patterns of change in marital status, and produced the findings shown in Fig. 3.7 (Bachman et al., 1997). Those data show sharp drops in proportions of heavy drinkers occurring during the 2-year interval in which respondents became married, in contrast to relatively little change during the 2-year intervals in which there was no change in marital status.

Engagement. Figure 3.7 also shows that the transition pattern from single to engaged to married tends to split the marriage effect on heavy drinking into two segments. The transition from single to engaged was accompanied by substantial reductions in proportions of heavy drinkers, suggesting some degree of what has been termed *anticipatory socialization.* Our regression analyses included a variable indicating engagement status;

the multivariate results for frequency of current drinking show an engagement effect nearly as large as the marriage effect (see Table A.6), and the results for heavy drinking tell a similar story (see Table A.7).[7]

Another perspective on engagement, distinguishing between those who were cohabiting at the time of follow-up and those who were not, is provided in Figs. 5.10 and 5.11. Current alcohol use (Fig. 5.10) shows only slight links with engagement, and only among women. However, heavy drinking (Fig. 5.11) shows several important differences linked with engagement. Among those cohabiting, being engaged is associated with a reduction in heavy alcohol use. The effect is not as large as the marriage effect, but it is actually larger than the decline in heavy drinking among those who were engaged but not cohabiting. (On the other hand, if we look at all singles, the relative engagement effect is fully as large as that observed when we look at all cohabitants.) The contrast between marrieds and singles remains the largest of all, consistent with our earlier comment that the engagement effect is in the same direction as the marriage effect, but not quite as large.

Divorce. There are modest "divorce effects" on current alcohol use, as shown in Fig. 5.12. The results in Fig. 5.13 are more dramatic, showing clearly that the transition from married to divorced is marked by an *increase* in proportions reporting heavy drinking, and that the increase is just about equivalent to the *decline* in proportions associated with becoming married. Among women especially, the shift is very much the same no matter what the previous (or subsequent) experience with respect to marital status, as can be seen in Fig. 3.7. These figures also illustrate, as first noted in chapter 4, that it would have been futile to include divorced among the predictors in our regression analyses; the marriage effects and divorce effects would neatly cancel each other, leaving those in the divorced category indistinguishable from other single individuals who had not been through the two transitions.

Figures 5.12–5.13 also show that among those divorced at both points in time, proportions of alcohol users and of occasional heavy drinkers are consistently high. The figures also show that the marriage effects decreasing the likelihood of alcohol use, or heavy use, were fully as large among those going from divorced to remarried as among those going from single to married. Finally, it should be noted that Figs. 5.12–5.13 show marriage effects and engagement effects, now measured over 2-year intervals between

---

[7]The reader who examines the data for engagement in Tables A.6 and A.7 will note an unmasking somewhat similar to that which appeared in Table A.5 (see footnote 4, chapter 4). We focus on the multivariate coefficients, because they contrast engaged individuals with other *single* individuals who are not engaged.

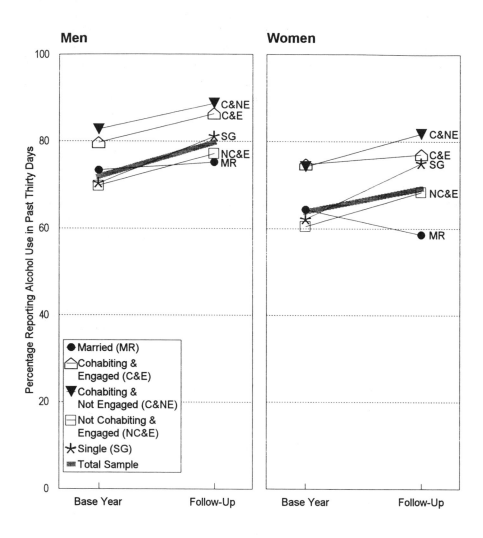

FIG. 5.10. Alcohol use in the past 30 days related to engagement, cohabitation, and marriage at time of follow-up. Percentages based on follow-ups 1–7, from classes of 1976–1994. In this figure, one person could contribute up to seven follow-up observations (see Analysis Issues and Strategy section in chapter 3). Approximate numbers of observations for men: 44,300, for women: 53,700.

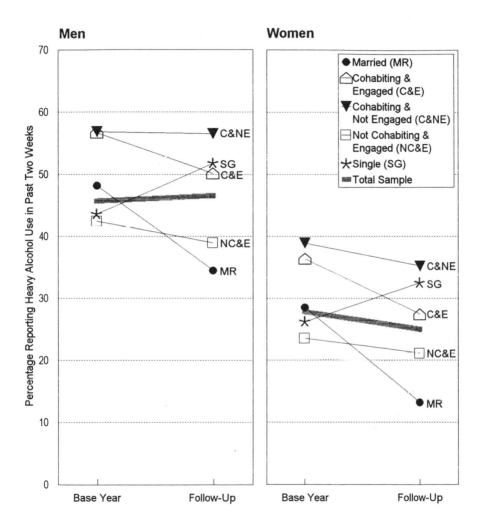

FIG. 5.11. Heavy alcohol use in the past 2 weeks related to engagement, cohabitation, and marriage at time of follow-up. "Heavy alcohol use" is defined as having five or more drinks in a row. Percentages based on follow-ups 1–7, from classes of 1976–1994. In this figure, one person could contribute up to seven follow-up observations (see Analysis Issues and Strategy section in chapter 3). Approximate numbers of observations for men: 45,800, for women: 56,200.

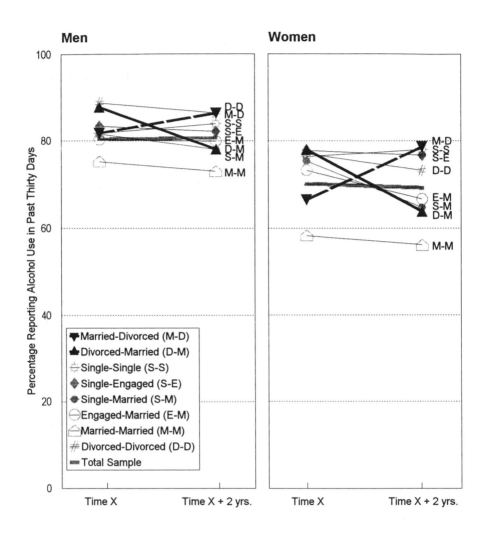

FIG. 5.12. Alcohol use in the past 30 days related to transitions in marital status. Percentages based on follow-ups 1–7, from classes of 1976–1994. Observations are drawn from two consecutive follow-ups, providing measures at two points in time that cover an interval of 2 years. That is, observations are based on individuals' data from follow-ups 1 and 2, follow-ups 2 and 3, follow-ups 3 and 4, and so forth. Note that an individual who participated in all seven follow-ups would contribute six observations. Approximate numbers of observations for men: 32,300, for women: 40,700.

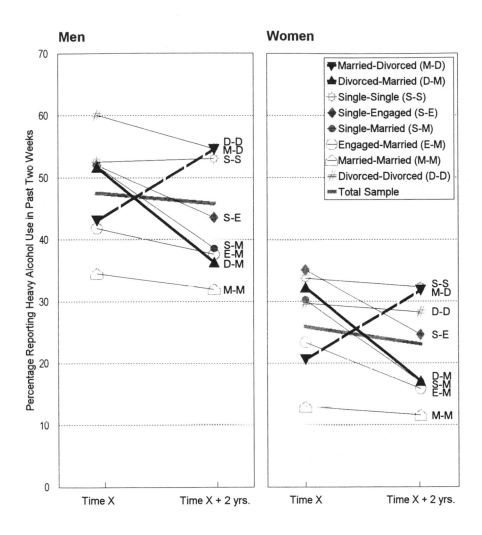

FIG. 5.13. Heavy alcohol use in the past 2 weeks related to transitions in marital status. "Heavy alcohol use" is defined as having five or more drinks in a row. Percentages based on follow-ups 1–7, from classes of 1976–1994. Observations are drawn from two consecutive follow-ups, providing measures at two points in time that cover an interval of 2 years. That is, observations are based on individuals' data from follow-ups 1 and 2, follow-ups 2 and 3, follow-ups 3 and 4, and so forth. Note that an individual who participated in all seven follow-ups would contribute six observations. Approximate numbers of observations for men: 32,400, for women: 41,100.

follow-ups, which are fully consistent with the results from base year to follow-up shown in earlier figures.

Implications for Interpreting the Marriage Effect.   All of the findings reported and summarized in this section are consistent with the following broad interpretation: it is the *present* condition of being unmarried, versus being married or engaged, not the long-term history of marital status, that is associated with major differences in alcohol use. This is not to say that the changes occur only after the exchange of vows, for the data on engagement clearly indicate the contrary. Rather, we believe that it is mutual commitment, as well as changes in social and recreational lifestyle, that generate most of the changes linked to marriage; many of these, of course, come into play at least to some extent during the months prior to the formal point of marriage.

CONCLUSIONS FROM MULTIVARIATE ANALYSES LINKING ALCOHOL USE WITH POST-HIGH-SCHOOL EXPERIENCES

The Appendix includes multivariate analyses linking post-high-school experiences with changes in frequency of current drinking (Table A.6) and frequency of heavy drinking (Table A.7). A number of important relationships are mentioned earlier in this chapter; in this section we consider ways in which those relationships seem to be unique or overlapping.

In the previous chapter on cigarette use, we noted that most effects were nonoverlapping and that the overall amount of variance explained was small. In the present chapter the story is quite different. There are larger amounts of variance explained, and some interesting overlaps are found between student status and living arrangements.

Explained Variance

The R-squared values in the Appendix show that about 3% of the variance for changes in frequency of heavy drinking is explainable by background factors, that fully an additional 2% is explainable by living arrangements, and that these basic patterns of results are much the same for men and for women (see Table A.7).

Changes in the frequency of current (30-day) alcohol use among men show much the same pattern as instances of heavy drinking—about 3% of the variance explainable by background factors and another slightly less than 2% explainable by living arrangements (see Table A.6). Changes in frequency of current alcohol use among women, however, was somewhat more strongly predictable, with about 4% being explainable by background factors and another nearly 6% being explainable by living arrangements (see Table A.6).

The larger amount of explained variance in the frequency of women's current alcohol use, compared with that of men, reflects at least three factors: (a) there was a very large pregnancy effect for women, with nothing comparable for men with pregnant spouses; (b) several other dimensions of living experiences (including engagement, marriage, and parenthood) showed slightly larger effects on the heavy drinking of women, compared with men; and (c) there were, on average, more women than men who were married, parents, or both at any time during the study, and this further heightened the relationships for women, compared with men.

The findings concerning pregnancy, in particular, serve to remind us that even when effects are quite large, they account for only limited amounts of variance if only a few individuals are affected—and, of course, only a relatively small proportion of women in our study were pregnant at any particular follow-up. We emphasize that the relationships displayed in the figures may be more meaningful than the relatively modest data on variance explained, reported in the Appendix, might suggest.

Overlaps Between Student Status and Living Arrangements

We noted earlier that college students were more likely than their age-mates to have increased their frequency of alcohol use and of heavy drinking, and we indicated that the explanation may lie in the living arrangements of college students. In particular, college students are less likely than average to marry in the first few years after high school, but they are more likely than average to leave their parents' homes. These kinds of living arrangements, as we have shown earlier, appear to contribute to increased alcohol use.

The multivariate analyses confirm that what we might call a "college effect" on alcohol use overlaps largely with other factors. First, there is a good deal of overlap with academic grades in high school and with college plans, both of which we treated as background factors. Second, there is a considerable overlap with the living arrangements noted earlier. Thus, as can be discerned from Tables A.6 and A.7, the dimensions of student and work experience make virtually no unique contribution to predicting or explaining variance in the alcohol use change scores once these other factors have been taken into account.

These multivariate findings are illustrated in Fig. 5.14, which shows relationships between student status and changes in heavy drinking focusing on the first 4 years after high school. The *unadjusted* data in the figure show that full-time students increased their instances of heavy drinking, whereas nonstudents did not. The *adjusted* data in the figure show that background factors and differences in living arrangements (using multiple regression analyses, as documented in Table A.7) fully account for the differences between students and nonstudents.

Figure 5.15 provides a similar look at relationships involving living arrangements during the same 4-year period after high school, and shows that adjustments for all other factors only modestly dampened those relationships. In particular, the substantial increases in heavy alcohol use associated with living in a dorm or in other arrangements remain strongly evident, as do the substantial decreases associated with being married.

Accounting for Age-Related Changes in Alcohol Use

Figure 5.1 indicated that the percentages of young adults reporting current alcohol use, and instances of heavy use, increased through age 22 and declined thereafter. Figure 5.16 shows that overall *frequency* of alcohol use rose substantially among men until age 22 and declined thereafter, and that among women it showed a smaller rise but an equally substantial decline. The adjusted data in Fig. 5.16 also show that to a considerable extent those age-related changes would be reduced if, in effect, there were no age differences in proportions living in dorms, married, pregnant, and so forth. Figure 5.17 tells a somewhat similar story for instances of heavy drinking. It shows the sharp decline that occurred among both men and women, and it suggests how much that age-related decline would be reduced if living arrangements and other factors were equalized across ages.

In summary, the multivariate analyses described in this section support the following interpretations of age-related changes in alcohol use: The *increases* in alcohol use between ages 18 and 22 resulted mainly from new freedoms in living arrangements on leaving parents' homes and moving into dormitories or dormitory-like housing shared with other young adults, as well as the freedom to purchase alcohol at age 21. The *reductions* in alcohol use between ages 22 and 32 largely reflect the impacts of new responsibilities associated with engagement, marriage, pregnancy, and parenthood.

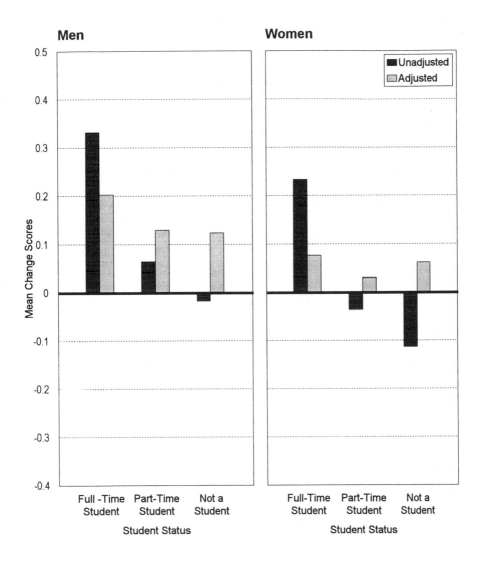

FIG. 5.14. Mean change scores in 2-week heavy alcohol use, unadjusted and adjusted, related to student status at time of follow-up (for follow-up respondents modal ages 19–22, only). The mean change score is the predicted amount of change in 2-week heavy alcohol use between base year and follow-up, where heavy alcohol use is defined as having five or more drinks in a row. The unadjusted mean change score only controls student status. The adjusted mean change score controls all the predictor variables. Positive change scores indicate an increase in use over time, and negative scores indicate a decrease. Calculation of change scores is discussed in detail in the Appendix.

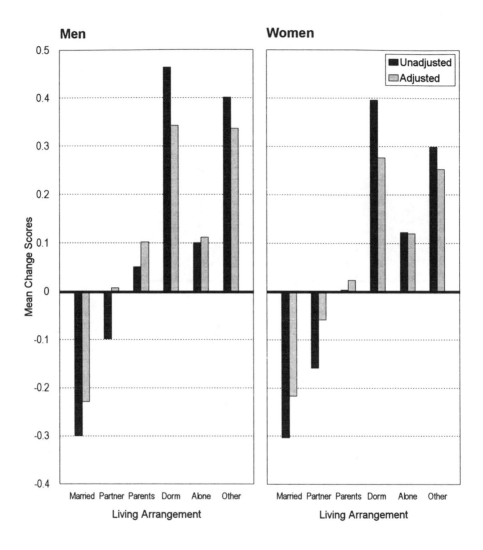

FIG. 5.15. Mean change scores in 2-week heavy alcohol use, unadjusted and adjusted, related to living arrangement at time of follow-up (for follow-up respondents modal ages 19–22, only). The mean change score is the predicted amount of change in 2-week heavy alcohol use between base year and follow-up, where heavy alcohol use is defined as having five or more drinks in a row. The unadjusted mean change score only controls living arrangement. The adjusted mean change score controls all the predictor variables. Positive change scores indicate an increase in use over time, and negative scores indicate a decrease. Calculation of change scores is discussed in detail in the Appendix.

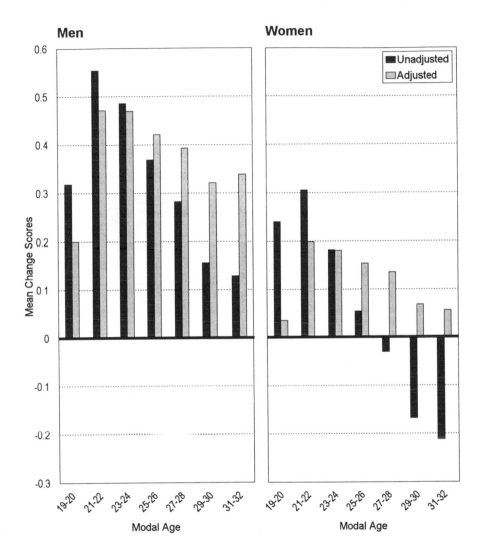

FIG. 5.16. Mean change scores in 30-day alcohol use, unadjusted and adjusted, related to modal age. The mean change score is the predicted amount of change in 30-day alcohol use between base year and modal age indicated. The unadjusted mean change score only controls the follow-up survey interval (or, modal age). The adjusted mean change score controls all the predictor variables. Positive change scores indicate an increase in use over time, and negative scores indicate a decrease. Calculation of change scores is discussed in detail in the Appendix.

109

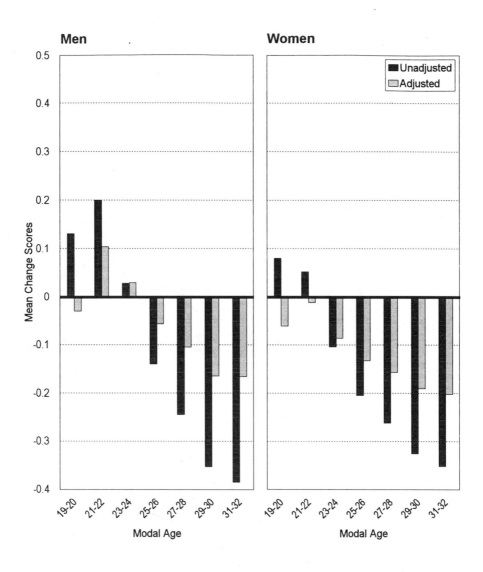

FIG. 5.17. Mean change scores in 2-week heavy alcohol use, unadjusted and adjusted, related to modal age. The mean change score is the predicted amount of change in 2-week heavy alcohol use between base year and modal age indicated, where heavy alcohol use is defined as having five or more drinks in a row. The unadjusted mean change score only controls the follow-up survey interval (or, modal age). The adjusted mean change score controls all the predictor variables. Calculation of change scores is discussed in detail in the Appendix.

6

Changes in Marijuana Use

We turn now to marijuana, the most widely used illicit drug in recent decades. At peak levels of use (1978–1979), about 60% of high-school seniors had used marijuana at least once in their lives, thus making it in some sense a normative behavior. Indeed, over one-third (37%) were active, current users. The rates gradually declined for each new graduating class throughout the 1980s and into the early 1990s, and in the class of 1992 only one-third reported having ever used marijuana. However, the graduating classes of 1993, 1994, and 1995 each showed an increase in proportions of marijuana users (see Johnston et al., 1997, for a full reporting of these trends in marijuana use).

Marijuana is not usually considered a "hard drug" in the same sense as other illicit drugs like cocaine and heroin, but its use nevertheless carries significant risks. Marijuana use has been identified as an important preceding step in the use of other illicit substances, and is closely tied to association with deviant peers and involvement in antisocial behavior. As an illicit substance, marijuana is also more widely disapproved in general than licit substances like tobacco and alcohol; marijuana use also carries the risk of incarceration, so it is less compatible with the assumption of adult social roles and may be more responsive to the socializing influence of adult roles and experiences.

Although overall rates of marijuana use have shifted quite a bit during the past two decades, individual differences in use (including nonuse) have shown a good deal of stability across time—not so stable as cigarette use, but just about the same as alcohol use. Specifically, after taking account of measurement reliability, we estimate the stability of marijuana use (annual measure) to be about .87 during the first year after high school, with annual stability then rising from about .92 to .95 during subsequent years. It thus seems clear that much of post-high-school marijuana use is influenced by factors present during high school. However, it is also true that considerable room remains for change, and we shall see evidence that many of the factors that influence alcohol use have similar impacts on the use of marijuana.

First, however, let us review some of the broad changes that have occurred in marijuana use.

PATTERNS OF CHANGE IN MARIJUANA USE

After rising during most of the 1970s, marijuana use among high-school students and young adults declined substantially and steadily throughout the 1980s and into the 1990s, a decline that we found to be closely linked to increases in perceived risks and disapproval (Bachman, Johnston, O'Malley, & Humphrey, 1988; Bachman, Johnston, & O'Malley, 1990; Johnston, 1985). Consistent with these earlier findings, the recent upswing in marijuana use is linked with attitude changes in the opposite direction (Johnston et al., 1997).

Cohort-sequential analyses of the interval from 1976 through 1986 indicated that the overall changes in marijuana use could be interpreted primarily as period effects (secular trends, or historical change) rather than as cohort differences (stable differences from one senior class to another); those analyses also revealed age-related shifts, with marijuana use increasing in the first few years after high school and thereafter decreasing (O'Malley et al., 1988a, 1988b). These age-related changes, of course, are an important focus of the present analyses, which examine whether post-high-school roles and experiences contribute to such changes in marijuana use.

The secular trends in marijuana use complicate our analysis of change to some extent. Figure 6.1 shows that increases in age were accompanied by substantial declines in proportions of marijuana users, both current (monthly) and annual. Frequency of use also declined with age, as can be seen in Tables A.8 and A.9. However, we believe that sizeable portions of those declines reflect the overall downward secular trend rather than any age-related process. In other words, although the figures provide an accurate description of the changes in marijuana use actually experienced by the cohorts covered in our panel analysis samples, our interpretation is that these changes reflect the joint effects of two distinctly different phenomena—(a) the overall historical decline in marijuana use (across various age groups) during much of the period; and (b) a separate set of age-related shifts (common to various class cohorts), many of which are linked to the post-high-school experiences examined in the present report.

Rates of Current and Annual Marijuana Use

Figure 6.1 shows time trends in marijuana use among those from the high-school classes of 1976–1981, tracking the same set of individuals from

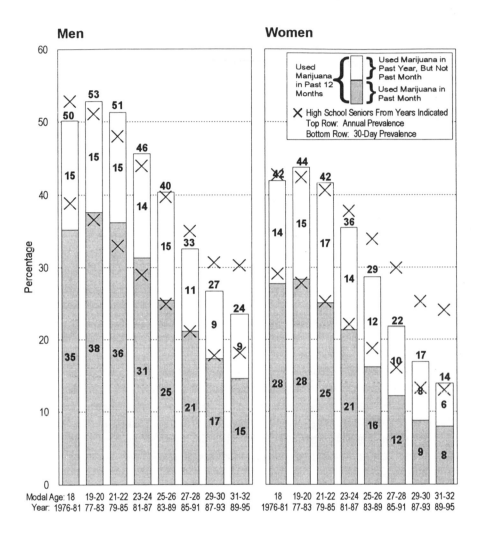

FIG. 6.1. Percentages of panel respondents who used marijuana in the past 12 months. Bar percentages are based on base-year (high-school senior) data, plus follow-ups 1–7, from classes of 1976–1981, only; one person could contribute up to seven follow-up observations (see Analysis Issues and Strategy section in chapter 3). Approximate numbers of observations for men: 22,300, for women: 26,800. Any apparent inconsistency between data labels in the bars and cumulative percent noted is due to rounding. High-school-senior percentages (x notations) are based on base-year data from sets of years indicated; senior samples include approximately 8,000 men and 8,000 women each year.

modal age 18 to modal ages 31–32.[1] These are the individuals who attended and graduated from high school when marijuana use was in its heyday. Fully half of the men and nearly as many of the women had used marijuana at least once during the year preceding graduation. Moreover, most of these annual users also used the drug at least once during the month preceding the senior-year survey. The figure shows that rates of monthly and annual marijuana use in these cohorts rose slightly during the first 2 years after high school, and then declined fairly sharply thereafter. Specifically, annual use among the men dropped from 53% at modal ages 19–20 to fewer than half that many (24%) by the time they reached modal ages 31–32, and monthly use dropped by a good deal more than half (from 38% to 15%). During that same 12-year time span (from ages 19–20 to ages 31–32), the proportions of women using marijuana declined by more than two-thirds—from 44% to 14% for annual use, and from 28% to 8% for monthly use.

As noted earlier, a considerable proportion of the decline shown in Fig. 6.1 can be attributed to the overall downward secular trend in marijuana use during most of the longitudinal period covered by the study. To help put this in perspective, we have added notations (xs) to Fig. 6.1 indicating prevalence rates for marijuana use among *high-school seniors* at each report-ing period; for example, the graduating classes of 1976–1981 reached modal ages 31–32 in the years 1989–1995, so the x shown above ages 31–32 indicates the prevalence rates for seniors averaged across the classes of 1989–1995. It is worth pointing out that the additional notations in Fig. 6.1 are derived from our total samples of high-school seniors, whereas the bars shown in the figure are based on only those who participated in the follow-ups; the differences at age 18 (i.e., the fact that the x notations are slightly higher than the tops of the bars) reflect panel attrition, which we judged small enough to not require a set of complicated corrections carried out through all analyses.

Looking again at Fig. 6.1, this time taking into account marijuana use among high-school seniors at the same historical intervals, we see that in their early twenties our panel respondents from the 1976–1981 cohorts were slightly more likely to use marijuana than were high-school seniors at the same points in time. By the time the women reached ages 23–24, however, the proportions of marijuana users dropped below the corresponding figures for female high-school seniors, and thereafter the gap widened. Among men this "crossover point" occurred later, and their proportions of users did not

---

[1]The measures of current (monthly) and annual marijuana use were based on the following questions: "On how many occasions (if any) have you used marijuana (grass, pot) or hashish (hash, hash oil) . . . during the last 12 months? . . . during the last 30 days?" The response scale is included in Table A.2 in the Appendix.

drop much below the rates for male high-school seniors at the same points in time. Thus, after taking account of secular trends, as represented by the data from high-school seniors in Fig. 6.1, our tentative conclusion is that some age-related declines in marijuana use remain during the midtwenties and beyond; however, they are much more modest than would be suggested by the overall downward shifts in Fig. 6.1, and in other figures in this chapter.[2]

ANALYSES LINKING MARIJUANA USE WITH POST-HIGH-SCHOOL EXPERIENCES

The analyses in this section focus on measures of current marijuana use (i.e., any use during the 30-day period preceding the survey). We conducted similar analyses using the 12-month measure, with closely parallel results. However, we opted to use the 30-day measure here for two reasons. First, it provides consistency with the reporting in the preceding chapters. The second and more fundamental reason is that the current measure deals with the very recent past, whereas the 12-month measure covers time that is more likely to have preceded the acquisition of the roles and experiences we are studying. Consider the example of a woman reporting being pregnant at time of follow-up; there is a fairly good chance that her drug use (or nonuse) during the preceding 30 days all took place while she knew she was pregnant (or perhaps was expecting to be pregnant), whereas her drug use during all of the preceding 12 months would necessarily include a considerable period during which she was not pregnant. Thus a better dependent variable, in terms of indicating pregnancy effects, would be the 30-day measure of drug use. The disadvantage of the 30-day measures, in comparison with the 12-month versions, is that the shorter intervals provide a more limited sample of any behavior that is somewhat rare, thereby introducing a greater degree of measurement error—not because of faulty recall (because recall is actually better for the shorter intervals), but rather because the limited time sample produces one form of sampling error. This does not represent a very serious problem for most of the figures shown in this chapter, because the errors cancel each other across the large numbers of respondents; however, it does substantially reduce explained variance in the *regression analyses*. For that reason the Appendix presents regression analyses for change scores based on both 30-day intervals (see Table A.8) and

---

[2]For further evidence of the secular trends in marijuana use, indicated not only by high-school-senior data but also by parallel trend data for young adults tracked across time, see Johnston et al. (1997), or prior reports in the same series.

12-month intervals (see Table A.9), so that interested readers may make comparisons between the two.

Student Status Related to Marijuana Use

Figure 6.2 shows that college students and nonstudents differed very little in likelihood of current marijuana use during the first few years *after* high school; however, *during* high school the college-bound were about one-third less likely to have been users. The results here are in some respects similar to those for heavy drinking shown in chapter 5 (Fig. 5.3)—the college students tended to catch up with their age-mates. The difference is that in heavy drinking the college students actually overtook and surpassed their age-mates, whereas in marijuana use they partly (but not completely) closed the gap (see also Schulenberg et al., 1994).

It is important to keep in mind the overall downward secular trend in marijuana use throughout most of the period studied. The modest decline in proportions of current users among the nonstudents is roughly in line with that secular trend, whereas the modest increase in current use among college students is counter to that secular trend and thus more noteworthy.

The "catching up" interpretation for college students also seems to be supported by the regression analysis results. Controlling for background factors alone reduced most of the student status regression coefficients to near zero. This occurred because those whose backgrounds during high school included academic success—those who got good grades and were planning to go to college—were lowest in marijuana use (as well as heavy drinking, smoking, and other drug use) while in high school.

Employment Status Related to Marijuana Use

Figure 6.3 displays proportions of current marijuana users (i.e., any use in the preceding 30 days) during high school and at the time of follow-up for the employment categories across the full set of panel responses (all seven follow-ups included).

Full-Time Civilian Employment.   Those in full-time civilian employment at the time of the follow-up showed no important departures from the overall average proportions of marijuana users, either in high school or at follow-up. It is the only category, however, for which this is true (except for the handful of men who identified themselves as full-time homemakers).

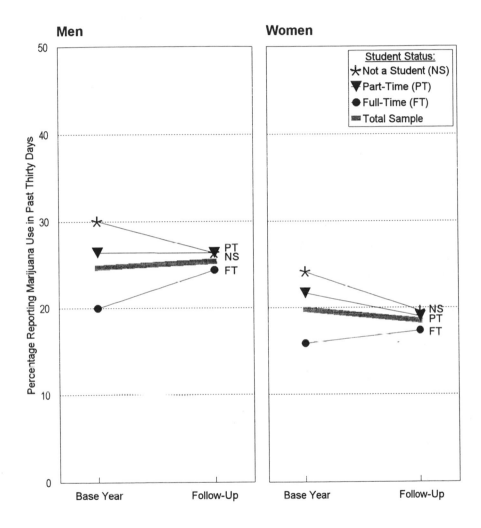

Men

Women

Student Status:
✱ Not a Student (NS)
▼ Part-Time (PT)
● Full-Time (FT)
▬ Total Sample

Percentage Reporting Marijuana Use in Past Thirty Days

50

40

30 — PT / NS / FT

20 — NS / PT / FT

10

0

Base Year   Follow-Up   Base Year   Follow-Up

FIG. 6.2. Marijuana use in the past 30 days related to student status at time of follow-up. Percentages based on follow-ups 1 and 2 (modal ages 19–22, only), from classes of 1976–1994. In this figure, one person could contribute up to two follow-up observations (see Analysis Issues and Strategy section in chapter 3). Approximate numbers of observations for men: 20,600, for women: 25,100.

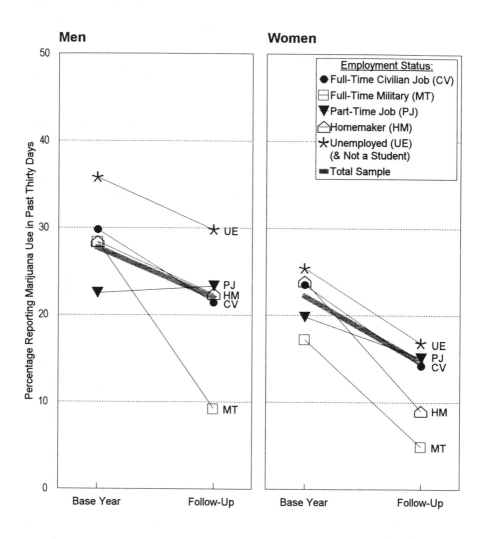

Men　　　　　　　　　**Women**

Percentage Reporting Marijuana Use in Past Thirty Days

Employment Status:
● Full-Time Civilian Job (CV)
▣ Full-Time Military (MT)
▼ Part-Time Job (PJ)
⌂ Homemaker (HM)
✶ Unemployed (UE)
  (& Not a Student)
▬ Total Sample

FIG. 6.3. Marijuana use in the past 30 days related to employment status at time of follow-up. Percentages based on follow-ups 1–7, from classes of 1976–1994. In this figure, one person could contribute up to seven follow-up observations (see Analysis Issues and Strategy section in chapter 3). Approximate numbers of observations for men: 47,200, for women: 57,700.

Part-Time Employment.   Here, as was true of cigarette use and alcohol use, the data for part-time employees might best be described as a slightly watered-down version of the data for full-time students. Their likelihood of being marijuana users was slightly below average when they were in high school, and equal to or slightly above average at the time of follow-up.

Military Service.   Although those in military service showed greater than average increases in cigarette use and in heavy drinking, their experiences with *illicit* drug use were quite another matter. Figure 6.3 shows dramatic declines in marijuana use among those in military service; indeed, the proportions of current users dropped to about one-third as many as had been current users as high-school seniors. It should be emphasized that the low rates of use among service personnel reflect *changes* rather than *selection effects.* Young men in military service were just as likely as their classmates to be marijuana users while in high school; the much lower rates of use emerged after they graduated. Among the smaller numbers of women in military service, the story is somewhat similar; however, it can be seen that their rates of marijuana use were somewhat below average even while they were still seniors in high school.

The regression results for current (30-day) as well as annual marijuana use, displayed in Appendix Tables A.8 and A.9, show that the sharp declines in marijuana use among service men and women are not at all reduced or explainable by background, marital status, or other factors included in the multivariate analyses. To the contrary, the findings very clearly and consistently suggest that the drastic reductions in marijuana use (quitting, in most instances) are attributable directly to some aspect(s) of the military service experience.[3]

Of course, quitting marijuana use need not have happened *after* entry into military service—in many cases, it probably happened after high school but prior to entry into the military. This seems especially likely in recent years, given that the armed forces now have strong anti- (illicit) drug policies backed by drug screening of recruits and current service personnel.

Homemakers.   The findings for marijuana use among female homemakers are in many respects similar to those for alcohol use and cigarette use.

---

[3]It should be noted that we have reported elsewhere (Johnston & O'Malley, 1997) a somewhat higher than average level of recanting of earlier reported drug use among follow-up respondents in military service, which we have interpreted as a higher level of denial of prior use due to the severity of consequences for being identified as a drug user in this environment. Nevertheless, it is hard to imagine that the very large declines in use reported here could be explained by this somewhat greater than average tendency to conceal past use.

Figure 6.3 shows a drop in marijuana use among homemakers twice as large as that for women on average.

The bivariate coefficients in Appendix Tables A.8 and A.9 tell a similar story, showing that marijuana use declined about twice as much among homemakers as among women as a whole. However, the multivariate coefficients with background and student status controlled were less than half as large, and once marital status, living arrangements, pregnancy, and parenthood were controlled, there was no independent "homemaker effect" at all. (The small numbers of men who reported being full-time homemakers did not differ significantly from average in marijuana use.)

Unemployment. Figure 6.3 shows that the proportion of current (monthly) marijuana users was about 8% higher among unemployed men than among men on average, but the same had been true when these individuals were high-school seniors. Among women there were smaller differences in the same direction at both points in time. The figure thus suggests that marijuana use during high school may be somewhat predictive of unemployment during the post-high-school years; however, it does not suggest that unemployment leads to notable increases in marijuana use. This somewhat counterintuitive finding replicates one reported much earlier, based on a national sample of young men in the Youth in Transition study (Johnston, 1973). Consistent with the data in Fig. 6.3, the regression analyses dealing with change scores in monthly and annual marijuana use show no significant relationships with unemployment (see Tables A.8 and A.9).

Living Arrangements and Marital Status Related to Marijuana Use

Because the stability levels of marijuana use are quite similar to those for alcohol, and because the frequencies of use are generally lower than those for alcohol, we judge that rather little of the marijuana use in our samples reflects chemical or psychological dependency. Thus, like alcohol use and in contrast to cigarette use, we expected marijuana use to be susceptible to changes in role responsibilities and social environments. A further reason for expecting such susceptibility is the fact that marijuana is an illicit substance; accordingly, its use is much less widely accepted than alcohol use, and less congruent with responsible adult roles.

Being Married. We expected that the responsibilities, mutual caring, commitments, intimacy, and adult contacts associated with marriage would reduce not only alcohol use but also the use of illicit drugs—especially when taken for recreational purposes. The results shown in Fig. 6.4 confirm those

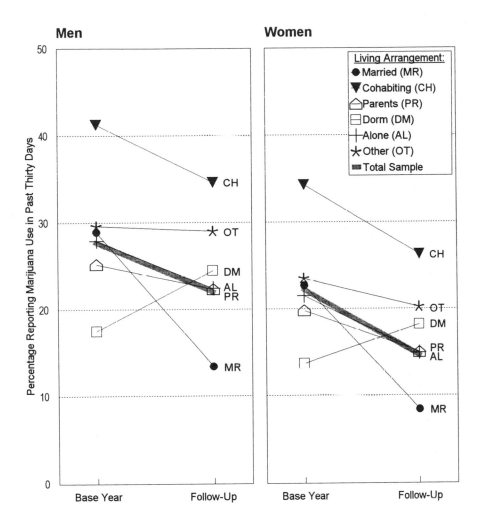

FIG. 6.4. Marijuana use in the past 30 days related to living arrangement at time of follow-up. Percentages based on follow-ups 1–7, from classes of 1976–1994. In this figure, one person could contribute up to seven follow-up observations (see Analysis Issues and Strategy section in chapter 3). Approximate numbers of observations for men: 47,200, for women: 57,700.

expectations with respect to current marijuana use. Just as was true for alcohol, those who were married by the time of follow-up were neither more nor less likely than their classmates to have been current marijuana users as high-school seniors, but those who had used were more likely to quit, and those who had not were less likely to initiate.

The bivariate coefficients in Appendix Tables A.8 and A.9 indicate that marijuana use declined two or three times as much among the married as among the unmarried. After controls for background factors, pregnancy, and parenthood (fourth column in the tables), the multivariate coefficients are smaller, but the effects remain important as well as statistically significant. Adding student and employment status as additional predictors (fifth column) produces virtually no change in the coefficient for marriage, indicating that the effects of marriage are independent of these other aspects of post-high-school experience. The comments in chapter 5 with respect to alcohol apply here as well; at least some of the changes in marijuana use *associated with* marriage may emerge before the formal exchange of vows, but probably subsequent to engagement or similar commitment to a future spouse.

Cohabiting.   We reported in previous chapters that high-school rates of smoking and drinking were higher than average among those who would later (at the time of follow-up) report living with a partner of the opposite sex. Figure 6.4 indicates that the cohabitants were also half again more likely than average to have been current marijuana users during high school. It seems increasingly clear that senior-year drug use is a predictor of later cohabitation (the next chapter provides further evidence of this relationship).

Figure 6.4 shows also that the proportions using marijuana decline between high school and follow-up among cohabitants, to much the same extent as for the sample as a whole. The bivariate coefficients in Appendix Tables A.8 and A.9 are also very low, telling much the same story with respect to overall changes in monthly and annual marijuana use. The *multivariate* coefficients, however, are slightly positive (and in some instances statistically significant). This unmasking occurs in the presence of an opposite effect associated with being engaged, as discussed later in the chapter.

Living With Parents.   As was the case for alcohol use, those who continued living with parents at follow-up had slightly lower than average rates of current marijuana use when they were in high school. Figure 6.4 indicates that at follow-up the proportions of users were at the average level, which would seem to indicate that those living with parents may not have decreased marijuana use as much as average. Figure 6.4, based on all seven follow-ups, may be misleading in this instance. Living with parents was most likely to occur during the first or second follow-up, so the general downward trend in marijuana use across time would have operated to a lesser extent for these cases. The regression analyses in Appendix Tables A.8 and A.9 show that with follow-up number and other factors controlled, those living with parents showed declines in marijuana use that did not depart significantly from average in most instances. More important, those analyses in Table A.8 that focused on just the first two follow-ups showed greater than average declines in marijuana use among those living with parents—both bivariately and with multivariate controls for all other predictors. Thus, with respect to marijuana, as with alcohol, continuing to live with parents during the first few years after high school seemed to have inhibited use.

Living in a Dormitory.   We saw in chapter 5 that alcohol use in general, and heavy drinking in particular, showed much larger than average increases among those living in a dormitory. The same can be said for marijuana use, as indicated in Fig. 6.4. Whereas marijuana use decreased among young adults in general, the proportions of current users increased among those living in dorms. The bivariate coefficients in Tables A.8 and A.9 tell the same story, although the multivariate coefficients with other factors controlled are substantially smaller. Here again, the most appropriate comparison is with individuals during the first and second follow-ups; these data show that significant dormitory effects remain after controls for all other factors.

Living Alone.   The young adults living alone (and not in a dormitory) did not differ significantly from the sample as a whole in terms of marijuana use, as can be seen in Fig. 6.4 and Appendix Tables A.8 and A.9.

Other Living Arrangements.   Figure 6.4 shows that the individuals in this category experienced rather little decline in marijuana use, in contrast to the overall downward trend. In fact, the coefficients in the right-hand portions of Table A.8 show that in the first 4 years after high school, frequency of current marijuana use actually increased among those in the other living arrangements category—and that remained true after multivariate controls.

We noted earlier that many of those in the other living arrangements category experience a social life similar to those living in a dormitory—albeit with fewer formal constraints on their behaviors. It is thus interesting to compare the marijuana using behaviors of the two groups. Figure 6.4 shows that *during their high-school years* those who later would be living in dormitories were far less likely than average to be marijuana users; that clearly was not the case among those destined for the other living arrangements category. The *bivariate* coefficients in the right-hand portions of Table A.8 show that among men during the first 4 years after high school, those in dormitories had larger increases in marijuana use than those in the other living arrangements category; among women, however, the two groups were virtually identical. More importantly, the *multivariate* coefficients indicate that after controls for other important factors, such as high-school grades and college plans, the other living arrangements seemed more likely than dormitory living to contribute to increased marijuana use.

Pregnancy and Parenthood Related to Marijuana Use

Pregnancy. In previous chapters we saw that pregnancy stood out as linked to reductions in cigarette use and in alcohol use. It would thus be surprising if pregnancy failed to have some impact on marijuana use. Figure 6.5 shows that only about 4% of pregnant women reported current marijuana use—about one-third as many as among the nonpregnant women. Here, as was the case for alcohol, the regression analyses show that most of the bivariate relationship between pregnancy and changes in current marijuana use remained in the multivariate coefficients after other factors, such as marriage, were controlled (see Appendix Table A.8).

Based on our earlier analyses showing that pregnancy was more strongly linked with current (30-day) alcohol use than with annual alcohol use, we expect similar findings for current and annual marijuana use. A comparison of Appendix Tables A.8 and A.9 reveals a similar finding for marijuana; although the *bivariate* coefficient for change in annual use (Table A.9) is larger than that for monthly use (Table A.8), the multivariate coefficient for the monthly change measure is larger than for annual change. Pregnancy is the only post-high-school predictor for which that is true; in every other instance (with one trivially small and nonsignificant exception) the coefficient is larger for change in annual marijuana use compared with change in current (30-day) use. The fact that the pregnancy relationship runs counter to this general pattern, here as in the case of alcohol use, provides further evidence for our straightforward *causal* interpretation: Being pregnant, and probably also preparing for pregnancy, causes young women to eliminate (or at least reduce) their use of marijuana.

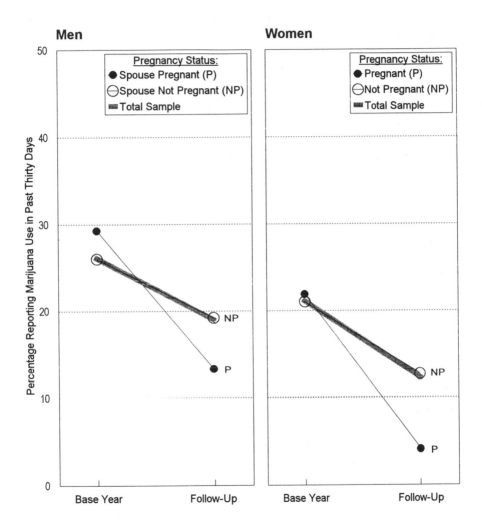

Men   **Women**

FIG. 6.5. Marijuana use in the past 30 days related to pregnancy status at time of follow-up. Percentages based on follow-ups 1–7, from classes of 1976–1994. The pregnancy item was not added to the follow-up questionnaire until 1984. In this figure, one person could contribute up to six follow-up observations (see Analysis Issues and Strategy section in chapter 3). Approximate numbers of observations for men: 39,200, for women: 48,200.

Were there similar effects for men with pregnant spouses? Although a first glance at Fig. 6.5 might suggest that, a look back at Fig. 6.4 shows that marriage is associated with just as large a decline in marijuana use. A look at the regression analyses confirms that simply having a spouse—pregnant or not—is what makes the difference for men; the substantial bivariate coefficients for "pregnant spouse" are reduced to nearly zero in the multivariate analyses, which include marriage as a strong predictor (see Appendix Tables A.8 and A.9).

Parenthood.   Among married men and women, parenthood was linked with greater than average declines in marijuana use. As was true for alcohol, however, most of these bivariate relationships were attributable to other factors, particularly marriage. Only small and nonsignificant multivariate coefficients remained for current marijuana use (Table A.8), although the coefficients for *annual* marijuana use (Table A.9) were larger (and reached statistical significance for the women).

Single mothers also showed greater than average declines in marijuana use, but not as much as married mothers. Although the bivariate coefficients were smaller for the single mothers, the *multivariate* coefficients were larger—presumably because the parenthood effect was not shared with any marriage effect (see Tables A.8 and A.9).

Among single fathers there is some evidence that parenthood was associated with greater than average declines in marijuana use. This stands in contrast to the lack of such findings for alcohol.

Further Findings on Marital Status and Marijuana Use

A prior analysis of Monitoring the Future data, introduced in chapter 3, contrasted earlier and later transitions into marriage. The findings for marijuana use are shown in Fig. 3.6, which clearly indicates that substantial reductions in proportions of annual marijuana users took place during the specific 2-year intervals in which respondents also changed their status from single to married (see also Bachman, Johnston, O'Malley, & Schulenberg, 1996).

Another prior analysis, introduced in chapter 3, produced results for marijuana that closely parallel those for heavy drinking shown in Fig. 3.7. Here again, the sharpest drops in marijuana use occurred during the 2-year interval in which respondents became married (see also Bachman et al., 1997). Still further evidence of the marriage effect on current marijuana use is included in Fig. 6.7 introduced later in the chapter; a substantial drop in proportions of current users occurred during the 2-year interval in which marriage occurred.

Engagement.   As was true with alcohol, the earlier analyses showed an engagement effect on marijuana use change scores similar to, but somewhat smaller than, the marriage effect (Bachman et al., 1997). The descriptive data shown in Fig. 6.6 also indicate engagement effects. Whether we look at those who were cohabiting or at those who were not, we find that those who were engaged showed greater drops in prevalence of marijuana use. The declines for engaged respondents in Fig. 6.6 are not as great as those for married respondents, no doubt because the data for those who were married also incorporate some effects of pregnancy, parenthood, and so forth. Indeed, when other factors are controlled in the multivariate analyses, in Appendix Tables A.8 and A.9, it appears that becoming engaged has almost as strong an effect in reducing marijuana use as becoming married.[4] Similar to our findings for cigarette use, engaged cohabitants were somewhat less likely than nonengaged cohabitants to have been marijuana users when they were seniors in high school.

Divorce.   Figure 6.7 suggests that divorce had the effect of increasing marijuana use. The increases were not as large as those for alcohol, but they ran opposite to the downward secular trend that was in effect during most of the period under study. The figure also shows that men who were divorced at both times were far above average in proportions of current marijuana users (this pattern was less strong for the women). Those who went from divorced to remarried showed marriage effects virtually identical to those who went from single to married.

Similar to the findings for cigarette use reported in chapter 4, our earlier analyses showed that marijuana use rates were above average among those who would later divorce (Bachman et al., 1997). Figure 6.7 shows that, compared with those who stayed married, those who made the transition from married to divorced were much more likely to have been current marijuana users while they were married. At least in part, this may reflect another aspect of the longstanding syndrome that includes poor grades in high school and few prospects for attending college (Schulenberg et al., 1994). However, it also seems possible that marijuana use itself, continued or initiated during young adulthood, may make a more direct contribution to the likelihood of divorce.

---

[4]Here again we focus on the multivariate coefficients because they contrast engaged individuals with other *single* individuals who are not engaged (see footnote 4, chapter 4).

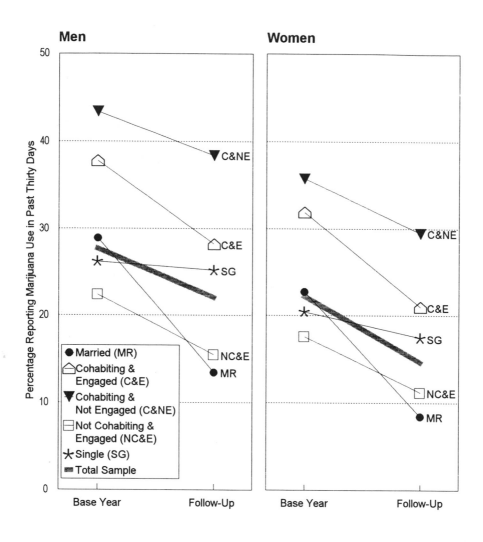

FIG. 6.6. Marijuana use in the past 30 days related to engagement, cohabitation, and marriage at time of follow-up. Percentages based on follow-ups 1–7, from classes of 1976–1994. In this figure, one person could contribute up to seven follow-up observations (see Analysis Issues and Strategy section in chapter 3). Approximate numbers of observations for men: 47,200, for women: 57,700.

Men

Women

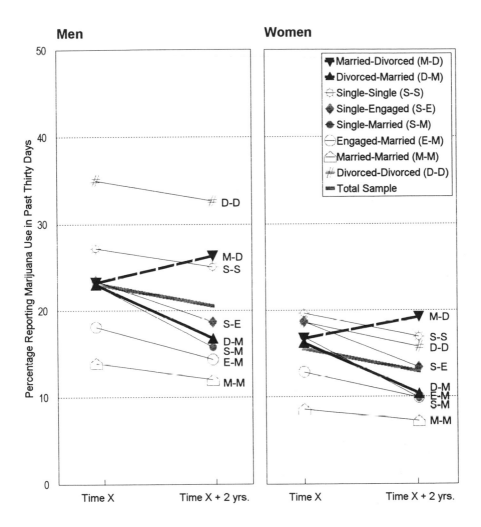

FIG. 6.7. Marijuana use in the past 30 days related to transitions in marital status. Percentages based on follow-ups 1–7, from classes of 1976–1994. Observations are drawn from two consecutive follow-ups, providing measures at two points in time that cover an interval of 2 years. That is, observations are based on individuals' data from follow-ups 1 and 2, follow-ups 2 and 3, follow-ups 3 and 4, and so forth. Note that an individual who participated in all seven follow-ups would contribute six observations. Approximate numbers of observations for men: 32,600, for women: 41,500.

CONCLUSIONS FROM MULTIVARIATE
ANALYSES LINKING MARIJUANA USE
WITH POST-HIGH-SCHOOL EXPERIENCES

At various points in this chapter we have noted key findings from the multivariate analyses of current marijuana use (Appendix Table A.8) and annual marijuana use (Table A.9). In this section we consider some additional findings from the regression analyses.

Explained Variance

Although patterns of findings were generally similar, our predictors were able to explain more variance in annual marijuana use change scores (Table A.9) than in monthly use change scores (Table A.8). This is not surprising, given that most respondents at the time of follow-up had not used the drug at all during the previous year, some had used but not in the past month, and many who did use in the past month did so only a few times. (Figure 6.1 shows marijuana use among those in the earliest cohorts; use was lower among those in later cohorts.) For a relatively infrequent behavior such as this, the 30-day time sampling unavoidably contains a good deal of random error—simply because the preceding month may or may not accurately represent a typical month for the respondent. Thus, we are referring here to a kind of *time-sampling* error rather than any error in *recall*.[5]

Interpreting amounts of explained variance in marijuana change scores is particularly complicated because of the downward secular trend that took place during most of the period under study. The background factors in the regression include a set of dummy variables for follow-up number; these explain a considerable amount of variance (see Tables A.8 and A.9), mostly reflecting the secular trend discussed at the start of the chapter. Because of this secular trend complication we do not want to place much emphasis on the overall amounts of explained variance with respect to changes in marijuana use.

One more general perspective on amounts of explained variance is worth recalling here. Our primary focus is on the *patterns* of change associated with certain post-high-school experiences; we have relatively little interest in total amounts of explained variance, except as they help us understand patterns of overlap among sets of predictors. The experiences associated

---

[5]It is worth noting that this sampling error problem with the 30-day marijuana use measure does not arise for Figures 6.1–6.7 shown earlier, because the figures are limited to summary descriptive data (percentages) based on large numbers of cases. Random sampling errors tend to cancel each other in such data.

with the most pronounced changes (declines) in marijuana use—most notably, military service and pregnancy—involve relatively small portions of our total cases, and thus contribute rather little to overall explained variance. However, there are substantial change scores and transition patterns associated with these experiences, and we judge those figures to be more relevant for present purposes than the overall portions of variance explained. That said, we now offer a number of observations based on our examination of the regression analyses.

Overlaps Between Student/Work Status and Living Arrangements

We noted earlier that being a full-time student was linked to slight increases in marijuana use, in contrast to modest downward shifts among those who were not students during the first few years after high school. We noted also that increases in marijuana use were more likely than average among those who as high school students had been least likely to use marijuana—that is, those with high grades and strong expectations of completing college. It is important to keep in mind that the latter background factors are also strong proxies for actual college entrance, so we do not interpret the regression results as indicating a complete lack of any "college attendance effect." Rather, our interpretation of the full regression results is that marijuana use did show a relative increase among *some* college students—specifically, those who lived in dormitories and those in the other living arrangements category. Moreover, consistent with our views expressed in earlier chapters, we judge that it was the living arrangements (and all of the social control and other social factors that are involved) rather than other aspects of the college experience that had the primary impact on drug use.

The one dimension of work status that showed a significant (indeed, undiminished) impact on marijuana use after controls for all other predictors was military service. Either shortly before or shortly after entrance into the armed forces, most of those who had been marijuana users in high school sharply reduced or eliminated their use. Women who were full-time home-makers also showed greater than average reductions in marijuana use, as indicated by the bivariate regression coefficients; however, the multivariate coefficients indicate that this can be attributed to other factors such as marriage and parenthood. Additionally, the impacts of living arrangements (including marriage), engagement, pregnancy, and parenthood are essentially the same whether or not student/work status variables are included in the equation.

Accounting for Age-Related Changes in Marijuana Use

Figure 6.8 displays change scores by age, shown unadjusted and adjusted for living arrangements and other factors. Here, in contrast to Figs. 5.16 and 5.17 for alcohol use, we see only small reductions in the age-related patterns after controls for living arrangements. Most of this decline in use, however, which happens to *correlate* with age, seems more appropriately interpreted as the result of the large overall downward secular trend in marijuana use during most of the historical period covered by these panel analyses. The notations in Fig. 6.1 are a useful reminder of how prevalence of current use among high-school seniors dropped by more than half. Although we have not attempted to quantify it precisely in this monograph, we believe that the secular trend accounts for most of the age-correlated decline shown in Fig. 6.8. Whatever decline remains we view as more "age-relevant"—and an appreciable proportion of *that* shift appears to be explainable in terms of the post-high-school experiences examined here.

If we thus think in terms of age-related *departures from the downward secular trend*, then the story for marijuana use becomes somewhat more similar to that for alcohol use, especially instances of heavy drinking. Specifically, increases in marijuana use (or smaller than average decreases) during the first few years after high school resulted from the new freedoms associated with leaving parents' homes and moving into dormitories or somewhat similar housing shared with other young adults. Decreases in marijuana use resulted from new responsibilities associated with engagement, marriage, pregnancy, and parenthood. One other factor limiting marijuana use could be described as new responsibilities, new constraints on freedom, or both; among the small proportions of men and very small proportions of women entering military service, marijuana use dropped dramatically.

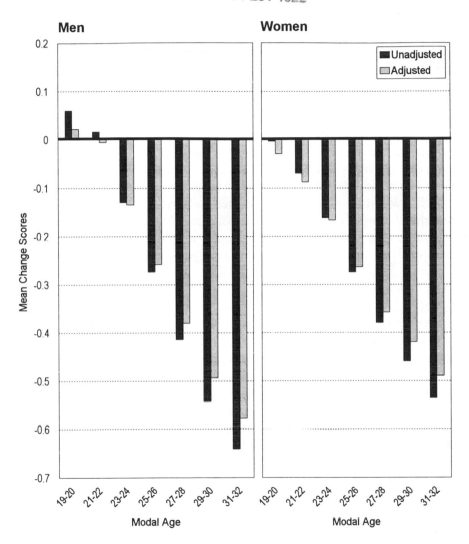

FIG. 6.8. Mean change scores in 30-day marijuana use, unadjusted and adjusted, related to modal age. The mean change score is the predicted amount of change in 30-day marijuana use between base year and modal age indicated. The unadjusted mean change score only controls the follow-up survey interval (or, modal age). The adjusted mean change score controls all the predictor variables. Positive changes scores indicate an increase in use over time, and negative scores indicate a decrease. Calculation of change scores is discussed in detail in the Appendix.

133

7

Changes in Cocaine Use

Cocaine is riskier, more widely disapproved, and more expensive than marijuana. It is not surprising, therefore, that cocaine is also less widely used than marijuana. Nevertheless, substantial minorities of our respondents used cocaine sometime during their lifetime. As recently as 1986, about one-third (32%) of all young adults in Monitoring the Future samples aged 19–28 reported having used cocaine during their lifetime.

PATTERNS OF CHANGE IN COCAINE USE

Unlike marijuana use, cocaine use did not decline significantly until after the 1986 Monitoring the Future surveys; thereafter it declined sharply, again linked to changes in perceived risk and disapproval (Bachman, Johnston, et al., 1990; Johnston et al., 1997). Also unlike marijuana use, the story involving changing attitudes and cocaine use includes a very obvious "smoking gun"—two of them, actually, in the form of cocaine-related deaths widely reported in the media. The first occurred in May 1986, when Len Bias, a college basketball star just drafted by the Boston Celtics, died as a result of cocaine use. Several weeks later, Don Rogers, a professional football star, also died as a result of cocaine use. These two deaths, coming in rapid succession, provoked extensive media coverage focusing on cocaine use and its risks. Moreover, the two young men were high achievers in prime physical condition—just the sorts of individuals with whom many high-school students and young adults might identify. The first Monitoring the Future surveys after the deaths of Bias and Rogers, conducted in the spring of 1987, revealed sharp increases in perceived risks and disapproval, and substantial reductions in reported use of cocaine.

With respect to marijuana use, other analyses demonstrated that changes over time could be interpreted primarily as secular trends (historical change) rather than as stable differences from one senior class to another (cohort effects; O'Malley et al., 1988a, 1988b). Similarly, we interpret the decline in cocaine use after 1986, which was observed for both high-school seniors

and young adults (Johnston et al., 1997), as a secular
for marijuana use, the secular trends in cocaine use ce
interpretations to some extent.

Our earlier cohort-sequential analyses showed substantial a
changes in cocaine use, with proportions of annual users roughly doub.
during the first 3 years after high school and then little in the way of further
change (O'Malley et al., 1988a, 1988b). That rise in cocaine use during the
first few years after high school was a more dramatic age-related shift than
we had seen with any of the other illicit drugs.

Our present panel analyses show a somewhat longer age-related rise in
cocaine use, extending through the midtwenties; this is followed by decreases in later years, which are partly attributable to the overall downward
secular trend after 1986, but which also reflect changes in family status and
living arrangements. Thus several factors seem to be involved in the
age-related changes in cocaine use; however, after taking account of secular
trends and impacts of new responsibilities, a strong rise in cocaine use during
early adulthood remains.

It should be noted that the data on cocaine use examined in this chapter
are different in several ways from the data reported in some of our other
publications. The cohort-sequential analyses designed to isolate age, period,
and cohort effects (O'Malley et al., 1988a), and our annual reports of trends
in drug use (e.g., Johnston et al., 1997), incorporate adjustments for panel
attrition that were neither practicable nor necessary for the present examination of impacts of post-high-school experiences. Additionally, those other
analyses focused exclusively on prevalence measures, whereas our present
analyses include *change* scores that take account of frequency of use. Finally,
we should emphasize that the analyses reported here cover a long period
during which overall usage rates of cocaine initially rose (during the late
1970s), remained relatively high through spring of 1986, and then declined
sharply. It is therefore important to keep in mind that the descriptions of
change presented in this chapter are an amalgam of these factors, and
cannot correspond precisely to our other reports of trends and changes in
cocaine use. Nevertheless, the present descriptions of change provide a
useful backdrop against which to consider the impacts of specific post-high-
school roles and experiences.

Rates of Current and Annual Cocaine Use

Figure 7.1 shows how prevalence of annual and monthly cocaine use
changed with increasing age among those from the high-school classes of

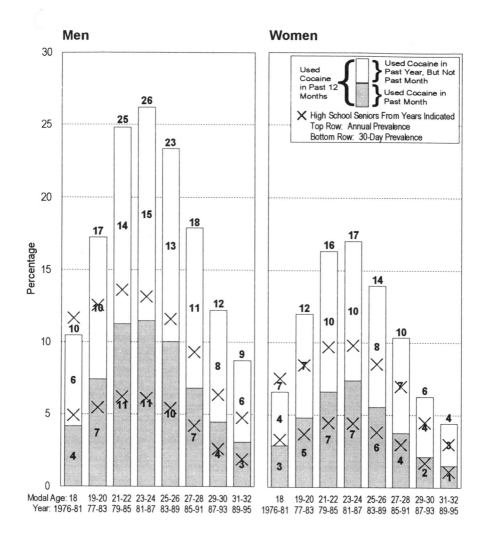

FIG. 7.1. Percentages of panel respondents who used cocaine in the past 12 months. Bar percentages are based on base-year (high-school senior) data, plus follow-ups 1–7, from classes of 1976–1981, only; one person could contribute up to seven follow-up observations (see Analysis Issues and Strategy section in chapter 3). Approximate numbers of observations for men: 22,800, for women: 27,200. Any apparent inconsistency between data labels in the bars and cumulative percent noted is due to rounding. High-school-senior percentages (x notations) are based on base-year data from sets of years indicated; senior samples include approximately 8,000 men and 8,000 women each year.

1976–1981.[1] Among men, proportions reporting any use during the past year rose from about 1 in 10 at age 18 (senior year of high school) to about 1 in 4 during the early twenties, with monthly rates less than half that large. Among women there were similar increases during the early twenties, although the proportions were about two-thirds the size of those for men. During this same period in history, cocaine use was rising among high-school seniors, but only modestly (as shown by the x notations included in Fig. 7.1).

Figure 7.1 also shows some substantial downward shifts. From their midtwenties onward, rates of cocaine use declined steadily among the members of the classes of 1976–1981. Similarly, each new graduating class, starting with 1987, showed lower rates of use. Importantly, and in contrast to the findings for marijuana use, prevalence of cocaine use among young adults even in their early thirties remained higher than the rates for high-school seniors during the same historical intervals.

Do these findings taken together indicate any age-related decline in cocaine use during the late twenties and early thirties, above and beyond secular trends, as we found for marijuana use? Such a conclusion is not easily derived from Fig. 7.1, because the declines in use with age (downward shifts of about two-thirds or even three-quarters between ages 23–24 and ages 31–32) are not drastically different from the declines (of roughly two-thirds) in seniors' annual prevalence during the same interval (comparing classes of 1981–1987 with classes of 1989–1995). We return to this question again at the end of the chapter, at which point we will have examined the impacts of post-high-school experiences, and can consider the results of our multi-variate analyses.

ANALYSES LINKING COCAINE USE WITH POST-HIGH-SCHOOL EXPERIENCES

In this section, for the same reasons as we outlined in the chapter on marijuana use, we focus on measures of current cocaine use (i.e., any use during the 30-day period preceding the survey), although analyses using the 12-month measure yielded generally similar results.

Student Status Related to Cocaine Use

Figure 7.2 reveals that during the first 4 years after high school, prevalence of cocaine use rose among full-time students, part-time students, and

---

[1]The measures of current (monthly) and annual cocaine use were based on the following questions: "On how many occasions (if any) have you used cocaine (sometimes called 'coke') . . . during the last 12 months? . . . during the last 30 days?" The response scale is included in Table A.2 in the Appendix.

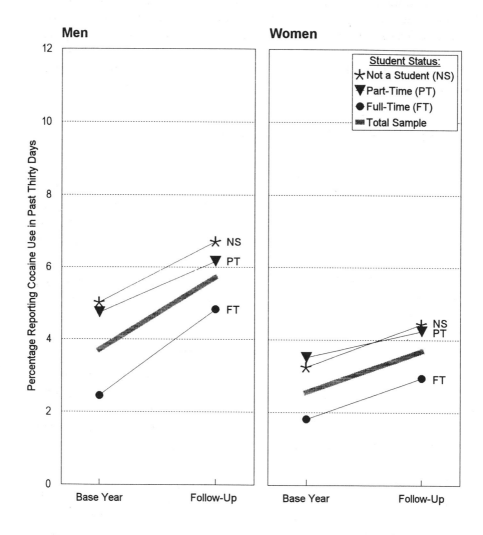

FIG. 7.2. Cocaine use in the past 30 days related to student status at time of follow-up. Percentages based on follow-ups 1 and 2 (modal ages 19–22, only), from classes of 1976–1994. In this figure, one person could contribute up to two follow-up observations (see Analysis Issues and Strategy section in chapter 3). Approximate numbers of observations for men: 20,900, for women: 25,400.

nonstudents. The sizes of shifts were not dramatically different and the regression analyses discussed later reveal no evidence of any "catching up" among college students. In fact, as we discuss later, the regression analyses actually indicate that students showed *lower* than average increases in cocaine use once their differences in living arrangements are taken into account. The most important differences among groups shown in Fig. 7.2 have to do not with *changes*, but with the consistent finding that those who went to college were less likely than their age-mates to be cocaine users; this was just as true while they were in high school as afterward.

Employment Status Related to Cocaine Use

Figure 7.3 shows only two employment categories in which current cocaine use was less prevalent than when the same individuals were high-school seniors—those in military service, and women who were full-time home-makers. For all other categories of employment status, likelihood of current cocaine use was greater at follow-up than in high school.

Full-Time Civilian Employment.   Here, as was true for marijuana use, those in full-time civilian employment were very close to the overall average prevalences of cocaine use both as seniors and at the time of follow-up.

Part-Time Employment.   As noted in previous chapters, many of those reporting part-time employment were also students, especially men. Thus it is not surprising to see the slightly lower than average proportions of cocaine users among part-time employed men, particularly during their senior year. The regression analyses, however, show no significant differences from average in the change scores of those in part-time jobs.

Military Service.   Just as we found for marijuana use, cocaine use dropped among both men and women who entered military service. It appears that the service-related differences reflect *changes* rather than *selection effects*, because the likelihood of cocaine use during the senior year of high school was not appreciably different from average.

Consistent with the findings for marijuana, the regression analyses presented in Appendix Tables A.10 and A.11 show that the downward changes in cocaine use among service personnel were not at all explainable by background, living arrangements, or other predictors included in the analyses. So we conclude again that illicit drug use declines due to some aspect(s)

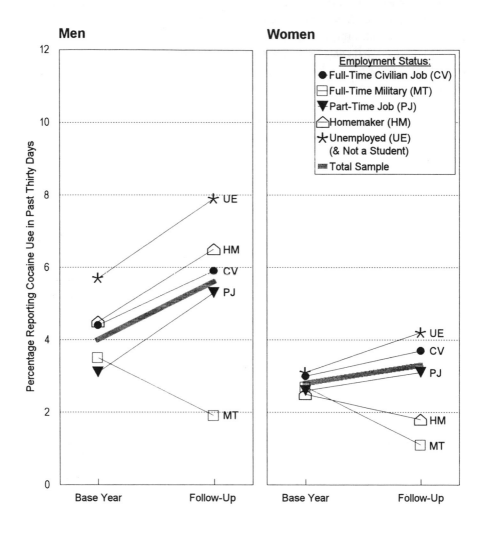

FIG. 7.3. Cocaine use in the past 30 days related to employment status at time of follow-up. Percentages based on follow-ups 1–7, from classes of 1976–1994. In this figure, one person could contribute up to seven follow-up observations (see Analysis Issues and Strategy section in chapter 3). Approximate numbers of observations for men: 47,900, for women: 58,400.

of military service; this includes, of course, those who quit use prior to entry so that they could pass the drug tests routinely administered to recruits.[2]

Homemakers.   Figure 7.3 shows a drop in prevalence of cocaine use among women who described themselves as full-time homemakers. Here again, as was true in each of the three preceding chapters, there is no independent homemaker effect. Rather, the decline in drug use is explainable in terms of other factors, including marital status, pregnancy, and parenthood.

Unemployment.   Figure 7.3 indicates that men who reported being unemployed at follow-up were about one-third more likely than average to be current cocaine users; however, the same was true when these individuals were seniors in high school. Among women, there are small differences in the same direction. The regression analyses show greater than average increases in annual cocaine use among unemployed men; this remains statistically significant after controls for background and student status, but is reduced a bit more (to nonsignificance) after further controls for marital status, living arrangements, and parenthood (see Table A.11 in the Appendix). That men's use of a costly drug like cocaine may increase during unemployment is interesting, especially given that their use of alcohol decreased, as seen in chapter 5. However, it should be kept in mind that the overall amounts of use and proportions of users remain quite low; it is the exception for anyone to use cocaine, including the unemployed.

Living Arrangements and Marital Status Related to Cocaine Use

The frequency levels for cocaine use reported by our panel respondents were generally quite low, suggesting that few of the users in our samples were chemically dependent on cocaine. Thus, like alcohol use and marijuana use, we expected cocaine use to be influenced by changes in role responsibilities and social environments.

Being Married.   Figure 7.4 shows that those who were married, in contrast to each of the other living arrangements shown, were less likely to use cocaine than when they were high-school seniors. The regression

---

[2]We note again, as in the previous chapter, that the degree of decline in use during military service may be exaggerated due to a greater than average tendency among those in the military to deny use (Johnston & O'Malley, 1997).

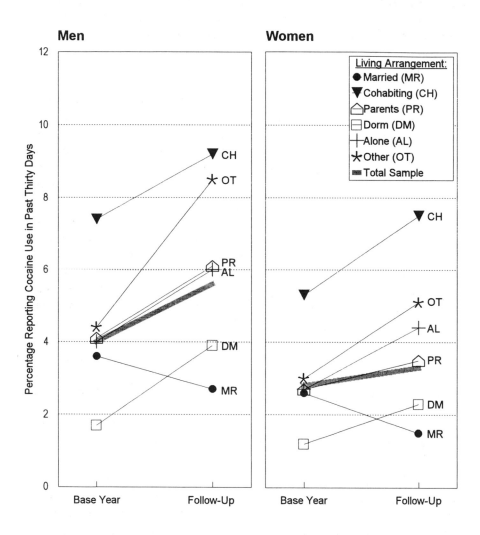

FIG. 7.4. Cocaine use in the past 30 days related to living arrangement at time of follow-up. Percentages based on follow-ups 1–7, from classes of 1976–1994. In this figure, one person could contribute up to seven follow-up observations (see Analysis Issues and Strategy section in chapter 3). Approximate numbers of observations for men: 47,900, for women: 58,400.

analyses in Appendix Tables A.10 and A.11 show bivariate and multivariate coefficients that are essentially equal, indicating that the effects of marriage on reductions in cocaine use are independent of other post-high-school experiences (and also independent of the background factors included in the analyses). Here again it is worth repeating the comment that some of the marriage effect on drug use may be anticipatory; indeed, the data on engagement reported later in this chapter suggest that was the case for cocaine use.

Cohabiting. Figure 7.4 again shows the distinctiveness of those who were cohabiting with a partner of the opposite sex at the time of follow-up. During their senior year of high school, these individuals were about twice as likely as their classmates to be current users of cocaine. The figure shows also that prevalence of monthly cocaine use increased much more than average among women who were cohabiting, although among male cohabitants the increases were not greater than those for men in general.

The multivariate analyses of changes in *frequency* of cocaine use are consistent with the prevalence data shown in Fig. 7.4; monthly use for cohabiting women increased significantly more than average, whereas that was not true for cohabiting men (Table A.10). For annual use, however, cohabitation was associated with significant increases in cocaine use among both men and women (Table A.11). Here again, as we found for marijuana use in chapter 6, the multivariate coefficients are a bit larger than the bivariate ones, and the unmasking occurs in the presence of a roughly equal and opposite engagement effect (to which we return later in this chapter).

Whatever the underlying dynamics, it seems clear that at least some of those who explore the alternative lifestyle of cohabitation show greater than average willingness to experiment with illicit drugs, including cocaine. That said, we should emphasize that the large majority of cohabitants were *not* current cocaine users at either senior year or follow-up.

Living With Parents. Figure 7.4 shows that those who were living with parents were just about average in proportions of cocaine users, both during high school and at follow-up. Appendix Tables A.10 and A.11 show that, with respect to changes in cocaine use, those living with parents did not depart at all from the overall means.

Living in a Dormitory. The findings for those living in a dormitory are fully consistent with the findings for full-time students in general. As can be seen in Fig. 7.4, those living in dorms were much less likely than average to have used cocaine, either during high school or at follow-up. With respect to *changes* in cocaine use, however, they did not depart from average in either direction, as can be seen in Appendix Tables A.10 and A.11. Apparently it is one thing for dorm students to involve themselves in heavy drinking and marijuana use, but quite another matter to get involved with cocaine use. These differences suggest that marijuana is viewed as a less risky, "casual" drug in the college student population, whereas cocaine is viewed as a much riskier, "hard" drug and thus is not as widely accepted.

Living Alone. Rates of current cocaine use rose moderately among those living alone; this increase was only slightly above the average for men, and a bit more above the average for women, as can be seen in Fig. 7.4. These findings are echoed in the regression analyses (Tables A.10 and A.11), which show increases only slightly greater than average (all except one were nonsignificant).

Other Living Arrangements. Those in this category were not different from average as high-school seniors, but at follow-up their prevalence of cocaine use was clearly above average (Fig. 7.4). The regression analyses showed consistent and significant increases in frequency of cocaine use associated with the other living arrangements category.

Pregnancy and Parenthood Related to Cocaine Use

Pregnancy. Figure 7.5 shows that fewer than 1% of pregnant women used cocaine during the preceding month, in contrast to about 3% of the other women. Among men with pregnant spouses, rates were lower than among other men, but no more so than would be expected from the impacts of marriage alone.

The multivariate analyses of changes in frequency of cocaine use (Tables A.10 and A.11) show fairly consistent findings. Among men there were small bivariate coefficients, but the multivariate coefficients were essentially zero, indicating that after controls for marital status there was no effect attributable to having a pregnant spouse. Among women the multivariate coefficients were distinctly lower than the bivariate ones (and nonsignificant), indicating that any relationship overlapped heavily with the marital status effect.

Parenthood. Among mothers, married and single, the multivariate analyses showed declines in annual cocaine use significantly greater than

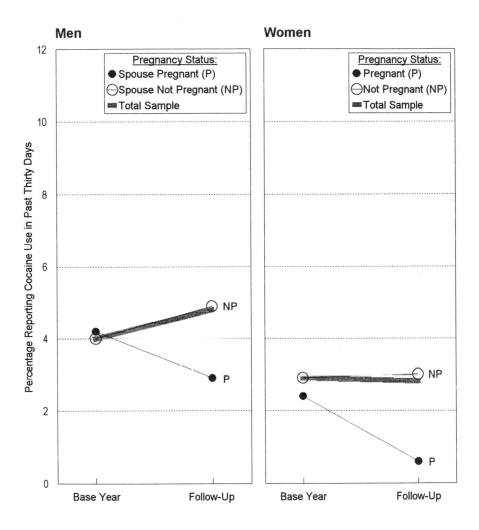

FIG. 7.5. Cocaine use in the past 30 days related to pregnancy status at time of follow-up. Percentages based on follow-ups 1–7, from classes of 1976–1994. The pregnancy item was not added to the follow-up questionnaire until 1984. In this figure, one person could contribute up to six follow-up observations (see Analysis Issues and Strategy section in chapter 3). Approximate numbers of observations for men: 39,700, for women: 48,700.

average, whereas among men the declines were smaller and nonsignificant (Table A.11). The changes in monthly cocaine use were too small to be significant (Table A.10).

Further Findings on Marital Status and Cocaine Use

Engagement.   Earlier analyses showed an engagement effect on cocaine use in the same (downward) direction as the marriage effect, albeit weaker (Bachman et al., 1997). Our present multivariate analyses show negative effects on cocaine use associated with engagement that are about as strong as those associated with marriage (see Tables A.10 and A.11).[3]

The descriptive data provided in Fig. 7.6 show that among those who were engaged at follow-up, cohabitants as well as those not cohabiting, there was virtually no increase in prevalence of current cocaine use (compared with rates as high-school seniors). Those who were not engaged (and not married) showed the largest increases in prevalence of cocaine use.

The data in Fig. 7.7, which show changes in proportions of current cocaine users over 2-year intervals between follow-ups, provide a different perspective because the comparisons do not involve the senior year of high school. Here again we see engagement effects that parallel and nearly equal marriage effects.

Divorce.   Our earlier analyses covering sets of three follow-ups showed that divorce was associated with increases in cocaine use; moreover, these increases equaled or exceeded the size of the decreases associated with marriage (Bachman et al., 1997). The same pattern is clear in the 2-year analyses shown in Fig. 7.7. It is no exaggeration to say that divorce has the effect of undoing the marriage effect on cocaine use.

Figure 7.7 shows patterns generally similar to those for the other drugs among those who were divorced at the start of the 2-year intervals. Those who remarried showed decreased likelihood of remaining current cocaine users. (Indeed, that drop appears dramatic among men, but we should recall that the numbers of cases are relatively small and the actual percentages are also small.) Those who remained divorced across both points showed above average percentages of users (but were not substantially different from those who were single at both times).

---

[3]Here once more we focus on the multivariate coefficients because they contrast engaged individuals with other *single* individuals who are not engaged (see footnote 4, chapter 4).

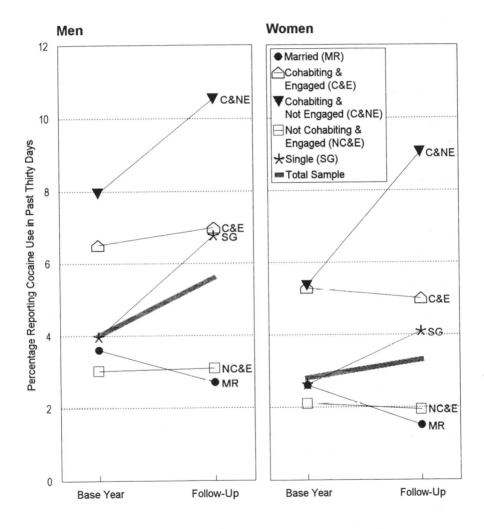

FIG. 7.6. Cocaine use in the past 30 days related to engagement, cohabitation, and marriage at time of follow-up. Percentages based on follow-ups 1–7, from classes of 1976–1994. In this figure, one person could contribute up to seven follow-up observations (see Analysis Issues and Strategy section in chapter 3). Approximate numbers of observations for men: 47,900, for women: 58,400.

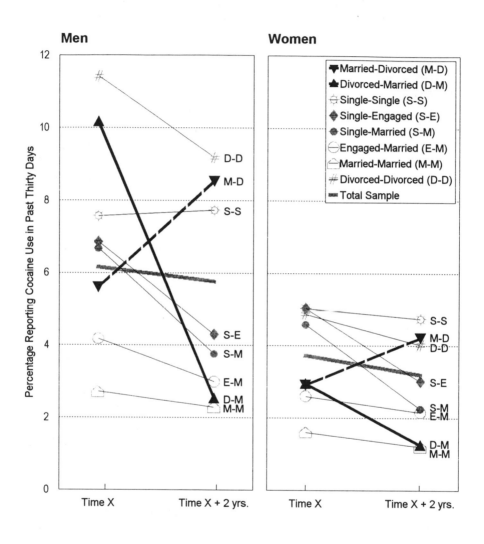

FIG. 7.7. Cocaine use in the past 30 days related to transitions in marital status. Percentages based on follow-ups 1–7, from classes of 1976–1994. Observations are drawn from two consecutive follow-ups, providing measures at two points in time that cover an interval of 2 years. That is, observations are based on individuals' data from follow-ups 1 and 2, follow-ups 2 and 3, follow-ups 3 and 4, and so forth. Note that an individual who participated in all seven follow-ups would contribute six observations. Approximate numbers of observations for men: 33,000, for women: 41,700.

CONCLUSIONS FROM MULTIVARIATE
ANALYSES LINKING COCAINE USE
WITH POST-HIGH-SCHOOL EXPERIENCES

Explained Variance

Comments in previous chapters concerning low amounts of explained variance in marijuana use change scores apply all the more to cocaine use. The majority of high-school seniors and young adults simply did not use cocaine at all, so for them the change scores for cocaine use were all zero. The variance in cocaine change scores derives from the minority of individuals who used the drug—the few who reported any use during the previous year, and the even smaller number who reported use in the past month. The related point made in the previous chapter about 30 days as a limited period for sampling relatively infrequent behavior, such as marijuana use, is even more applicable to cocaine use. Accordingly, we focus attention primarily on the 12-month data shown in Appendix Table A.11.

Overlaps Between Student/Work Status and Living Arrangements

Being a full-time student showed no bivariate relationship to changes in frequency of cocaine use during the past year; however, the multivariate analyses controlling for living arrangements, parenthood, and other factors revealed a significant negative impact associated with being a full-time student. This provides an interesting contrast to marijuana use and heavy drinking, where we interpreted our findings as indicating that students caught up with their age-mates (and surpassed them, in the case of alcohol) primarily because students were less likely to marry and more likely to leave their parents' homes—changes in living arrangements generally associated with increased drug use. With respect to cocaine use, however, we conclude that being a college student tended to hold down the use of the drug. The negative relationship between military service and cocaine use is enhanced with controls for living arrangements, as can be seen in Table A.11.

In the case of women who were full-time homemakers, however, it appears that the bivariate relationship is fully explainable in terms of living arrangements. Consistent with our findings for other forms of drug use, it appears that homemakers showed lower use because they were married and often mothers, not because of other aspects of the home-maker role.

Living arrangements (including marriage), engagement, pregnancy, and parenthood all showed essentially the same impacts on cocaine use, whether student/work status variables were included in the equation or not (as we found for marijuana use).

In summary, it appears that there are significant effects associated with student status and military service, both of which tend to inhibit cocaine use. It also appears that these effects are essentially independent of other significant inhibiting effects associated with the responsibilities of engagement, marriage, and motherhood, as well as the enhancing effect associated with the freedom of being in other living arrangements.

Accounting for Age-Related Changes in Cocaine Use

Figure 7.8 presents mean changes in current (30-day) cocaine use by age, both unadjusted and adjusted for living arrangements and all other predictors. The figure shows moderate reductions in the age-related patterns when the other predictors are included—a higher proportionate reduction than we found for marijuana (see Fig. 6.8), but less than the reduction for the alcohol use measures (see Figs. 5.16 and 5.17).

We argued in the previous chapter that much of the residual age-related pattern for marijuana was attributable to the downward secular trend in use of that drug. A similar argument can be made for cocaine, although the secular trend is not simply downward (as can be seen from the high-school-senior data points included in Fig. 7.1). As in the case of marijuana, we believe that beyond the overall secular trend there remain changes in cocaine use, or age-relevant shifts, that are explainable in terms of the post-high-school experiences we have been examining. We believe that the age-related departures from the secular trend in cocaine use are influenced both by the new freedoms of young adulthood—especially leaving parents' homes—and by new constraints and responsibilities—including, most notably, military service, engagement, marriage, and parenthood.

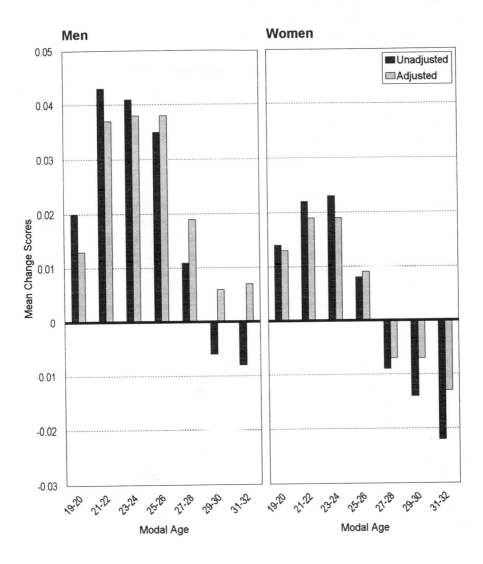

FIG. 7.8. Mean change scores in 30-day cocaine use, unadjusted and adjusted, related to modal age. The mean change score is the predicted amount of change in 30-day cocaine use between base year and modal age indicated. The unadjusted mean change score only controls the follow-up survey interval (or, modal age). The adjusted mean change score controls all the predictor variables. Calculation of change scores is discussed in detail in the Appendix.

8

Summary, Conclusions, and Implications

This book has explored the developmental period following high school, from the late teens to the early thirties. We looked for both change and stability in patterns of drug use, and found some of each. Much of the change proved to be linked to the new freedoms and responsibilities that accompany—indeed, define—the transition from adolescence to adulthood.

Our search was made possible by an extraordinary set of panel data generated by the Monitoring the Future project—data that are nationally representative, cover a developmental span of up to 14 years, involve high-school cohorts extending over nearly two decades, and include large numbers of individuals surveyed at multiple points in time. Using these data, we examined young adults' use of four drugs—tobacco, alcohol, marijuana, and cocaine. Many important differences among these drugs were documented; however, we also saw that certain experiences, such as marriage and pregnancy, can lead to stopping or reducing the use of all four substances. These and other role experiences can explain at least some of what has been described as "maturing out"—in this case, reductions in substance use among young adults after their early twenties.

We examined these relationships separately for men and for women, and found the patterns to be fundamentally similar, with the notable exception of pregnancy. In addition, the impacts of key role transitions on drug use were found to be much the same whether the transitions occur earlier or later in young adulthood. These and other consistencies leave us increasingly confident of the soundness and generalizability of these findings.

What are the experiences of young adulthood that seem to matter most in terms of changes in drug use? Marital status and other aspects of living arrangements are especially important. Some arrangements, such as leaving parents' homes and moving into dormitories or similar housing among other unrelated young adults, lead to increases in alcohol and other drug use. Other arrangements, such as becoming married (i.e., living with a spouse), are associated with substantial reductions in such use. More complex, in terms of implications for substance use, is life in a military environment:

Consumption of cigarettes and alcohol increase, whereas illicit drug use drops sharply.

Most of this chapter is devoted to a summary and integration of the findings presented in this volume, after which we offer some conclusions and implications. Before undertaking the summary, however, it is useful to set the stage in two ways. First, we provide some historical and developmental context for understanding drug use during the transition to young adulthood. Second, we highlight differences, similarities, and interrelationships among the drug using behaviors we have examined.

PLACING THESE FINDINGS IN CONTEXT

Why do some young adults smoke cigarettes, some drink excessively, and some use illicit drugs? Why do some substantially change their patterns of drug use after high school, whereas others do not? These two questions overlap a great deal, but they are not identical. In this book we have focused primarily on the second question, considering specifically how the new freedoms and responsibilities of young adulthood lead to changes in drug use. However, other factors are involved in answering these questions, especially the first one; before reviewing our present findings, it may be useful to consider briefly some of the other influences we know have contributed to the drug use of young adults during the past several decades.

New Perspectives on the Drug Problem in the United States

In recent decades there has been a substantial change in the nation's views about drug use and abuse. During the 1940s, 1950s, and early 1960s, the "drug problem" was seen largely in terms of relatively small numbers of people, mostly in inner cities, who were addicted to hard-core illicit drugs such as heroin, and who led lives of crime in order to support their drug habits. By the 1970s, it was clear that use of illicit drugs had become widespread, and data from large-scale nationwide surveys showed that majorities of the nation's youth and young adults were involved on at least an occasional basis. The realization that many high-school students had tried marijuana, that substantial numbers were using it on a regular basis, and that other illicit drug use was widespread, prompted redefinitions of the drug problem. In addition to the problem represented by hard-core addicts, there was the new mainstream problem of occasional recreational use. A further evolution in thinking about the drug problem among youth, as well as adults, was the recognition that problems of substance abuse are by no means limited to illicit drugs such as marijuana, cocaine, and heroin; to the contrary, tobacco and alcohol, two substances legally purchased (by adults), came to be seen as very much a part of the nation's drug problem. Indeed, it is now widely understood that in terms of illness, injury, and death, the costs of tobacco and alcohol use far outweigh those attributable to illicit drug use.

The Monitoring the Future project in general, and the present monograph in particular, focus primarily on the mainstream drug problem. The present analyses included only individuals who remained in high school through the end of their senior year, and who were willing to participate in our panel surveys extending into young adulthood. People living lives of crime, in prison, or on the street, were less likely to be reached by our mail survey attempts and less likely to complete and return questionnaires. Thus this study does not cover all youth and young adults, and most likely the individuals we missed were disproportionately involved in heavy drug use and other problem behaviors.

Although the sample employed in this study is not *entirely* representative, it is fair to describe it as *broadly* representative. We believe that the drug-using and -abusing behaviors examined here constitute a very important portion of the nation's drug problem, and that the processes whereby a great many of the nation's young adults "mature out" of youthful drug use and abuse are valuable topics for study and for further research. Our study does not represent all of the young adults who have become habituated to cigarette use, but it includes a substantial proportion. Similarly, our samples do not capture all who occasionally drink to excess, but many of them are included, some of whom eventually become chronic alcohol abusers. Without a doubt our research underrepresents those who are deeply involved in the illicit drug subculture, but it does include a great many who use illicit drugs (particularly marijuana) on at least an occasional basis and often on a more than occasional basis.

Secular Trends (Period Effects) in Drug Use

How likely is it that a certain young adult uses a particular drug? A large part of the answer, of course, depends on which drug is being considered. Another part of the answer, as we have documented here, depends on how

old the individual is, whether he or she is married,
pregnant. A third part of the answer has to do with w
asked, because there have been dramatic changes in dru
decades. The average young adult in 1980 was more tha
be a current marijuana user as the average young adu
analyses of Monitoring the Future data have documented these substantial
secular trends in marijuana use and in cocaine use, as well as modest secular
trends in alcohol use (see O'Malley et al., 1984, 1988a, 1988b, for detailed
analyses of such trends; see also Johnston et al., 1997, for the most recent
updates of these trends).

So one important determinant of drug use among young adults—or
adolescents or older adults, for that matter—is simply the historical period
in which they live. Especially with respect to illicit drugs, the probability of
use has a great deal to do with the rise and fall of a drug's popularity. In the
present book we have treated such period effects as context, to be taken
into account as necessary, while we have focused primarily on other factors
that seem to influence individuals in essentially the same fashion whether
a drug's popularity is waxing or waning. Put another way, we have concentrated on what often are called *age effects*—changes with age, and the
experiences correlated with aging, that tend to be common across cohorts
and across recent historical periods.

Perceptions and Attitudes About Drugs

Among the most important determinants of the popularity of illicit drugs in
recent years has been disapproval of their use, and perceptions that their
use is risky. In other analyses we have tracked these attitudes and perceptions
over 20 years, and have shown that they correspond very closely with (and
sometimes slightly precede) changes in drug use (Johnston et al., 1997, and
earlier volumes in the same series). We have also demonstrated in greater
detail that increased disapproval and perceptions of risk largely account for
the overall declines in marijuana use during much of the 1980s (Bachman
et al., 1988; Johnston, 1982), and later declines in cocaine use (Bachman,
Johnston, et al., 1990).

It should come as no surprise that at the individual level of analysis, a
person's perceptions and attitudes with respect to specific drugs are strongly
correlated with his or her use of those drugs. If our purpose in this book had
been simply to see how much variance in drug use we could predict or
explain, then certainly such attitudinal measures would have been included
as predictors. We chose instead to focus on the impacts of post-high-school

oles and experiences; an exploration of the ways in which perceptions and attitudes about drugs may be involved as intervening variables is a large and complex project that we have left for future analyses.[1]

Stability of Drug Use During Young Adulthood

If one really wants to predict the drug use of a young adult, nothing is likely to work better than knowing that individual's use of the same drug a year or two earlier. We have found high cross-time correlations for our measures of drug use, even though such correlations are diminished by unavoidable measurement errors. These errors are increased, to some extent, when we focus on a limited time interval such as 2 weeks (for our measure of heavy drinking) or 30 days (for the other drugs). By keeping to fairly short intervals we are able to increase accuracy *in the aggregate* (because there is less forgetting, blurring of dates, or other distortions; see Bachman & O'Malley, 1981/1989); however, *at the individual level* we are left with a kind of time sampling error because we lack precision in measuring behaviors of those who engage in the behavior only occasionally (e.g., "binge" only every few weekends). Fortunately, when measurements are available from three or more time points, it is a fairly straightforward matter to estimate measurement errors; we reported some such estimates based on early Monitoring the Future data (O'Malley et al., 1983), and we recently conducted new analyses covering the full range of panel data examined in this book. When measurement errors are estimated and taken into account (i.e., removed statistically), we are able to estimate the actual *stability* of drug use, defined as the correlation between two *true* (i.e., error-free) variables assessed at different points in time.[2]

Use rates for each of the drugs covered here have shown very high levels of stability, especially over 1-year intervals. Annual stability estimates for each are shown in the upper portion of Fig. 8.1. Four important points are worth noting, based on these annual stability estimates. First, stability rates for all drugs during the first year after high school are quite high. Second, stability rates grow higher as individuals grow older; we believe this increas-

---

[1]In addition to adding a complex new set of analyses, an exploration of perceptions and attitudes as intervening variables would have reduced our sample sizes by a factor of about five, because most of these measures appear on only one or another of the five (and, in recent years, six) different questionnaire forms used in the Monitoring the Future surveys. All variables used in the present analyses appear in all questionnaire forms.

[2]This definition of stability in terms of the consistency of differences among individuals across time (e.g., consistent rank orderings) is not at all the same as constancy in mean levels. In the aggregate, mean levels of most licit and illicit drug use drop considerably after the first few years of young adulthood; however, as we show later, the stability of ordering among individuals remains quite high.

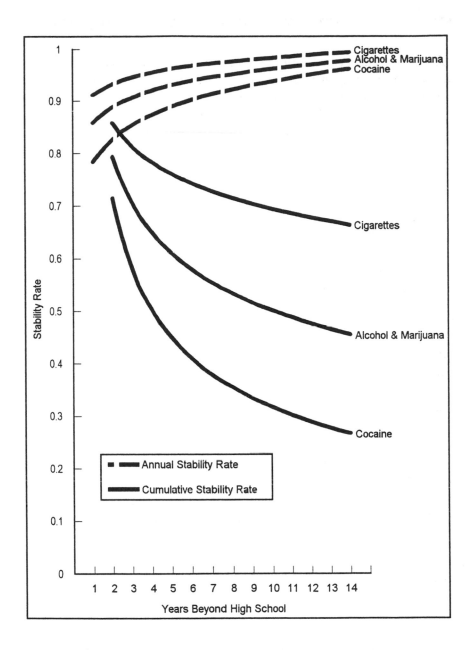

FIG. 8.1. Stability rates of drug use. Stability rates are estimated correlations between "true" (i.e., error-free) variables assessed at different points in time. The dashed lines show that annual stability rates (consistency over a 1-year interval) increase gradually with age. The solid lines show that correlations with senior-year drug use grow smaller as age increases. The estimates shown are idealized patterns based on extensive preliminary analyses. A more complete report (by O'Malley and others) is forthcoming.

ing stability reflects the fact that the rate of change in new roles, freedoms, and responsibilities gradually decreases with increasing age. Third, the stability rates for cigarette use are distinctly higher than those for the other drugs; this is consistent with our findings that roles and responsibilities have a very limited impact on cigarette use, and with the fact that so many individuals find the cigarette habit very difficult to break. Fourth, the stability rates for alcohol use, instances of heavy drinking, and marijuana use are so closely similar that they can be summarized with a single trend line, indicating that these drugs are all roughly similar in their susceptibility to change. (Stabilities for the less commonly used cocaine are slightly lower.)

Lest we be misled by these very high *annual* stability rates, and conclude that there is rather little room for change, Fig. 8.1 includes *cumulative* stability rates extending to the 14-year span covered by our panel analyses. The figure shows that estimated 14-year stabilities are about .65 for cigarette use, about .45 for alcohol use and marijuana use, and only about .25 for cocaine use. It can also be seen that 5-year stabilities, between modal ages 18 and 23, are about .75 for cigarette use, about .45 for cocaine use, and about .60 for the other drugs. It thus seems clear that change during any one year is fairly limited, probably involving only a limited portion of young adults; however, with each additional year the changes aggregate. This pattern of very high short-term stability coupled with larger cumulative changes over longer intervals closely matches the gradual shifts across time in the proportions of young adults assuming the roles of spouse (see Fig. 3.4) and parent (Fig. 3.5).

DIFFERENCES, SIMILARITIES, AND INTERRELATIONSHIPS AMONG DRUG-USING BEHAVIORS

In the preceding four chapters we examined usage of cigarettes, alcohol, marijuana, and cocaine, focusing on one drug in each chapter. We do not repeat our descriptions of the individual drug use patterns here; rather, we now contrast the four drugs, noting differences, similarities, and interrelationships in usage.

Several distinctions in usage patterns for the four drugs are worth keeping in mind. One distinction is that historical trends in use have varied considerably from drug to drug. Another distinction is that the different drugs have shown various patterns of age-related change, with all eventually declining in use by the time young adults reach their late twenties and early thirties. Perhaps the most fundamental distinction is simply that the proportions of users, and amounts of use, differ dramatically from one drug to another. For example, in 1995 more than two-thirds of young adults were current alcohol users (defined as use in the past month), whereas fewer than 2% were current cocaine users (Johnston et al., 1997). Far fewer young adults smoke than drink; however, the sheer numbers of cigarettes consumed vastly outstrip the numbers of drinks consumed. Most young adult alcohol users drink on a less-than-daily basis, and most who use illicit drugs do so infrequently, but the typical young adult smoker lights up 10 or more times per day. These high levels of cigarette use, and the high stability of smoking behavior across long intervals, testify to the strength and persistence of most cigarette habits.

These differences among drug use patterns are some of the reasons we chose to examine each of the drugs separately in this book, rather than combining them into a single composite measure of "drug use in young adulthood." Still another reason for treating the drugs separately is that the various post-high-school experiences we have examined do not seem to affect all kinds of drug use in exactly the same ways.

There are, nevertheless, a number of important similarities across the different drugs in the ways that use seems to be linked with post-high-school experiences. In the present chapter we focus mostly on those similarities and common patterns. As a first step, we briefly illustrate the extent to which the use of each of the drugs correlates with use of each of the others. These intercorrelations help to indicate the extent of the similarities and differences among the drug-using behaviors studied here.

Smoking Correlated With Other Drug Use

Figure 8.2 shows proportions of alcohol users, marijuana users, and cocaine users among the young adult cigarette smokers and nonsmokers in our study.[3] Clearly, smoking was positively correlated with use of other drugs. The majority of both smokers and nonsmokers were current alcohol users; nevertheless, among nonsmokers about one-quarter of the men and more than one-third of the women were nondrinkers, compared with only about half as many of those who were smokers. The more serious type of alcohol use, five or more drinks in a row, was reported by substantially more smokers

---

[3]The figures in this chapter are based on all follow-up data from all available cohorts, and represent averages across the nearly 20-year span included in these analyses. It should be kept in mind that rates of use for marijuana and cocaine shifted considerably from 1977 through 1995 (see notations in Figs. 6.1 and 7.1). However, even though the proportions of users shifted over time, other analyses (not shown) confirm that usage rates for these drugs were positively and similarly intercorrelated across all years and all ages studied.

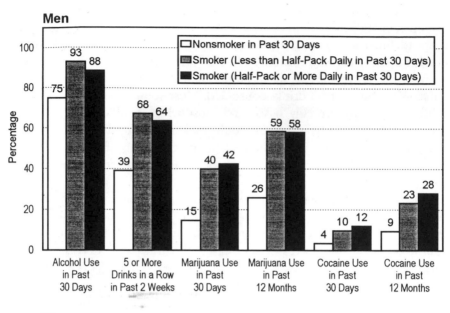

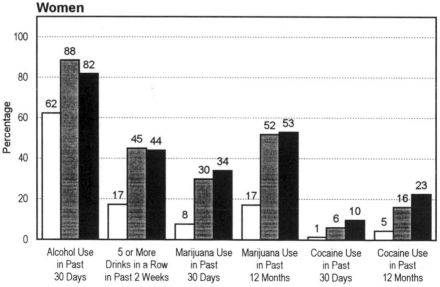

FIG. 8.2. Alcohol, marijuana, and cocaine use related to cigarette use by young adults (all follow-up data from all cohorts).

160

than nonsmokers—more than twice as many among the women, and more than half again as many among the men. Marijuana use and cocaine use were also two to four or more times more likely among smokers than nonsmokers.

Alcohol Use Correlated With Other Drug Use

Figure 8.3 distinguishes three levels of alcohol users, showing that use of other drugs differed sharply among them. Among the rather small portion of the total sample who reported no alcohol use during the past 30 days, relatively few smoked cigarettes (13–14%), even fewer used marijuana in the past year (8–9%), and very few used cocaine in the past year (about 2%). Compared with these very low rates among nondrinkers, rates of smoking and illicit drug use were 2 to 4 times higher among those who reported some alcohol use in the past 30 days but no instances of heavy drinking during the past 2 weeks, and rates were 2 to 3 times higher again among those who did report instances of heavy drinking. Thus, compared with those who used no alcohol during the past month, those who reported having five or more drinks in a row during the past 2 weeks were about 6 times more likely to have used marijuana during the past year, and about 10 to 12 times more likely to have used cocaine.

Marijuana Use and Cocaine Use Correlated With Other Drug Use

The next two figures show the high levels of overlapping drug use from the perspective of marijuana users and nonusers (Fig. 8.4) and cocaine users and nonusers (Fig. 8.5). The similarities between the two figures are considerable, but there are some interesting differences. Although occasions of heavy drinking are common among current marijuana users (76% of the men and 56% of the women), such occasions are even more common among the current cocaine users (85% of the men and 67% of the women). Moreover, whereas nearly all cocaine users reported being marijuana users (see Fig. 8.5), the majority of marijuana users did not report any cocaine use in the past year (see Fig. 8.4). These findings indicate that the use of one illicit drug, marijuana, did not necessarily lead to the use of the more serious illicit drug, cocaine; however, looked at the other way, the findings show that about 9 out of 10 cocaine users were also using marijuana.

Panel research with adolescents has shown that early drug use experiences with cigarettes and alcohol almost universally precede illicit drug use

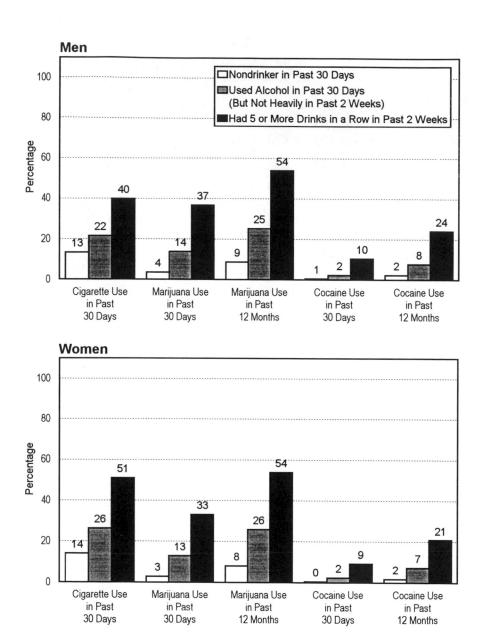

FIG. 8.3.   Cigarette, marijuana, and cocaine use related to alcohol use by young adults (all follow-up data from all cohorts).

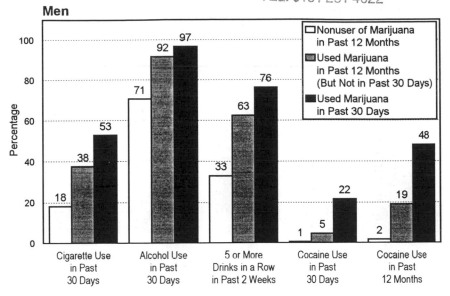

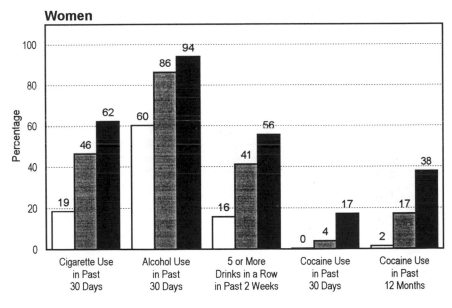

FIG. 8.4. Cigarette, alcohol, and cocaine use related to marijuana use by young adults (all follow-up data from all cohorts).

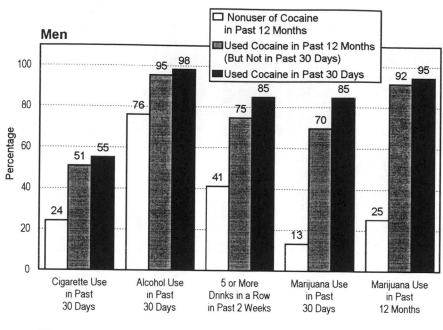

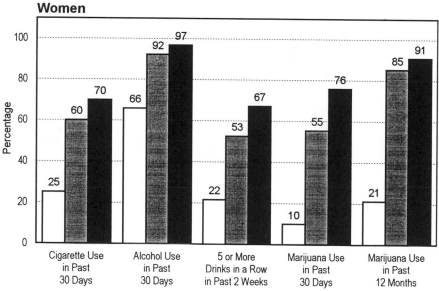

FIG. 8.5. Cigarette, alcohol, and marijuana use related to cocaine use by young adults (all follow-up data from all cohorts).

(Kandel et al., 1992). The correlational data for young adults, presented earlier, extend those findings by showing that virtually all current users of marijuana or cocaine were also current alcohol users, most had used alcohol heavily during the past 2 weeks, and most were current cigarette users. Do illicit drugs eventually become substitutes for licit drugs? There is certainly no indication in these data that use of illicit substances lessens the likelihood of using licit substances such as cigarettes and alcohol. (Incidentally, we examined 2-year change scores—i.e., change from one follow-up to the next—for the several dimensions of drug use studied here; all are positively correlated, which provides further evidence that use of these substances tends to rise and fall together.)

LINKING DRUG USE WITH POST-HIGH-SCHOOL EXPERIENCES: SUMMARIZING AND INTERPRETING OUR FINDINGS

Causal Assumptions and the Limitations of Observational Studies

Our panel data stretching from the senior year of high school to as much as 14 years later (modal ages 18–32) provide rich opportunities for examining how changes in role statuses, and corresponding changes in freedoms and responsibilities, are linked with changes in substance use. Our analyses and reporting were guided by our fundamental assumption that these changes in roles and experiences contribute, both directly and indirectly, to changes in levels of post-high-school drug use. However, we recognize that most such causal assumptions are simplifications, and that there are interesting and important exceptions in which changes in drug use may precede and contribute to changes in role status. We noted in chapter 1 the difficulties of studying causal relationships in natural settings, and it is worth stressing again that correlational studies cannot prove causation—even when the analyses employ panel data spanning a number of years. Nevertheless, panel data can be very helpful in demonstrating when there are correspondences between one kind of change and another, thereby narrowing the range of plausible causal interpretations. Moreover, panel data can play a very important role in sorting out the effects of *selection* (i.e., preexisting differences) from those of *socialization*, and we have seen at least one clear example of post-high-school differences (the relatively low smoking rates observed among college students) that seem to be no more than a continuation of distinctions that were in place well before the end of high school. When at times we speak of the "impacts" or "effects" of post-high-school roles and experiences on drug use, it should thus be understood that we are not asserting that our panel data analyses have *proven* the causal interpretation, but that we consider it to be the most *plausible* interpretation in light of our extensive panel data.

Disentangling the Effects of Post-High-School Experiences

After graduation from high school, most young adults embark on one of two primary paths—many become full-time college students, and most others enter full-time employment. This key decision has many important correlates; most notably, the full-time college students tend to defer marriage, and parenthood, and many of them leave their parents' homes somewhat earlier than their age-mates who do not go to college. We recognize that the causal processes can be complex; the willingness or unwillingness to defer marriage or leave one's hometown may help some young people to decide in favor of college and help others to decide against it. Nevertheless, we think that the primary decision for most young people is whether or not to go to college; then, flowing from that fundamental decision, come the further decisions having to do with employment, living arrangements, and the timing of marriage. This perspective is similar to the differential socialization hypothesis (cf. Chassin et al., 1992; Schulenberg et al., 1994; Yamaguchi & Kandel, 1985b) that early academic success and college attendance represent primary selection factors that channel young adults toward specific socialization experiences.

It should, of course, be noted that our regression analyses take a "main effects" or "additive" approach to the impacts of the several post-high-school experiences examined here, rather than seeking interactions. This is consistent with our prior experience that the effects studied here are, in fact, additive. A few exceptions are worth noting. First, some patterns are somewhat different for men than for women, especially the impacts of single parenthood and the distinction between pregnant women and men with pregnant spouses. Our use of separate analyses for men and women permitted these and other gender-related interactions to emerge, of course, but the impressive finding shown in the figures and tables is that the results for men and women are closely parallel, with few interactions other than those just mentioned. One other interaction involved the distinction between single and married parents, but we took account of that by distinguishing these two kinds of parenthood in our regression analyses.

In the following sections we summarize how changes in drug use are linked with a variety of post-high-school experiences—college, military service, and other employment; engagement, cohabitation, marriage, pregnancy, parenthood, divorce, and other aspects of living arrangements. Throughout this summary we offer our interpretations of the causal relationships, bearing in mind that correlations cannot prove causation, but also that panel data can provide stronger support for some interpretations than for others.

Student Status Related to Drug Use

A majority of our panel respondents were full-time students during the first 2 years after high school, and many continued to be full-time students for the next year or two (see Fig. 3.2). As we have noted, this fundamental decision to invest the first few years after high school in higher education has implications for many other aspects of lifestyle. What can be said about the impacts of college attendance on drug use? The first thing to be said, based on our longitudinal analyses, is that the impacts are both more and less than cross-sectional data alone might lead one to believe—more with respect to alcohol and marijuana, and less with respect to cigarettes.

College students are far less likely than their age-mates to be daily cigarette smokers, but this cross-sectional difference in smoking rates has relatively little to do with their experiences in college. Our panel analyses reported here (see Fig. 4.3) and earlier (Bachman et al., 1984; see also Bachman et al., 1978) show that most college students never became regular smokers while they were in secondary school. Thus college attendance is related to large and important differences in *levels* of smoking, but little in the way of post-high-school *changes* in smoking, and that is consistent with a selection effect interpretation. That said, we should note that our regression analyses of change scores revealed that during the first 4 years after high school, cigarette consumption increased two to three times as much among nonstudents as among full-time students (see Table A.5).

How should we account for this differential change in cigarette use linked to student status? We believe that both selection and socialization effects may be involved to some extent. First, recalling that fewer of the college students were regular smokers during high school (see Fig. 4.3), and that most of the post-high-school increases in smoking involved higher rates of use by those already habituated to cigarette use, some differential change might amount to a sort of "delayed-action" selection effect; that is, preexisting differences (in proportions of smokers) led to differential change.

Second, the smaller increases in smoking among college students may also reflect some socialization effects; the college environment, with its very low proportions of smokers, probably discourages students from initiating or increasing the consumption of cigarettes (Chassin et al., 1992; Schulenberg et al., 1994).

Earlier analyses of Monitoring the Future panel data (Bachman, Schulenberg, et al., 1990; Schulenberg et al., 1994), as well as the earlier Youth in Transition study (Bachman et al., 1978), add further support to our preferred interpretation of the negative relationship between college attendance and smoking, which can be summarized as follows: (a) Those who are academically successful in high school (and earlier) are unlikely to become smokers during adolescence, and these same individuals are likely to go to college. (b) Because cigarette smoking is such a difficult habit to break, the differences in smoking rates linked to earlier educational success persist during and beyond the college years. Thus educational accomplishments probably do influence smoking behaviors; however, most such effects involve educational successes and failures that occur far in advance of college attendance.

When it comes to alcohol use, especially occasional heavy drinking, the impact of college attendance is quite another matter. Here, indeed, the effects are greater than would be suggested by a simple cross-sectional comparison of young adults in their first years after high school, because such cross-sectional data would fail to capture the substantially higher than average *increases* in heavy drinking among college students, as can be seen in Fig. 5.3. During high school, those headed for college are less likely than average to indulge in occasional heavy drinking; accordingly, some of the change on entering college might be viewed as a kind of "catching up" or "closing the gap" with their age-mates who do not go on to college. However, the college students, especially the women, do more than close the gap—they actually reverse it. Thus here it appears that socialization effects are at work (see also Schulenberg et al., 1994).

What is it about the college experience that causes college students to show greater than average increases in alcohol use and especially heavy drinking? It seems clear that the primary reason has to do with living arrangements. Compared with their age-mates, full-time students are much less likely to be married, but more likely to have left their parents' homes and to be living in dormitories or other housing involving roommates. We have found that being unmarried and leaving the parental home are factors associated with greater than average increases in alcohol use and heavy drinking. Our findings also suggest that the contribution of student status to increased alcohol use, including heavy drinking, is entirely indirect via these living arrangements, because when the living arrangements (plus marital and parental status) are included in the regression equations, the impact of student status is reduced essentially to zero. In other words, the effects of student status on alcohol use overlap completely with the effects of these other factors, so that student status shows no independent (i.e., direct) effect. Our interpretation of these findings is that student status does indeed contribute to increased alcohol use, but only indirectly via the marital status and other living arrangements that generally go along with being a college student.

The college students also "closed the gap" with respect to marijuana use. As can be seen in Fig. 6.2, during the first 4 years after high school marijuana use rose slightly among college students, whereas it declined slightly among nonstudents. Because the noncollege bound were about half again as likely as the college bound to have been current marijuana users when they were high-school seniors, the result is a convergence (but no reversing of the gap, in this case).

College students were only about half as likely as their age-mates to have been current cocaine users during high school, but here the similarity with marijuana use and heavy drinking ends. Figure 7.2 shows no convergence or "catching up" among college students; moreover, the regression analyses (Tables A.10–A.11) indicate that students showed lower than average increases in cocaine use once differences in living arrangements were taken into account. It thus seems that the influences of college student living arrangements extend to use of the illicit drug marijuana, but these environ-ments do not support initiation or increases in use of cocaine.

Employment Status Related to Drug Use

Analyses of post-high-school work status are unavoidably complicated by the fact that some individuals are not considered to be in the workforce due to their status as students or homemakers, whereas others may be included as part of the workforce even though they are currently unemployed. We made a number of distinctions in employment experiences, as summarized in the following paragraphs, but we found clear and consistent differential changes in drug use linked to only two categories of individuals—those who were full-time homemakers, and those in military service.

Full-Time Civilian Employment. By modal age 23 the majorities of men and women in our samples were in full-time civilian employment, and by their later twenties that was true of two-thirds of the women and nearly all of the men (see Table 3.1). It is thus not surprising that drug use among the full-time employed did not depart significantly from average—they *were* the average.

Part-Time Employment.   Most part-time employment was reported during the first 4 years after high school, and most part-time employees were also full-time students. We described the drug use data for part-time employees as a slightly watered-down version of the data for full-time students, and our regression analyses showed no significant relationships between drug use and part-time employment once student status was controlled.

Military Service.   Serving in the armed forces was strongly linked with changes in drug use, and in this case our multivariate analyses showed these relationships to be largely independent of either background or other role statuses and responsibilities. Most interestingly, and in contrast to virtually all other effects reported in this book, the effects we found for military service were in sharply opposite directions, with licit substance use increasing and illicit substance use decreasing. These findings are consistent with other recent studies by Bray et al. (1991) and by Kroutil et al. (1994).

In the present analyses, those in military service showed greater than average increases in cigarette smoking (see Fig. 4.4) and in instances of heavy drinking (Fig. 5.5). Controls for marital status, living arrangements, pregnancy, and parenthood had little effect on these relationships (see Tables A.5 and A.7), so we conclude that aspects of the military service itself contributed to the increases in smoking and drinking. Recent efforts by military leadership to reduce alcohol abuse may eventually influence the pattern just described, so we will continue to monitor this relationship.

The patterns of change were dramatically different for use of the illicit drugs marijuana (see Fig. 6.3) and cocaine (Fig. 7.3); both dropped sharply among those who entered military service. The differences related to military service emerged largely after high school, suggesting the effects of socialization rather than selection. Our regression analyses (see Tables A.8–A.11) showed that these relationships were not at all diminished by controls for background or living arrangements, so again it seems clear that the effects are directly attributable to aspects of military service—most notably, the vigorous anti- (illicit) drug policies initiated by the armed forces in recent years, including preenlistment drug testing as well as random drug testing after enlistment.

Homemakers.   Women who described themselves as full-time homemakers were less likely than average to increase their smoking (see Fig. 4.4), and they were more likely than average to decrease alcohol use (Fig. 5.4), heavy drinking (Fig. 5.5), marijuana use (Fig. 6.3), and cocaine use (Fig. 7.3). Although these relationships are surely genuine, our regression analyses (Tables A.5–A.11) led us to interpret these changes in drug use among full-time homemakers as little more than a reflection of the fact that nearly all were married, many were parents, and some were pregnant at the time of the follow-up survey. In other words, there is little evidence to suggest any separate homemaker effect above and beyond the effects of marriage and parenthood. (Because we consider that marriage and parenthood generally lead to the full-time homemaker status, rather than vice versa, we do not interpret these relationships as indicating any sort of indirect effect of homemaker status.)

Unemployment. Those who reported being unemployed at the time of follow-up were more likely than average to have been drug users during their senior year of high school (as well as afterward); specifically, they were more likely to have been half-pack or more smokers (see Fig. 4.4), marijuana users (Fig. 6.3), and cocaine users (Fig. 7.3). We did not, however, find clear and consistent evidence of differential *changes* in drug use linked with unemployment (see Tables A.5–A.11). This is not to say that becoming unemployed does not have impacts on drug use, but rather that any such effects were not strong enough, or not consistent enough in direction, to be discerned reliably in the present analyses. These findings are consistent with those from our earlier nationwide study of young men followed from modal ages 16 to 24 (Bachman et al., 1978; Johnston, 1973). Other longitudinal research in this area (Kandel & Yamaguchi, 1987; Newcomb & Bentler, 1985; Yamaguchi & Kandel, 1985b) also has favored a selection interpretation, linking early drug use to later job instability but finding no causal link from unemployment to adult substance use.

Living Arrangements and Marital Status Related to Drug Use

Much of the drug use that occurs in early adulthood is heavily influenced by social contacts. For that reason, our categorization of living arrangements focused, directly or indirectly, on the *interpersonal* aspects of our respondents' lives. Individuals sharing a residence are usually in daily contact, have many opportunities to be aware of each other's behaviors, and often influence each other's behaviors. Thus we expected and found that living arrangements during the post-high-school years are linked with changes in the use of alcohol (see Figs. 5.6–5.7), marijuana (Fig. 6.4), and cocaine (Fig. 7.4).

Cigarette use (Fig. 4.5) is the one exception, showing fewer and generally smaller effects; however, this too is consistent with our expectations in view of the facts that (a) smoking habits are generally well established before the end of high school and very resistant to change, (b) smoking does not result in the kinds of "highs" (or intoxication) that the other drugs can produce, and (c) smoking habits, once established, seem not to require social facilitation or encouragement, and are often practiced in private.

Being Married.   Arguably the most fundamental and pervasive distinction among living arrangements has to do with whether or not an individual is married. Not only do married couples ordinarily share living quarters, they also share long-term commitments to each other and, if they become parents, to their children. We therefore judged marriage to be preeminent among living arrangements in terms of potential for influencing drug use, and we included it as the first category in our classification. Our results fully support this analysis decision. Marriage, and the anticipation of being married (i.e., becoming engaged), are accompanied by significant reductions in use of alcohol, marijuana, cocaine, and even cigarettes (see Figs. 4.5, 5.6, 5.7, 6.4, and 7.4, and Tables A.5–A.11). Being married involves new sets of responsibilities, mutual caring, intimacy, and increased adult contacts, as well as less time spent in bars and at parties frequented by singles—the "singles scene," where a lot of smoking, drinking, and illicit drug use tend to take place. All of these lifestyle changes seem likely to reduce heavy drinking and the recreational use of illicit drugs.

These findings add strength to the consistent body of evidence concerning the influence of marriage. By contrasting the effects of marriage and engagement with a variety of other significant roles and experiences in young adulthood, these results underscore the strength and importance of the marital relationship in altering adult behavior. In addition, the anticipatory effects shown for engagement add to the relatively little research showing premarriage reductions in substance use (Yamaguchi & Kandel, 1985b).

It is important to keep in mind that other related factors such as pregnancy and parenthood can make their own contribution to reducing drug use; however, the regression analyses controlling these factors clearly indicate that marriage itself plays an important role in limiting the use of drugs. This is consistent with other recent findings demonstrating the primary influence of the marital role (Burton et al., 1996). To be sure, some of the marriage effects documented here are actually anticipatory; nevertheless, the fact remains that the total effects of marriage, including some factors that often precede the actual exchange of vows, are generally in the direction of constraining drug use and abuse.

Although married couples ordinarily share living quarters, one exception to the rule involves military service: Many married individuals in the service do not live with their spouses. We have relatively few such cases in our study, but Bray, Kroutil, and Marsden (1995) reported that married members of the service who were living with their spouses were, relative to unmarried service personnel, much lower in alcohol and illicit drug use; those who were married but not living with their spouses had alcohol and illicit drug use rates just about midway between the other two groups. This suggests that there are some effects based on mutual commitments and caring, but that these effects may be diminished when the living arrangements do not provide further reinforcement.

Cohabiting.   The data for cohabitation show selection effects and socialization effects. With respect to selection effects, those who were cohabiting during a follow-up were distinctly more likely than average to have been drug users during high school. Specifically, as high-school seniors they were half again more likely than average to have been regular cigarette smokers (see Fig. 4.5), they were somewhat more likely to have been alcohol users (Fig. 5.6) and occasional heavy users (Fig. 5.7), they were half again as likely to have been current marijuana users (Fig. 6.4), and they were twice as likely to have been current cocaine users (Fig. 7.4).

At the time of follow-up, cohabitants in general were more likely than average to have increased their use of cigarettes and cocaine, suggesting some socialization effects. However, more detailed distinctions (see Figs. 4.7 and 7.6, as well as 5.10, 5.11, and 6.6) revealed that those cohabitants who were engaged did not show this pattern of greater than average increases (or lower than average decreases) in drug use. We should note also that the majority of all cohabitants were not (and had not been as seniors) daily cigarette smokers or current (i.e., monthly) users of either marijuana or cocaine. In other words, although cohabitants were more likely than average to be users of each of these three substances, only a minority of them did so.

These mixed findings are consistent with earlier studies that provide evidence of selection into cohabitation based on early substance use and unconventional beliefs (DeMaris & MacDonald, 1993; Newcomb, 1987; Nock, 1995; Thornton et al., 1992; Yamaguchi & Kandel, 1985a), as well as socialization influences of cohabitation (Axinn & Thornton, 1992; Bachman et al., 1984; Newcomb, 1987). This suggests lines for future analyses that extend well beyond the scope of those reported here. It may be interesting to consider the different ways in which cohabitation fits into the life course of many contemporary young adults. For some it may be a rather normative precursor to marriage, for others it may be a longer term alternative, and for still others it may be a limited involvement with little in the way of mutual commitment. Cohabitation followed by a period of being single would seem to be quite different from cohabitation followed by marriage (and perhaps parenthood), and we suspect that the sequences of drug use associated with these two patterns would be different as well.

Living With Parents.   During a period when many of their age-mates undergo large, often profound, changes in living arrangements, young adults who continue to live with their parents are much less likely to experience dramatic changes in interpersonal contacts and social activities. They also showed close to average levels of change in all four categories of substance use, both bivariately and after other factors were controlled. In effect, these individuals are not as exposed to the new freedoms from constraints (as well as the additional peer pressure) that often accompany life in dormitories or apartments, but neither are they involved in the new commitments and responsibilities of marriage. The result seems to be that their drug use change patterns fall neatly in between the patterns for others with different mixes of freedoms and responsibilities.

Living in a Dormitory.   College students living in dormitories, like college students in general, were much less likely to have been cigarette smokers in high school, and also less likely to have smoked during young adulthood. On the other hand, alcohol use, especially instances of heavy drinking, showed substantial increases among those living in dormitories, even after student status and other factors were controlled; comparisons of bivariate and multivariate coefficients (see Tables A.6–A.7) indicate that roughly two-thirds or more of these "dormitory effects" on drinking were independent of the other factors examined here. Also, whereas rates of marijuana use held roughly steady among most young adults during the first 4 years after high school, marijuana use increased somewhat among those in dorms. Although less than half of this dormitory effect remained after other factors were controlled, it was still sufficient to be statistically significant (see Table A.8). With respect to cocaine, however, there was no such effect at all (see Table A.10). As we noted in chapter 7, apparently it is one thing for students living in dormitories to involve themselves in heavy drinking and (perhaps) marijuana use, but quite another matter to get involved with cocaine use.

Important socialization effects of dormitory living also have been suggested by other researchers as a potential explanation for consistent findings of higher substance use, particularly alcohol use, among college students. The freedom from constraints in the social lives of dormitory residents leaves the door open to greater use; moreover, dorms often provide distinct opportunities for substance-use socialization in the form of dorm parties and drinking games (Brennan et al., 1986; Wechsler, Dowdall, Davenport, & Castillo, 1995).

Living Alone.   The relatively small numbers of young adults who reported living alone (and not in a dormitory) showed slightly greater than average increases in cigarette smoking and alcohol use, but were not consistently different from average in their use of marijuana or cocaine. Our findings have certain parallels with the selection effects found by Newcomb and Bentler (1985), indicating that adolescent cigarette and alcohol use was associated with living alone in young adulthood, but illicit drug use was not. This relatively independent lifestyle may be associated with some new freedoms that accommodate increased use of licit substances, but living alone may provide fewer external social influences that might lead to greater illicit substance use (e.g., attending fewer parties where drugs are shared and greater isolation from other people who possess drugs).

Other Living Arrangements.   "Other living arrangements" is a residual analysis category that included those living in apartments or houses shared with several others, those living with a partner of the same sex, and military personnel living in barracks or in shared off-base housing. Individuals in this category showed increases in alcohol use and instances of heavy drinking that were roughly comparable to the increases associated with living in a dorm; there was also a fairly close correspondence with dorm residents in terms of changes in marijuana use (after other factors were controlled—see Tables A.8–A.9). These similarities in findings are consistent with our view that for many young adults these other living arrangements involve a social life somewhat similar to that in a dormitory; indeed, many students chose these other living arrangements as an alternative to living in dormitories. However, the other living arrangements category also included many non-students, which no doubt contributed to the higher smoking rates in this category compared with those living in dormitories. We also found significantly greater than average *increases* in cigarette use among those in this category (see Table A.5).

The great majority of all respondents reported no use of cocaine, and this was true also of those in the other living arrangements category. Nevertheless, those in this category did show greater than average increases in cocaine use (see Fig. 7.4 and Tables A.10–A.11). It is in this respect that at least a subset of those in the other living arrangements category seem most clearly different from those living in dormitories.

Pregnancy and Parenthood Related to Drug Use

As noted in chapter 4, we treated pregnancy status and parenthood status as two distinct dimensions (using two sets of dummy variables) in these analyses, while recognizing that they are closely related. In particular, any effects of pregnancy on drug use that led to more permanent changes in drug-use behavior would emerge in analyses as "parenthood effects."

Pregnancy.   A very encouraging finding is that being pregnant was associated with dramatically lowered levels of alcohol use (see Figs. 5.8–5.9) and marijuana use (Fig. 6.5). Particularly noteworthy is the fact that pregnant women were the only subgroup to show a net reduction in proportions of half-pack-a-day smokers between senior year and follow-up (see Figs. 4.3–4.7, especially Fig. 4.6).

Although panel analyses cannot demonstrate conclusively that pregnancy or the anticipation of being pregnant *caused* these women to cut down on their use of drugs, the evidence in support of that interpretation is compelling. First, we should note that most people, and especially women who are pregnant or anticipating pregnancy, are aware of the risks that a pregnant woman's substance use can pose for a developing fetus. Certainly prenatal care now includes strong cautions against alcohol use, cigarette use, and the use of other drugs. In addition, there has been widespread coverage of these issues in the media. One of the effects of that coverage is that pregnant women are aware that the risks are known by most others who may be observing their behavior, and that awareness of potential disapproval may have an additional deterrent effect.

A significant further piece of evidence is our present finding that the annual marijuana use measures, although in most respects showing slightly stronger relationships than the monthly use measures, show slightly weaker relationships with respect to pregnancy (and the same was true for monthly vs. annual alcohol use, although the annual use data are not reported in this volume). Because pregnancy (and often any planning or anticipation of pregnancy) would not span the full 12-month interval reflected in our annual drug-use measures, it follows that genuine pregnancy effects should be weaker ("noisier") when annual data are used—exactly what we found.

Based on this evidence, our interpretation is straightforward and parsimonious. We believe that pregnancy—perhaps including the intention or anticipation of becoming pregnant—does indeed cause women to cut down and in many cases eliminate their use of cigarettes, alcohol, marijuana, and even (for the much smaller numbers of women involved) cocaine.

The story for men is less dramatic and more complicated. Husbands with pregnant spouses showed no reduction in use of cigarettes (at either bivariate or multivariate levels of analysis). We did find lowered levels of other drug use among men with pregnant spouses; however, that seemed to be attributable to the fact that these men were married, because there was little evidence in the multivariate analyses of any additional "pregnant spouse effect" once the effect of marriage was controlled.

These significant reductions in the use of cigarettes, alcohol, and other drugs by pregnant women, and some reduction in use by spouses of pregnant women, are consistent with previous research (Fried et al., 1985; Ihlen et al., 1990; Yamaguchi & Kandel, 1985b). Further, the present results add strength to the causal interpretations in other studies by testing this relationship in a national sample while controlling other significant adult roles.

Parenthood.   Although most parents in our study were married, a significant proportion were not. We analyzed the two categories separately in searching for parenthood effects because we considered the social environments of married and single parents to be different in potentially important ways, and also because most single fathers do not live with their children.

Being a married parent was associated with declines in use of alcohol and illicit drugs, although some of these declines seem due to marriage rather than parenthood per se. Nevertheless, for married mothers significant negative coefficients remained for alcohol, marijuana, and cocaine, and for married fathers the coefficient for current alcohol use remained significant (see Tables A.6–A.11). For single mothers negative coefficients were found that were similar to those for married mothers; however, for single fathers the only significant negative coefficient was for annual marijuana use (see Table A.9).

The findings for cigarette use are more complex (see Table A.5). Those who were single fathers or mothers at the time of follow-up were more likely than average to have been smokers as high-school seniors, and they were also more likely to have increased their use of cigarettes. Being a married father showed no significant effect on smoking. Being a married mother, however, was associated with statistically significant reductions in smoking, even with other factors controlled. At least in part, that finding may reflect that some women who managed to quit smoking during pregnancy were able to resist the urge to resume smoking. We cannot guess to what extent such continued abstention results primarily from a desire to protect children from passive smoke, or for personal health or other reasons; indeed, sometimes the answer to that question may not be known to the mothers themselves.

Despite the considerable stresses of parenthood (Belsky & Pensky, 1988; Cowan et al., 1991; Ruble et al., 1988), in no case was parenthood associated with increases in substance use among married parents. However, the mixed results shown for single parents suggest that single mothers experience constraints on substance-use behavior similar to married mothers when it comes to intoxicating drugs (e.g., alcohol, marijuana), but both single mothers and single fathers have fewer constraints in their cigarette use. These parents may be under considerably greater stress than married parents (Brooks-Gunn & Chase-Lansdale, 1995; McLoyd & Wilson, 1991); also, they may have fewer social supports for any efforts to quit smoking, and thus experience greater difficulty breaking the cigarette habit. Single parents were much more likely than average to have been smokers in the first place (i.e., during high school), so here again we may be observing a kind of "delayed action" selection effect akin to that found for those who did not go on to college.

Further Findings on Marriage, Engagement, Divorce, and Drug Use

Earlier in this chapter we contrasted married respondents with those in other living arrangements, and summarized strong and consistent marriage effects, especially with respect to reduced frequency of heavy drinking, marijuana use, and cocaine use. However, focusing on current marital status as one of several living arrangements omits two other potentially important aspects of marital status—engagement and divorce.

Engagement. Earlier analyses of Monitoring the Future data, reported elsewhere (Bachman et al., 1997), focused on 4-*year* patterns of change in marital status and their effects on drug use. In general, those analyses showed that respondents who reported being single at one follow-up, then engaged 2 years and one follow-up later, and then married 2 years after that, had total declines in drug use over the 4 years roughly equal to the declines that occurred for other respondents whose transition from single to married took place within a 2-*year* interval. It is not surprising that the overall change from single to married should show much the same effects, in terms of drug use, irrespective of whether an intermediate follow-up survey happened to occur during the interval in which a respondent was engaged. What was not obvious, until we conducted the analyses, is that when we were able to observe that intermediate point we would find an engagement effect amounting to half or more of the total marriage effect. Prompted by earlier findings, we included engagement status as one of the measures in our present regression analyses, and we conducted new descriptive analyses of changes in drug use as related to both engagement and cohabitation.

Our analyses showed that engagement tended to decrease drug use, both among those cohabiting and among those not. With respect to smoking, there were only small effects and only among women (Fig. 4.7 and Table A.5). However, each of the other drug-use measures showed clear engagement effects (see Figs. 5.10–5.11, 6.6, and 7.6); moreover, regression results showed significant effects of engagement similar to the marriage effects, although generally somewhat smaller (see Tables A.6–A.11). These effects shown for engagement may be due to changes in the social environment (e.g., new social contacts, time spent with future spouse rather than friends), and they could also reflect deep psychological commitments to the new partnership (Dickens & Perlman, 1981); in any case, it seems clear that important social changes occurring prior to the wedding have impacts on drug use.

Divorce.   Divorce marks an ending of the mutual commitment involved in engagement and marriage. The impacts of divorce on drug use were dramatic, as can be seen in Figs. 4.8, 5.12–5.13, 6.7, and 7.7. Without exception, the transition from married to divorced was marked by an increase in the proportions using all four substances—tobacco, alcohol, marijuana, and cocaine. Moreover, and again without exception, the figures show that the transition from divorced to remarried was marked by a decrease in proportions of drug users. Among the obvious possible reasons for these divorce effects are the following: Divorce severs many of the social ties established in marriage; this often reduces constraints on behavior, especially for nonparents or noncustodial parents. Divorced singles may be likely to reenter the "singles scene"—the world of bars and parties frequented by singles. Divorce is often accompanied by emotional distress (Aseltine & Kessler, 1993), which may precipitate a return of earlier patterns of higher substance use; this "rebound" is entirely consistent with other evidence of an increase in use following divorce (Hanna, Faden, & Harford, 1993; Hallberg, 1992).

Interpreting the Marriage Effect on Drug Use.   The findings summarized in this section, along with other analyses illustrated in Figs. 3.6 and 3.7, suggest that rather than the long-term history of marital status, it is the *present* condition of being engaged or married, versus being unmarried or divorced, that has the primary effect of restraining drug use. Certainly there is more involved in the marriage effect than simply living together, because engagement effects were equally evident among cohabitants and among those not cohabiting. A more significant clue is the finding that something nearly as large as the marriage effect seems to result from engagement alone; this finding suggests that mutual commitment and the corresponding changes in social and recreational lifestyle, all of which occur among engaged couples as well as married ones, may be among the most important causes of lowered drug use during young adulthood.

CONCLUSIONS AND IMPLICATIONS

Imagine two young women who graduate from high school at the same time. Imagine that they are identical, except that one enters college and lives in a dormitory, whereas the other takes a job, marries, and soon becomes pregnant. This premise that two otherwise identical people would choose such vastly different life paths is nonsensical, of course. Two women headed in such different trajectories are likely to differ in many other fundamental ways—backgrounds, past accomplishments, and established patterns of behavior. This, in a nutshell, illustrates the problem of studying real people making real choices about what kinds of environments they will experience during young adulthood—what kinds of new freedoms and responsibilities will be theirs.

Young adulthood is especially interesting to researchers because of the great diversity of choices and resulting experiences available during this portion of the life span. Experiences during the high-school years seem almost uniform and lockstep in comparison with the wider range of opportunities that opens on graduation. In addition to being interesting, the young adult period is especially challenging to researchers; the challenges arise not only because of the new diversity of options, but also because the choices among these options are not made entirely—or even mostly—at random.

Stability Versus Change—Selection Versus Socialization

One of the challenges facing researchers is that of distinguishing between the preexisting differences that lead different individuals to choose different environments on the one hand, and the actual impacts of the new environments on the other hand. Here is where longitudinal panel data are especially valuable. Such data, although not necessarily definitive, enable us to sort through many of the competing explanations for why different individuals in different environments behave differently.

In a much earlier longitudinal project, which was in many ways the predecessor to this one, we tracked young men from about age 16 to age 24, focusing on the correlates of their educational attainments. We concluded that many of the differences at age 24, along dimensions ranging from self-esteem to cigarette use, were clearly in evidence before the end of high school (Bachman et al., 1978). In other words, that earlier examination of change and stability led us to emphasize stability; we saw more dramatic evidence of selection effects than of socialization effects.

Our first major panel analyses based on Monitoring the Future data, extending to only 3 years after high school, was also concerned with stability and change. Based on those initial analyses, we offered two broad conclusions: first, that the most important predictor of drug use in the first years after graduation is drug use during high school; second, that the different living arrangements after high school lead to important shifts upward or downward in drug use (Bachman et al., 1984).

In the analyses reported in this book, with panel data now extending as far as 14 years, we have returned once more to the complementary themes of change and stability. Once again we have found evidence for both, but this time our emphasis is on change—on socialization effects. We still see strong evidence of preexisting differences, especially with respect to educational attainment; most notably, the differences in smoking between those who do and do not enter college were large before they left high school, and may last throughout their lifetimes. We also see very high estimates of stability from one year to another in all dimensions of drug use analyzed here. Nevertheless, when we track individuals over longer intervals of time, we find that more and more of them move into the adult roles of marriage and parenthood; and we find that with each passing year the similarities with youthful patterns of drug use grow weaker.

Two Directions of Change in Young Adulthood

As young men and women leave high school and move into the new experiences of adulthood, it is a useful simplification to speak of two directions of change—one involving new freedoms and the other involving new responsibilities. As we have seen, these two kinds of role change imply two different directions of change in drug use as well.

New Freedoms and Increases in Drug Use.   In the first few years after graduation, many young adults leave their parents' homes, and all leave the "in loco parentis" controls imposed by high schools. These newly emerging adults are freer than they were a few months or years earlier—freer to smoke when (if not always *where*) they wish, freer to stay out late and go to parties, freer (especially after age 21) to buy alcohol and consume it in bars and restaurants, and freer to keep supplies of illicit drugs away from the watchful eyes of parents.

Not all of these young adults treat their new freedoms as opportunities to initiate the use of various drugs. On the contrary, most who were nonusers during high school remain nonusers in the years immediately thereafter. However, among those who had developed patterns of drug use while still in high school—and this includes the majority of all young people when it comes to the use of alcohol, and substantial minorities for the use of cigarettes and the use of marijuana—the new freedoms accompanying these first years of adulthood provide opportunities for increasing use, and we have seen considerable evidence of such increases.

New Responsibilities and Decreases in Drug Use.   As can be seen in Figure 3.4, the proportions of young men and women who are married increase with each additional year after high school, reaching about two-thirds by modal age 32. We have seen clearly that those in our study who were married were less likely than average to be occasional heavy drinkers (Fig. 5.7), current users of marijuana (Fig. 6.4), or current users of cocaine (Fig. 7.4). We have even seen evidence that those who were married were less likely than average to increase cigarette consumption (Table A.5; see also Fig. 4.5).

It is safe to say that being married is the most important of the new responsibilities contributing to declines in drug use—most important in that this new responsibility is widely experienced and shows substantial impacts consistent across all of the substances we have been examining. Moreover, as we noted earlier in this chapter, the evidence for marriage effects is pervasive, extending to those who become engaged, and showing up in reverse among those who become divorced.

Whereas marriage is the most pervasive factor contributing to stopping or reducing drug use, pregnancy is the most dramatic. In terms of declines in percentages of users, the impacts of pregnancy on alcohol use, illicit drug use, and even the hard-to-break habit of cigarette use, are unmatched by any other factor we studied. Women who are pregnant have profoundly important responsibilities to their unborn children, and our evidence suggests that most of them take these new responsibilities very seriously. In most cases, the responsibilities of pregnancy arise only after marriage, thus placing them a bit later in the typical progression through early adulthood.

Freedoms and Responsibilities: The Shifting Balance. First come the new freedoms, then the new responsibilities. It is hardly that simple, of course; there are a great many exceptions. Nevertheless, the sequence experienced by most young adults is an opening up of new freedoms soon after completing high school, followed in most cases by the gradual assumption of an increasing number of new responsibilities. Most importantly, as we have illustrated, these responsibilities involve other people—fiancees, spouses, and children. Commitments to a college education or to a job, which really amount mostly to commitments to self, may also matter; however, in our findings they appear less central than the interpersonal factors.

Accounting for Age-Related Differences in Drug Use by Young Adults

We argued earlier that there is a typical age-related pattern of change during young adulthood, shifting from a period dominated by new freedoms to one dominated by new responsibilities. Given that new freedoms tend to provide new opportunities for drug use, whereas new responsibilities tend toward the inhibition of drug use, we might expect that the overall patterns of age-related changes in drug use would involve first an increase and then a decrease. To a considerable extent, that is what we found. Smoking rates increased during the first few years after high school, and then showed very modest declines among men and slightly greater declines among women (see Figs. 4.1 and 4.9). Much the same can be said for current alcohol use and instances of heavy drinking; however, the declines were more pronounced than for smoking, especially with respect to instances of heavy drinking (see Figs. 5.1, 5.16, and 5.17). Marijuana use and cocaine use also showed initial increases and later decreases, although these were complicated by secular trends as discussed in chapters 6 and 7.

Can the increases in drug use during early adulthood, and the subsequent gradual decreases, be attributed directly to the new freedoms and responsibilities we have been studying? In particular, are marriage effects and pregnancy effects large enough to explain the "maturing out" that began to occur by the time our respondents reached their midtwenties? Our analyses here are not definitive, but they are strongly suggestive. Let us look first where the light is clearest—which means focusing on cigarette use and alcohol use, where secular trends have not been so large as to be seriously confounded with age-related changes.

The results with respect to smoking are summarized in Fig. 4.9, which presents results from our regression analyses showing age-related changes in cigarette use both unadjusted and after taking account of marital status, living arrangements, pregnancy, and all other predictors. For the men it can be seen that the adjustments make virtually no difference at all; although smoking rates (compared with senior year of high school) reached their peak during the midtwenties and dropped off a bit thereafter, it appears that those shifts had little to do with the new responsibilities we measured. Among women, on the other hand, it appears that an appreciable proportion of the drop-off is attributable to factors that we included in our regression analyses.

With respect to alcohol use the results are stronger; moreover, the effects of the adjustments for post-high-school experiences are nearly as large for men as for women, as can be seen in Figs. 5.16–5.17. Figure 5.16 shows clearly that frequency of current alcohol use (use in the past 30 days) rises until ages 21–22. A considerable portion of that rise remains after adjustments for post-high-school experiences, but that is not at all surprising given that age 21 is the threshold for legal drinking. After ages 21–22, the unadjusted data in Fig. 5.16 show that overall frequency of alcohol use declined substantially among our respondents; indeed, a decade later (at ages 31–32) the men were drinking only slightly more often than when they were high-school seniors, and the women actually were drinking less than as seniors. Put another way, the decline from ages 21–22 to ages 31–32 was about half of a point on our roughly logarithmic scale, where a decrease of one full point would represent cutting drinking in half. However, after adjustments for the effects of living arrangements, marriage, pregnancy, and so forth, this decline was only about one-third as large as it was before the adjustments.

Figure 5.17 shows that during the decade from ages 21–22 to 31–32, instances of heavy drinking (five or more drinks in a row in the past 2 weeks) declined by more than half a scale point among men (unadjusted), and the decline among women was nearly as large. After adjustments these differences were only about half as large.

The results for marijuana use, shown in Fig. 6.8, are complicated by the large downward secular trend during much of the period under study. As we argued in chapter 6, a considerable portion of the declines *correlated* with age seem not to be "age relevant." Nevertheless, the figure does show that some portion of the overall decline, and perhaps a substantial portion of the age-related departures from the downward secular trend, was reduced by adjustments for the effects of living arrangements, marriage, pregnancy, and so on.

As discussed in chapter 7, and shown in Fig. 7.8, our interpretation of the cocaine data is similar to that for the marijuana data. Even though the secular trend for cocaine is more complex, we find that there remain age-relevant shifts in cocaine use that are explainable in terms of the post-high-school experiences we examined.

What do we conclude, then, about whether changes in drug use during young adulthood can be attributed to new freedoms and responsibilities? In the case of cigarettes, we think that the increases during the first several years after graduation are attributable fairly directly to the fact that young smokers escape the close constraints on smoking imposed by high-school attendance. Turning to the declines observed from the early twenties onward in consumption of alcohol, marijuana, cocaine, and even (among women) cigarettes, we think they are caused in considerable measure by the shifting balance between freedoms and responsibilities—the fact that increasing proportions of young adults assume new obligations, especially to spouses and children, as they move through their twenties and into their thirties.

Implications of Findings on Age-Related Changes in Drug Use

Nearly all young people experiment with cigarettes and alcohol before they leave high school. Fortunately, the majority of them do not develop daily smoking habits, although a tragically large minority do—tragic because so many will suffer health consequences. Many high-school seniors, and even larger portions of young adults, occasionally drink large quantities (five or more drinks) of alcohol in a single sitting, and thereby endanger themselves and others. Fortunately again, most survive that period of earliest adulthood, and as they grow older they engage in such behaviors less and less often. Similarly, use of marijuana and use of cocaine both show age-related declines before young adults reach their thirties.

Thus, although large majorities of "mainstream" youth and young adults experiment with drug use, sometimes in risky ways, most of them mature out without becoming addicted to alcohol or to illicit drugs. We think there is room for encouragement in such findings because they suggest that much of the drug-using behavior of young adults is responsive to social environments—especially to new responsibilities.

The implications of this general finding are broad indeed. This responsiveness to the social environment suggests that efforts at intervention in young adulthood are not swimming against the tide. To the contrary, it suggests that efforts to promote positive adjustment in many areas of life, such as improving chances for success in work, education, and family life, are targeting the very processes that help to reduce substance use in adulthood.

The findings concerning cigarette use are less reassuring, although the damage from this form of drug use usually emerges many years past young adulthood. There is at present little reason to doubt that substantial numbers of those unwilling or unable to break their smoking habits during young adulthood will continue smoking throughout an adulthood that will, for significant numbers of them, be prematurely terminated as a direct consequence of smoking. It has been encouraging to see that significant proportions of pregnant women seem able to stop their cigarette use, at least temporarily. It remains to be seen whether further research on the impacts of passive smoking, especially its impacts on children, will lead to more smoking cessation by young mothers and fathers.

Implications for Future Analyses

It is perhaps a cliche to end research reports with statements that more research is needed. Popular variations on that basic theme include calls for replication using larger and nationally representative samples, or using panel data to sort out causal relationships. Well, the present analyses have used panel data and large nationally representative samples; moreover, the central findings show a high degree of consistency and generality across two decades. So, in at least a partial departure from the usual cliche, we do *not* place so high a priority on further replication of what we have found and reported here. Instead, we think the present findings point toward new lines of investigation—some using Monitoring the Future data, and others based on more in-depth and qualitative studies.

The analyses completed here focused on the major roles and experiences that define young adulthood; we set out to determine whether these new freedoms and responsibilities relate to—and perhaps contribute to—drug use and changes in drug use. A primary purpose was to analyze such effects *in combination*; the strategy for examining multiple roles and experiences simultaneously was to look at changes between an initial "before" measurement point (the base-year surveys in the senior year of high school) and a number of "after" points (the follow-up mail surveys). We could thus treat individuals as fundamentally similar at the end of high school (because we limited our analyses to the very large majority of them who were unmarried, childless, and still living with their parents). Then, when we focused on their post-high-school roles, we were actually measuring two aspects of their experience simultaneously: (a) their current situations as young adults, and (b) changes from their prior circumstances as high-school seniors. We could then link these new roles and role changes to the ways their drug use changed between senior year and follow-up.

What have we learned from these analyses? Our conclusions, as summarized in this chapter, are that several aspects of post-high-school experience have particularly important impacts on drug use, and that such effects are partially or mostly independent of the effects of other factors. Having carried out what might be termed a broad-brush approach to these relationships, it now seems promising to move toward finer grained analyses of important factors, particularly marital status, pregnancy, and other aspects of living arrangements. In particular, we now feel justified in looking at certain areas of post-high-school experience *separately*, without the complexities of dealing simultaneously with multiple other factors.

Indeed, we were able to make a start in this direction in the present volume. After our basic regression analyses demonstrated powerful effects of marital status even when other factors were controlled, we then could concentrate on marital status and explore it in greater detail. We undertook analyses focusing on 2-year shifts between follow-ups (as illustrated in Fig. 5.13, for example), and extended the analyses to include the effects of divorce.

The present analyses have shown that some post-high-school freedoms and responsibilities have substantial effects on drug use, but many questions remain about *why* or *how* these effects occur. In some instances the regression analyses clearly indicated that certain effects are indirect via other effects—most notably, it appears that the impacts of college attendance on drug use occur almost entirely via marital status and living arrangements. The analyses also indicated that some of the effects of marriage are anticipatory, and occur by the time individuals are engaged. More generally, the use of panel data has made it clear that most of these impacts can be characterized as socialization effects rather than selection effects. Nevertheless, there remain many questions to be answered about just why it is that certain post-high-school roles and experiences cause increases in drug use, whereas others cause decreases.

A few central questions cut across all the findings: What are the sources of change? What processes explain change? Are similar processes in action for the different role effects? What accounts for why some individuals do not follow the typical patterns—individuals whose drug-using behaviors are contrary to what would be expected given their adult roles and experiences? We hope to address some of these questions in our own future work using Monitoring the Future data. However, there are many issues that can be illuminated with data derived from more narrowly focused and intensive research yielding in-depth qualitative information. The following paragraphs offer examples of specific questions that could be pursued.

Leaving Parents' Homes.   Consider the increases in drug use that typically occur when individuals move from their parents' homes and live in dormitories or in other housing involving unrelated young adults. We have speculated that changes in the frequency of evenings out for recreation, time spent in bars and at parties, and the reduction or removal of parental monitoring may all contribute to such increases. However, some young adults leave parents' homes and do not increase drug use, so it would be of interest to explore what factors seem to protect such individuals. Future analyses of Monitoring the Future data will examine some of these questions, but many could also be approached using more qualitative data than our closed-ended questionnaires provide.

Engagement and Marriage.   Another promising area for further exploration involves the decreases in drug use linked with marriage, including the anticipatory effects linked with engagement. We and others have suggested a number of possible processes mediating how and why marriage has such effects, most of which are not mutually exclusive. Marriage could change behavior patterns (going to parties and bars, spending time with single friends), motivations for drug use/nonuse (linked to approval/disapproval by fiance or spouse), opportunities for drug use (with less time available to get high because of added responsibilities), self-concepts (from fancy-free youth to responsible adult), or any of a number of other possible mediating factors. Some of these processes might be examined in a fashion similar to that used in this report, or with analytic techniques that could more thoroughly differentiate individual longitudinal trajectories (for example, via latent growth curve analysis, or event history analysis). Here again there is much that might be gained from smaller scale studies and qualitative analyses. Interview studies, possibly including multiple members of social networks (e.g., both spouses, interviewed separately), could help get at the roots of the social processes involved.

Divorce.   The rise in drug use after divorce has been clearly demonstrated, but questions remain. Is the rise linked primarily to lifestyle changes, such as going out more, spending more time with single friends, or decreasing contact with family members, or is it linked more to psychological distress—regression to less mature behavior patterns, self-medication, or coping? What factors might mitigate such effects of divorce? Are there differences in impacts depending on whether there are children involved, and whether the divorced parent remains in frequent and active contact with the children? Here again there seems much to be gained from in-depth interview studies.

Cohabitation.   We found marriage effects to be consistent throughout young adulthood; they are much the same whether marriage occurs early or later. Our analyses thus far have suggested the same is true for cohabitation, but there is room for closer scrutiny. Other questions, better addressed by more qualitative data, could focus on whether the effects of cohabitation vary depending on the degree of commitment or the conventionality of the people involved.

Pregnancy.   Our data show that drug use drops sharply during pregnancy; the contrast between monthly and annual drug use data indicates that for at least some women the shift occurs fairly close to the time of becoming pregnant. Nevertheless, finer grained data would help indicate whether the changes associated with pregnancy are generally sudden, or gradual. Interviews of women during or after pregnancy might be helpful in learning what proportions cut drug use in anticipation of pregnancy, and what proportions reduce use only after positive pregnancy tests. Interview studies could also address the following questions: Do women get information about drug-related pregnancy risks from their physicians, friends, family, the media, or a combination thereof? Do they perceive others as actively discouraging drug use by pregnant women? Are husbands of pregnant women aware of drug risks, and do they encourage their wives to reduce use? Do pregnant wives pressure their husbands to reduce use? Why do some women *not* reduce or eliminate drug use when pregnant? Exploring these questions might help to identify the mechanisms underlying the dramatic decreases in drug use among pregnant women, which in turn might help shape further efforts to discourage drug use while pregnant.

Parenthood.   Parenthood shows smaller and more mixed effects than does pregnancy; nevertheless, there is enough evidence to encourage further examination of the factors underlying the effects of parenthood on drug use. For example, single mothers showed effects similar to those for married mothers, but it would be worth exploring how alike (or different) the underlying processes are. Another interesting question would be to what extent mothers perceive their lower drug use as a carryover from pregnancy. In particular, when mothers who stop smoking during pregnancy are able to continue abstention, do they attribute that mostly to concerns for their children (passive smoke effects, negative parental role modeling), or do they see the primary motivation as caring for their own health? The answers to such questions would help sort out the effects of pregnancy versus motherhood, and also provide valuable information for designing drug prevention segments of prenatal care and parenthood classes.

Next Steps. The aforementioned questions illustrate the kinds of further research that may reveal the processes underlying the basic findings reported here. For our part, we expect to pursue a number of these questions in future analyses of Monitoring the Future data. However, some answers will remain beyond our grasp; thus, we encourage others to address these questions, and particularly to undertake more qualitative investigations.

Concluding Comments on Young Adulthood, New Freedoms, and New Responsibilities

This study has demonstrated many ways in which new freedoms and new responsibilities have significant impacts on drug use during young adulthood. It would be nice at this point to draw some clear and practical policy implications for possible use in drug abuse prevention efforts. Alas, the most important post-high-school roles and experiences we have identified, in terms of their impacts on drug use, are not ones that we could—or should—be eager to manipulate. We would not discourage young adults from leaving home and going to college, even though we have shown that it may increase their risks of alcohol abuse. Nor would we recommend a tour of military service as a means of reducing illicit drug use—especially because a side effect might be increases in licit drug use! Neither would we recommend early marriage and frequent pregnancy as means for reducing drug use, even though those effects have been demonstrated here.

During young adulthood, especially the first few years, many individuals move away from the social controls exerted by high schools and parents, and their new freedoms place them at increased risk for alcohol abuse and other forms of drug use. Although eventually most young adults take on the responsibilities of marriage and parenthood, those fundamental role changes must come in their own good time. Meanwhile, the first years of young adulthood remain ones of increased risk. Our findings suggest that such risks are reduced when young adults are in social roles and situations that keep them in close contact with other people—parents, fiances, spouses, children—with whom there are strong shared commitments, and toward whom the young adults feel a sense of responsibility.

Appendix

This Appendix provides three kinds of supplementary material. First, it presents information on sampling and data-collection procedures used in the Monitoring the Future project. Second, it discusses the validity of drug-use self-reports. Third, it presents results of multiple regression analyses (in Tables A.5–A.11) and a description of the reporting format and guidelines for interpreting the regression results.

SAMPLING AND DATA-COLLECTION PROCEDURES

A separate technical report spells out the design and procedures for the Monitoring the Future project, and includes considerable detail on sampling methods, response rates, measurement content, and issues of validity in self-reports of drug use (Bachman, Johnston, & O'Malley, 1996). The annual monographs on trends in drug use and related factors (e.g., Johnston et al., 1997) provide considerable detail on methods. Our discussion here is limited to key features of the design, plus matters specific to the present analyses.

Sample Design and Methods

From its outset, the Monitoring the Future project was designed with two interrelated components: (a) annual nationwide surveys of high-school seniors using group-administered questionnaires, and (b) periodic follow-up questionnaires mailed to subsamples of each senior-class cohort. This cohort-sequential design (Labouvie, 1976; Schaie, 1965) permits a wide range of analyses, including the study of longitudinal changes reflecting the differential impacts of various post-high-school environments and role transitions.

Multistage Samples of High-School Seniors.   Samples of seniors are drawn by a multistage procedure: the first stage consists of geographic areas (the Survey Research Center's primary sampling areas located throughout the coterminous United States); the second stage is the selection of one or more schools in each primary sampling area (generating a total of 130 to 140 schools); and the third stage is the random selection of up to about 350 seniors per school (yielding nationally representative cross-sections totaling about 16,000 to 18,000 high-school senior respondents each year).

Follow-Up Samples of Young Adults.   For reasons of cost control and sampling efficiency, only a subset of each senior class sample is selected for follow-up. Two subsamples from each senior class are drawn, each numbering about 1,200; members of one group are invited to participate in a follow-up survey 1 year after graduation, and every 2 years after that; those in the other group are invited to participate 2 years after graduation, and every 2 years after that. The follow-up samples are drawn using stratified random procedures; they are self-weighting, with one important exception as noted in the following section.

Use of Sample Weights in These Analyses.   Because the primary focus of the Monitoring the Future project is drug use, those who used illicit drugs as seniors are oversampled by a factor of 3 to 1. Our analyses assign a weight of $\frac{1}{3}$ to each of these individuals (with all others weighted 1), thereby removing any bias that would have resulted from the oversampling. The numbers of cases reported herein are always the weighted Ns, which we consider to be a reasonably good indicator of the levels of accuracy provided by these samples.

There is room for argument about whether weighted or unweighted data should be used in multivariate relational analyses (e.g., Andrews, Morgan, Sonquist, & Klem, 1973; Lee, Forthofer, & Lorimor, 1989). On the one hand, use of weights generally reduces systematic biases in representing the sampled population. On the other hand, if the data set includes a few cases with especially large weights, the danger exists that random idiosyncratic data for some such cases would influence the patterns of findings disproportionately. The present analyses involve no such large weights, because the large majority of cases are weighted 1, and all others are $\frac{1}{3}$. In other words, we are using what might best be described as samples that are largely self-weighting (i.e., largely unweighted), with the exception that there is a modest degree of additional accuracy for those individuals in the stratum consisting of senior-year illicit drug users. (It may be helpful to consider the alternative strategy of randomly discarding two-thirds of the cases in that illicit stratum. We could then analyze the data completely unweighted, but the results would differ in only very small and entirely random ways from the present analyses—such differences would reflect slightly reduced accuracy, nothing more.)

One further consideration is that stratified samples are generally less accurate than simple random samples of the same size. This is indeed the case for samples of high-school seniors because of the relatively large numbers of cases clustered in each sample school and the variation in sample weights; however, the follow-up surveys involve distinctly smaller numbers of cases per school and little variation in weights associated with schools. Thus it is estimated that the present follow-up samples have levels of accuracy fairly comparable to simple random samples of the same size.[1]

Samples Included in These Analyses.   Extensive follow-up data are available from all senior-class cohorts from 1976 onward. At the time the final sets of analyses were initiated, the 1995 follow-up data were the latest available. We chose to analyze up to seven follow-ups (if available) for each cohort. Accordingly, the present analyses include the senior classes of 1976 through 1994, with each class followed for up to 14 years but no later than 1995, as shown in Table A.1.

In summary, these analyses made use of all of the follow-up data available at the time they were completed. As discussed in chapter 3, the decision to use all available panel data means that there is a 13- or 14-year follow-up span for the classes of 1976 through 1982, whereas for each successive class the available span is smaller.

Focus on Unmarried Seniors Living With Parents.   For reasons discussed in chapter 3, a small portion of the cases for whom we had data were excluded from the present analyses. Specifically, we restricted these analyses to include only those who *as seniors* were unmarried, living with parents (or guardians), and not living with any children of their own. This had the effect of excluding fewer than 7% of the follow-up cases, as detailed in Table A.1.

Representativeness of Samples.   We have already noted that the samples used for these analyses were restricted to fall short of representing the full cohorts of young adults in the periods studied. First, the base-year data collections sampled high-school seniors, and thus omitted individuals who left high school before the end of the senior year. Second, we could not include a full 13- or 14-year span of follow-up data for later cohorts, simply because those data were not yet available. Third, we excluded from the present panel analyses those few who as seniors were already married, had children, were no longer living with parents or guardians, or any combination thereof.

---

[1]For further discussion of sample accuracy and design effects in the Monitoring the Future study, see the Appendix material in volumes reporting questionnaire responses from high-school seniors (e.g., Johnston, Bachman, & O'Malley, 1995).

TABLE A.1

Number of Observations Available for Analysis, by Class Year, for Classes 1976–1994

Class Year	76	77	78	79	80	81	82	83	84	85	86	87	88	89	90	91	92	93	94	95	Ns of Observations	Weighted Ns of Observations	Weighted Ns of Observations with Exclusions
76	BY	FU1	FU2	FU3	FU4	FU5	FU6	FU7													11,340	8,805.33	8,087.00
77		BY	FU1	FU2	FU3	FU4	FU5	FU6	FU7												12,473	9,429.00	8,621.33
78			BY	FU1	FU2	FU3	FU4	FU5	FU6	FU7											12,634	9,549.33	8,867.67
79				BY	FU1	FU2	FU3	FU4	FU5	FU6	FU7										12,569	9,431.67	8,827.00
80					BY	FU1	FU2	FU3	FU4	FU5	FU6	FU7									12,633	9,513.00	8,920.33
81						BY	FU1	FU2	FU3	FU4	FU5	FU6	FU7								12,455	8,695.00	8,194.00
82							BY	FU1	FU2	FU3	FU4	FU5	FU6	FU7							11,121	8,379.00	7,766.33
83								BY	FU1	FU2	FU3	FU4	FU5	FU6	FU7						10,156	7,728.00	7,224.00
84									BY	FU1	FU2	FU3	FU4	FU5	FU6	FU7					9,262	7,400.67	6,926.67
85										BY	FU1	FU2	FU3	FU4	FU5	FU6	FU7				8,290	6,578.00	6,132.33
86											BY	FU1	FU2	FU3	FU4	FU5	FU6	FU7			7,327	5,973.00	5,623.00
87												BY	FU1	FU2	FU3	FU4	FU5	FU6	FU7		6,436	5,358.00	4,983.67
88													BY	FU1	FU2	FU3	FU4	FU5	FU6	FU7	5,926	5,010.67	4,688.00
89														BY	FU1	FU2	FU3	FU4	FU5	FU6	5,021	4,289.67	4,038.33
90															BY	FU1	FU2	FU3	FU4	FU5	4,089	3,562.33	3,340.33
91																BY	FU1	FU2	FU3	FU4	3,427	3,016.33	2,801.33
92																	BY	FU1	FU2	FU3	2,664	2,383.33	2,193.67
93																		BY	FU1	FU2	1,677	1,482.33	1,373.33
94																			BY	FU1	878	751.33	705.33

Total: 150,378 117,335.99 **109,313.65**

Observations excluded because data missing on gender: -734 -563.33 (-0.5%)

Observations excluded because respondents were not living with a parent at BY: -7,712 -5,532.67 (-4.7%)

Observations excluded because respondents were married at BY: -1,631 -1,319.00 (-1.2%)

Observations excluded because respondents had children at BY: -772 -607.33 (-0.5%)

Total Eligible: 139,529 **109,313.66 (93.2%)**

Notes: "BY"= Base Year. "FU"= Follow-Up. "Base Year" is the senior year survey administration. "FU1" is the first follow-up survey administration, "FU2" is the second, and so forth. All analyses are based on weighted N with exclusions. 109,313.66, less the appropriate exclusions for the specific analysis. The inconsistency between the "Total Eligible Weighted N" and "Total Weighted N with Exclusions" is due to rounding.

In addition to the aforementioned systematic exclusions from the samples, representativeness is affected by nonparticipation at several points in the sampling process. First, about 25–30% of the schools initially invited to participate in the surveys each year declined to do so; however, in almost every such instance a similar school was recruited as a replacement. Second, about 15–20% of sampled seniors in participating schools did not complete questionnaires; this was largely due to absenteeism, and other analyses indicated that this produced only modest amounts of bias in estimates of drug use (Johnston et al., 1997). Third, some individuals targeted for follow-up either could not be reached or did not choose to participate. At the first follow-up, fully 80% returned completed questionnaires. By the seventh follow-up (13–14 years after high school), the total panel retention remained quite high, at about 67%. Nevertheless, this panel attrition generated a degree of bias. Fortunately, along most background dimensions the bias was small, as documented in Bachman, O'Malley, et al. (1996), and we suspect that any bias in *relationships* is even smaller. (For more extensive treatments of Monitoring the Future participation rates, representativeness, and validity, see Bachman, Johnston, & O'Malley, 1996; Johnston et al., 1997.)

Any nonparticipation in sample surveys is regrettable, of course; nevertheless, it should be noted that the sample losses described earlier are generally lower than those reported for most panel studies of drug use in adolescence and young adulthood. Moreover, although the sample losses among seniors and the panel attrition during follow-ups did produce some distortion, the panels still retain a broad range of variation on all of the measures examined here, giving us considerable confidence that overall patterns of relationships are well represented in these samples.

In summary, there are limitations to our ability to generalize because (a) several restrictions had to be imposed in defining target samples, (b) there were some losses sustained in the senior-year surveys, and (c) there was panel attrition. Nevertheless, the panel data cover a broad spectrum of the high-school-senior population and a wide range of post-high-school behaviors. Moreover, the numbers of cases are sufficiently large that we are able to analyze subgroups constituting small proportions of the total samples. Obviously, it is impossible for small subgroups to account for large portions of the total variance in drug use; nevertheless, we report a number of instances where the findings for such subgroups stand in sharp contrast to the rest of the sample. Our analysis methods were designed to take advantage of the sample size and to display subgroup differences clearly.

Survey Methods

Questionnaires.   All of the Monitoring the Future surveys use self-completed questionnaires that are formatted for optical scanning. Although multiple questionnaire forms have been used each year in order to broaden the total coverage, only items that appear in all forms were used in the present analyses. The specific measures used are introduced in appropriate chapters; for further details on questionnaires and measurement content, see Bachman, Johnston, and O'Malley (1996).

Base-Year Surveys of High-School Seniors.   Each spring the surveys of seniors are administered during regularly scheduled class periods by locally based Institute for Social Research representatives and their assistants. Respondents are asked to provide their names and addresses on forms that are then separated from the questionnaires (but linkable by code numbers accessible only to research staff).

Follow-Up Surveys of Young Adults.   Follow-up questionnaires, similar in most respects to the base-year questionnaires, are sent in the spring by certified mail accompanied by a respondent payment check (initially $5, increased to $10 beginning in 1992). Additional reminder mailings are sent to nonrespondents, and after several weeks attempts are made to telephone all outstanding cases to encourage their participation.

VALIDITY OF SELF-REPORTED DRUG-USE MEASURES[2]

The question always arises whether sensitive behaviors like drug use are honestly reported. Like most studies dealing with sensitive behaviors, we have no direct, totally objective validation of the present measures; however, the considerable amount of inferential evidence that exists strongly suggests that the self-report questions produce largely valid data. A more complete discussion of the contributing evidence that leads to this conclusion is found in other publications (Johnston & O'Malley, 1985; Johnston, O'Malley, & Bachman, 1984; Wallace & Bachman, 1993); here we only briefly summarize the evidence.

First, early analyses we undertook using a three-wave panel design established that the various measures of self-reported drug use have a high degree of reliability—a necessary condition for validity (O'Malley et al.,

[2]This section is adapted from Johnston et al., 1997.

1983). In essence, this means that respondents were highly consistent in their self-reported behaviors over a 3- to 4-year interval. Second, we find a high degree of consistency among logically related measures of use within the same questionnaire administration. Third, the proportion of seniors reporting some illicit drug use by senior year reached two-thirds of all respondents in peak years and nearly 80% in some follow-up years, which constitutes *prima facie* evidence that the degree of underreporting must be very limited. Fourth, the seniors' reports of use by their unnamed friends—which they would presumably have less reason to distort—has been highly consistent with self-reported use in the aggregate in terms of both prevalence and trends in prevalence. Fifth, we have found self-reported drug use to relate in consistent and expected ways to a number of other attitudes, behaviors, beliefs, and social situations—in other words, there is strong evidence of *construct validity*. Sixth, additional strong evidence of construct validity is provided in the present volume, which shows that many shifts in post-high-school drug use are linked logically and consistently to new roles and responsibilities that were expected to influence drug use. Seventh, the missing data rates for the self-reported use questions are only slightly higher than for the immediately preceding nonsensitive questions, in spite of the instruction to respondents to leave blank those drug use questions they felt they could not answer honestly.

This is not to argue that self-reported measures of drug use are valid in all cases. In the Monitoring the Future study we have gone to great lengths to create a situation and set of procedures in which students feel that their confidentiality will be protected. We have also tried to present a convincing case to respondents about why such research is needed. We think the evidence suggests that a high level of validity has been obtained. Nevertheless, insofar as there exists any remaining reporting bias, we believe it to be primarily in the direction of underreporting. Thus, we believe our estimates to be lower than their true values, even for the obtained samples, but not substantially so.

MULTIPLE REGRESSION ANALYSES
PREDICTING CHANGES IN DRUG USE

In chapter 3 we discussed our reasons for using multiple regression analysis as a method for dealing simultaneously with a complex array of factors that might be related to drug use among young adults. We introduced each of those factors and showed some of the ways in which they are interrelated, and we discussed our decisions to (a) pool data across multiple cohorts and

(b) pool data across multiple time intervals, but (c) present analyses separately for men and for women. In this portion of the Appendix we provide additional information about our regression analysis strategy, we define the drug use change scores, and we provide guidelines for interpreting the multiple regression tables.

Variables Used in the Regression Analyses

Multiple regression is designed to focus on one "dependent variable" at a time, and examine the "effects" on that variable of a number of "independent variables" or "predictors." We placed quotation marks around these terms because analyses of survey data, even longitudinal panel data, involve our *assumptions* about causal directions—assumptions that seem obvious for some variables, quite plausible for others, but sometimes debatable with respect to the post-high-school roles and experiences that are the focus of these analyses. Indeed, although the analysis methodology supposes only one direction of causation, our view of the underlying reality is sometimes more complex. However, having acknowledged that this approach involves assumptions and simplifications, we should add that it generally serves quite well as a means of summarizing complex relationships, and we have not felt inhibited from considering more complex causal interpretations than those implied by the terminology.

Dependent Variables: Drug Use Change Scores.   The dependent variables in these regression analyses consist of changes in drug use. Chapters 4 through 7 deal with monthly use of four different substances: cigarettes, alcohol, marijuana, and cocaine. Additionally, chapter 5 includes a measure of instances of heavy drinking (five or more drinks in a row) during the past 2 weeks, and chapters 6 and 7 deal with annual use of marijuana and cocaine. For each form of drug use presented in the regression analyses, respondents were asked about their frequency of use during the past 30 days (or 2 weeks, for heavy drinking). The response scales and scoring are shown in Table A.2.

Every follow-up survey generated a change score for each of the dimensions in Table A.2. Change scores were calculated in a straightforward manner: the earlier, or "before," measure of use (always based on the senior-year survey) was subtracted from the later, or "after," measure of use (based on the follow-up survey). Positive scores indicate an increase in use over time, and negative scores indicate a decrease. The interval of time can range from 1–2 years (between senior year and the first follow-up) to as high as 13–14 years (between senior year and the seventh follow-up).

TABLE A.2

Drug-Use Response Scales

Score	Cigarette Use (30 Days)	Alcohol, Marijuana, Cocaine Use (30 Days or 12 Months)	5 Drinks in a Row (2 Weeks)
1	Not at all	None	None
2	Less than 1 cigarette per day	1-2 occasions	Once
3	1-5 cigarettes per day	3-5 occasions	Twice
4	About ½ pack per day	6-9 occasions	3-5 times
5	About 1 pack per day	10-19 occasions	6-9 times
6	About 1½ packs per day	20-39 occasions	10 or more times
7	2 packs or more per day	40 or more occasions	

It is important to note that each of the response scales in Table A.2 is roughly logarithmic rather than reflecting equal intervals; specifically, an increase of one scale unit indicates approximately a doubling of use, whereas a decrease of one scale unit indicates a reduction by about one-half. Accordingly, the change scores derived from these scales also are roughly logarithmic, and we consider that to be quite useful. For example, we would judge a change in alcohol use from 2 occasions to 4 occasions per month to be a more substantial increase than a change from 22 to 24 occasions; the change involves an increase of only 2 occasions in each case, but the proportional shifts are very different. The change score calculations used here do, in fact, treat an increase from 2 to 4 occasions as equivalent to an increase from 8 to 16, or an increase from 15 to 30; in each case the change score would be +1 and would reflect roughly a doubling in frequency of use.

Predictor Variables: Post-High-School Roles and Experiences. The predictor variables of greatest interest in this book are post-high-school roles and experiences measured at the same time as the after portion of the dependent-variable drug use change score. In one sense, these post-high-school roles and experiences are after measures only, but in another very important sense they represent changes, because some very important before characteristics as of the senior year in high school have been held constant across all respondents included in these analyses. Recall that these analyses exclude the small numbers of those who, at the time of the initial survey at the end of their senior year, indicated that they were already married, were not living in the home of one or both parents or guardians, were already parents, or any combination thereof. It follows, then, that a respondent who was married at the time of a follow-up survey could also be considered as having made a particular change in marital status during the before–after period being examined. A respondent living in a dormitory at the time of follow-up could be considered to have made a particular change in living arrangements, whereas a respondent living with parents at the time of follow-up could be considered as not having changed living environments. These interpretations of before–after change are, of course, great simplifications. Nevertheless, as discussed in chapter 3, our strategy of treating all respondents as basically alike along key dimensions in their senior year enables us to examine simultaneously a complex mix of post-high-school experiences and role responsibilities.

The specific post-high-school roles and experiences used as predictor variables in the regression analyses match those treated in the figures and text in chapters 4 through 7. They are grouped into two sets for the regression analyses. The first set consists of student status plus work status; in a sense, these two dimensions in combination represent the young adults' primary job environment. For many the job environment simply corresponds to their employment in the work force; for many others during the first few years after high school, the real job consists of being a student; and for some the primary job consists of being a full-time homemaker. The second set of roles and experiences consists of living arrangements including marital status, combined with engagement status, pregnancy status, and parenthood status. Taken together, these dimensions capture much of the social environment of many young adults.

Additional Predictors: Control or Background Factors.   Several other predictor variables were included in our regression analyses primarily as *controls*. Although the use of change scores reduces the need for controlling background factors, we view the inclusion of such variables as important safeguards—especially because the boundary between background and contemporaneous influences cannot always be clearly drawn. Several background factors, measured at the end of senior year, were included primarily as control variables in these analyses: race, region, urbanicity, high-school grades, college plans. Race may seem to be clearly a background factor, yet social environments often differ considerably by racial subgroup and such differences do not end with graduation from high school. Similarly, region and urbanicity relate to differing social contexts, and although some individuals move to different locations after high school, many do not—so these background factors may reflect contemporaneous influences as well as those in effect during high school. High-school grades and senior-year plans for college reflect a complex mixture of endowment, ambition, and achievement, all of which can have continuing impacts on individuals.

Two other variables, grouped with the background variables for analysis purposes, were included in part for "housekeeping" purposes, although they are also of substantive interest. The first and more important of these variables is the distinction between follow-up surveys, which serves as an indicator of the number of years post-high-school as well as a close proxy for age (e.g., the first follow-up occurred 1 or 2 years after high school when the modal age of respondents was 19 or 20, and the seventh follow-up occurred 13 or 14 years after high school when modal ages were 31 or 32). The second variable represents a further refinement, and distinguishes whether the first of the (otherwise biannual) follow-ups occurred 1 or 2 years after high-school graduation.

Conventions Followed in Conducting and Reporting Regression Analyses

All of the multiple regression analyses reported here were carried out in a manner consistent with usual conventions. That leaves room for many choices and options, and some of those we chose may be unfamiliar to some readers. In this section we provide an overview and rationale for the choices we made in developing these regression analyses. In the next section we provide specific detailed guidelines for interpreting the tables.

Numbers of Cases Specified for Regression Analyses. We observed in chapter 3 that our fictional John Jones would have generated seven different change scores (per drug) because he participated in seven different follow-up surveys; and we noted (footnote 6 in chapter 3) that these seven change observations would not be strictly independent of each other, because they are all from the same individual. This means that (a) the change scores from any single individual share a common before measure (based on the drug use reported as a high-school senior) and (b) the after measures are not entirely independent of one another. Therefore, rather than base tests of statistical significance on the total number of *observations*, the numbers of *cases* we specified in the regression analyses approximated the total numbers of *separate individuals* (further decreased by weighting, as discussed earlier in this Appendix). Thus, the numbers of cases specified were 12,000 for men and 15,000 for women.

Pair-Wise Deletion, Missing Data on Pregnancy. Pair-wise deletion was used in the regression analyses. In general, there was very little missing data, with one noteworthy exception. The measure of pregnancy was incorporated into follow-up surveys beginning in 1984. A glance at Table 3.1 will confirm that this represents the majority of all follow-ups included in these analyses; therefore, for purposes of these regression analyses, we were willing to treat the follow-ups from 1984 onward as representing the full set of analysis cases with respect to pregnancy.

Dummy Variables and Continuous Variables.   Nearly all of the predictor variables used in these analyses are categorical rather than continuous, and many (such as work status and living arrangements) cannot be treated as ordinal variables in any meaningful sense. Accordingly, we used a number of sets of dummy variables, which had the additional advantage of giving us detailed data on each of the predictor categories, as discussed later. Three of the background predictors—urbanicity, high-school grades, and college plans—were treated as continuous variables to simplify interpretation (and conserve degrees of freedom):

1. *Urbanicity* (based on residence during senior year of high school) was a five-category variable, scaled as follows: 1 = *lived on a farm,* 2 = *lived in the country but not on a farm,* 3 = *lived in a (small) city (non-SMSA),*[3] 4 = *lived in a (larger) city (SMSA, not self-representing),* 5 = *lived in a (very large) city (self-representing SMSA).* For the sample as a whole, the mean score on the urbanicity scale was about 3.75.

2. *High-school grades* were reported on a 9-point scale ranging from 1 = D, to 9 = A. For women the mean was 6.25, and for men it was 5.72 (with 6.0 equal to a B).

3. *College plans* were responses to a question asking "How likely is it that you will . . . graduate from college (4-year program)?" with the following response alternatives and codes: 1 = *definitely won't,* 2 = *probably won't,* 3 = *probably will,* 4 = *definitely will.* For women the mean was 2.81, and for men it was 2.85.

Special Format for Reporting Regression Analyses.   We report the findings from the regression analyses in the form of *unstandardized* regression coefficients, so that sizes of effects (i.e., changes in drug use) can be interpreted directly. Moreover, unstandardized regression coefficients make it easy to observe when relatively rare situations (such as pregnancy) have impacts that equal or exceed more common situations (such as being married), even though the latter may account for more in the way of explained variance. This emphasis on unstandardized coefficients is not out of the ordinary. What is unusual, however, is the way we have chosen to report regression coefficients based on sets of dummy variables. In place of the common practice of excluding one category of the predictor, and displaying regression coefficients as departures from that "omitted" category treated as a reference point, our approach is to make the mean for the overall sample our reference

---

[3]SMSA is the acronym for *Standard Metropolitan Statistical Area* and is defined by the Census Bureau. For details, see appendix B of Johnston et al. (1997).

point and treat *all* categories of the predictor in terms of departures from that mean.[4]

For those familiar with Multiple Classification Analysis (Andrews et al., 1973), we note that our format for presenting regression findings was inspired by some of the features found in that form of regression analysis—features that make the output easier and more straightforward to interpret than is true of typical multiple regression output, especially when dummy variables are involved. In broad outline, the format used in our regression tables has the following characteristics:

1. The starting point is a *constant* that consists of the mean of the dependent variable (i.e., the mean change score for the drug in question) calculated across all respondents (i.e., all male cases, or all female cases). In effect, this constant represents our best guess about the dependent variable for any respondent if we knew nothing about any of the predictors.

2. For each of the three predictor variables treated as interval scales (i.e., urbanicity, high-school grades, and plans to complete college), the format presents a coefficient indicating the change or difference in the dependent variable that is associated with a 1-point shift in the predictor variable. It is important to note that to calculate the effect associated with any particular point on these three predictor dimensions, one must first calculate the difference between that point and the mean for all respondents for that predictor dimension, and then multiply that difference by the coefficient. (Although that may seem a bit awkward, it has the important advantage of maintaining the overall constant as a meaningful value, rather than a largely arbitrary one. Because there is little need to make the actual calculations for the three control variables in question, we considered the trade-off worthwhile.)

3. For each of the categorical predictors consisting of a set of dummy variables, the format provides a corresponding set of coefficients—one for each dummy variable category (including the "omitted" category). Each such coefficient indicates the extent of departure from the overall mean (i.e., the constant) associated with being in that category. Both bivariate and multivariate coefficients are displayed. Each bivariate coefficient indicates the average deviation from the overall mean for all cases in that particular category, without taking other variables into account. The multivariate regression coefficients show adjustments to the overall mean with all other predictors in the column included.

4. Summary statistics consist of the usual Multiple-R and R-squared values, as well as an R-squared value adjusted to take account of degrees of freedom.

---

[4]We are indebted to our colleague, Willard Rodgers, for his contributions to developing and describing this form of presentation combining dummy variable and ordinary variable multiple regression analysis (see especially Rodgers & Bachman, 1988; also Bachman et al., 1992).

Detailed Guidelines for Interpreting Regression Tables[5]

Tables A.5 through A.11 are identical in the sets of predictor variables used, and almost identical in format; they have different dependent variables. For illustrative purposes we concentrate on Table A.6, in which the dependent variable is change in alcohol use (during the past month) between senior year and follow-up.

Each of the tables consists of two parallel parts, reporting results separately for women and for men. They are arranged on facing pages to permit easy comparison. Our illustrations focus on the data for women.

Columns 1–5: Analyses Using All Available Cases. The first five columns of data in both the female and male portions of each table are based on analyses using the full set of available cases across up to seven follow-ups. The entries in the first column are unstandardized bivariate regression coefficients, showing relationships between each predictor and the dependent variable, while taking no account of relationships with other predictor variables. The entries in the next four columns are unstandardized multiple regression coefficients, showing relationships between certain predictors and the dependent variable with certain other predictor variables included in the equation. The second column is limited to the background predictor variables; the third column includes background predictors, plus student status and work status; the fourth column includes background predictors, plus living arrangements (the first category of which is married), engagement status, pregnancy status, and parenthood status; and the fifth column includes all of the above variables. Comparisons among the third, fourth, and fifth columns permit an exploration of overlapping relationships between student/employment status on the one hand, and an extended set of living arrangements and parenthood status on the other hand. Comparisons involving the second column permit an understanding of overlaps with predictors we treat as background factors.

Columns 6–7: Analyses Using the First Two Follow-Ups Only. The sixth and seventh columns are based on analyses using only the first two follow-ups, corresponding to the first 4 years after high school.[6] These data are particularly relevant for relationships involving student status, because relatively few respondents were students beyond the second follow-up. The sixth column is analogous to the first, showing unstandardized bivariate

---

[5]Most of the material in this section has been adapted directly from pp. 143–144 of Bachman et al. (1992), which was drafted originally by Willard Rodgers.

[6]These analyses were not carried out for the annual (12-month) marijuana and cocaine change scores.

regression coefficients. The seventh column is analogous to the fifth, showing unstandardized multiple regression coefficients with all predictors included in the equation.

Constant. The constant shown at the top of each column is the *mean* change score on the dependent variable. For the first five columns in the female portion of Table A.6, that value is 0.124, indicating that across the full set of seven follow-ups used to calculate change scores, the average increase for women was 0.124 on the 7-point scale measuring alcohol use. (For the last two columns in the female portion of Table A.6, the constant value is 0.271; the difference between the two constants occurred because during the earliest years of adulthood captured by the first two follow-ups, the average increase in alcohol use among women was larger than during the longer interval.) It should be recalled that these means for changes in alcohol consumption were computed across *all* cases, not just those who were alcohol users. Thus the increases *among alcohol users* were somewhat larger than those shown for the total sample.

Coefficients for Predictors Treated as Interval Scales. The coefficients for interval-scaled predictor variables are conventional unstandardized bivariate (columns 1, 6, 8, and 13) and multiple (columns 2–5, 7, 9–12, 14) regression coefficients. (Tables A.9 and A.11 are slightly different in format; the bivariate regression coefficients appear in columns 1 and 6, and the multiple regression coefficients appear in columns 2–5 and 7–10). These regression coefficients indicate the deviation from the average change on the dependent variable associated with a unit change on the predictor variable. For example, the coefficient for High-School Grades in the first column of Table A.6 is 0.105, indicating that with each increase of one unit on the scale (e.g., from B to B+) the average reported increase in 30-day alcohol use is 0.105 *higher* (based on the full set of cases from follow-ups 1–7). To calculate the overall mean change scores for women who had straight-A grade averages in high school, three steps are necessary: First, determine how much the straight-A grade (coded 9) deviates from the overall mean for women. Table A.3 provides the overall means for each of the interval-scaled predictor variables. The overall mean of High-School Grades for women, based on the full set of cases, is 6.252, and so the straight-A deviation from the overall mean is +2.748 (i.e., 9.000 − 6.252). Second, multiply this deviation by the coefficient to determine that straight-A female students had alcohol change scores which deviated by +0.289 (i.e., 2.748 × 0.105) from the overall change scores for women. Third, combine that value with the overall female constant of 0.124 to determine that, on average, women who were straight-A students in high school

TABLE A.3

Means of Interval-Scaled Predictor Variables

Variable	WOMEN		MEN	
	Based on Cases from Follow-Ups 1-7	Based on Cases from Follow-Ups 1-2	Based on Cases from Follow-Ups 1-7	Based on Cases from Follow-Ups 1-2
High School Grades (D=1, A=9)	6.252	6.241	5.721	5.727
R will attend 4 yr. college? (Definitely won't=1, Definitely will=4)	2.809	2.905	2.846	2.910
Urbanicity (Farm=1, Very large city=5)	3.761	3.796	3.745	3.766

increased their rates of monthly alcohol use by 0.413 (i.e., 0.289 + 0.124) on the 7-point scale.

The preceding exercise calculated the predicted change based on the simple bivariate association between high-school grades and change in 30-day alcohol use. The subsequent columns (2–5) provide the multiple regression coefficients for the predictor, taking into account the other variables for which coefficients are shown in that particular column. The statistical significance for each of these multiple regression coefficients is assessed by the t-ratio (not shown), and if the null hypothesis of no linear relationship can be rejected, the coefficient is marked by one asterisk (.05 level) or two asterisks (.01 level).

Coefficients for Categorical Predictors.   The table entries for categorical predictors are less conventional, but more readily interpretable than those for the interval-scaled predictors. The coefficient shown for each value of a categorical variable is the predicted extent to which respondents in that category deviate from the overall average (i.e., deviate from the constant). For example, for women who were pregnant at follow-up, the coefficient in the first column is ⁻1.147, indicating a dramatic decrease in alcohol use in contrast to the small increase in the overall average; after combining with the constant of 0.124, we see that their overall change was ⁻1.023—still a very large decrease. Columns 2–5 show that multivariate controls for other factors had little effect on this large and statistically significant relationship.

Multiple-R and Multiple-R-Squared Values.   The bottom rows of entries in each of the tables consist of multiple-R and R-squared values, the latter indicating the amount of variance explained by the various sets of predictor variables. The adjusted R-squared value takes account of degrees of freedom, and provides an unbiased estimate of the population value.

Comparing the *R*-squared values among columns permits an assessment of unique and overlapping explained variance. Such assessments with respect to changes in cigarette use are discussed in the final portion of chapter 4, and similar discussions with respect to the other drugs appear at the end of chapters 5–7.

TABLE A.4

Weighted Ns of Observations by Variable Subgroup

| | WEIGHTED Ns of OBSERVATIONS | | | |
| | WOMEN | | MEN | |
VARIABLE	Full Set of Cases from Follow-Ups 1-7	Cases from Follow-Ups 1 and 2	Full Set of Cases from Follow-Ups 1-7	Cases from Follow-Ups 1 and 2
SET#1 RACE				
WHITE	49,285	20,932	41,812	17,805
BLACK	5,551	2,554	3,385	1,596
OTHER	5,009	2,553	4,272	2,184
SET#2 REGION				
NORTHEAST	13,726	5,859	11,298	4,776
NORTH CENTRAL	18,501	7,805	15,501	6,592
SOUTH	17,966	8,079	14,644	6,513
WEST	9,653	4,296	8,027	3,704
HIGH SCHOOL GRADES	58,952	25,640	48,248	21,058
R WILL ATTEND 4YR COLLEGE	57,657	25,072	46,944	20,499
URBANICITY	59,845	26,039	49,456	21,582
SET#3 FOLLOW-UP NUMBER				
FU #1	14,127	14,127	11,696	11,696
FU #2	11,913	11,913	9,890	9,890
FU #3	9,974		8,241	
FU #4	8,204		6,691	
FU #5	6,595		5,443	
FU #6	5,174		4,285	
FU #7	3,859		3,223	
SET#4 ADMINISTRATION OF FIRST FOLLOW-UP				
ONE YEAR AFTER HIGH SCHOOL	31,354		26,044	
TWO YEARS AFTER HIGH SCHOOL	28,490		23,425	
SET#5 STUDENT STATUS AT FOLLOW-UP				
FULL-TIME STUDENT	15,858	13,007	13,770	10,780
PART-TIME STUDENT	5,594	2,195	4,615	1,786
NOT A STUDENT	38,393	10,837	31,084	9,020
SET#6 WORK STATUS AT FOLLOW-UP				
FULL-TIME CIVILIAN JOB	31,092	9,163	29,305	8,051
MILITARY SERVICE	400	196	2,465	1,244
PART-TIME JOB	12,567	8,086	7,685	5,486
HOMEMAKER	4,428	1,011	147	76
NONSTUDENT, NOT EMPLOYED	2,977	1,218	2,247	958
OTHER	8,380	6,366	7,619	5,771
SET#7 LIVING ARRANGEMENT AT FOLLOW-UP				
MARRIED	21,333	3,785	13,727	1,644
PARTNER	4,763	1,826	3,152	985
PARENT(S)	16,170	10,917	15,025	9,789
DORM	4,748	4,548	3,865	3,582
LIVE ALONE	3,805	754	4,384	885
OTHER	9,024	4,209	9,317	4,701
SET#8 ENGAGEMENT STATUS AT FOLLOW-UP				
ENGAGED	5,192	2,905	3,404	1,547
NOT ENGAGED	54,653	23,134	46,065	20,039
SET#9 IS R PREGNANT AT FOLLOW-UP?				
YES	2,770	671	1,718	264
NO	47,147	17,454	39,184	14,522
SET#10 PARENTHOOD STATUS AT FOLLOW-UP				
MARRIED PARENT	12,338	1,474	7,911	708
SINGLE PARENT	3,742	1,016	1,931	518
NOT A PARENT	43,764	23,549	39,626	20,360
TOTAL OBSERVATIONS	59,845	26,039	49,469	21,586

Notes: Sets #1 and #2 were measured at Base Year;
Sets #3 and #4 were determined by timing of follow-up;
Sets #5 - #10 were measured at follow-up.

Regression Analyses Linking Post-High-School Experiences to Changes in 30-Day
Cigarette Use

VARIABLE	BIVARIATE COEFF.	BKGD.	BKGD.+ STUD./WORK	BKGD.+ LIV. ARR.	ALL SETS
		REGRESSION COEFFICIENTS FOR WOMEN			
		Based on Full Set of Cases from Follow-Ups 1-7			
CONSTANT	0.093	0.093	0.093	0.093	0.093
SET#1 RACE					
WHITE	-0.008	-0.010 *	-0.009 *	-0.004	-0.004
BLACK	0.103	0.094 **	0.090 **	0.046	0.042
OTHER	-0.036	-0.010	-0.009	-0.009	-0.008
SET#2 REGION					
NORTHEAST	-0.075	-0.057 **	-0.058 **	-0.069 **	-0.070 **
NORTH CENTRAL	0.033	0.038 **	0.038 **	0.036 *	0.036 *
SOUTH	0.055	0.031 *	0.030	0.041 **	0.040 **
WEST	-0.057	-0.048 *	-0.046 *	-0.046 *	-0.044 *
HIGH SCHOOL GRADES[a]	0.010	0.006	0.007	0.008	0.010
R WILL ATTEND 4YR COLLEGE[a]	0.021	0.022 *	0.026 **	0.005	0.016
URBANICITY[a]	-0.042	-0.039 **	-0.038 **	-0.044 **	-0.042 **
SET#3 FOLLOW-UP NUMBER					
FU #1	0.023	0.021	0.036	-0.024	-0.003
FU #2	0.046	0.046 *	0.053 **	0.015	0.029
FU #3	0.034	0.034	0.027	0.029	0.019
FU #4	0.002	0.003	-0.008	0.027	0.012
FU #5	-0.046	-0.045	-0.055 *	-0.003	-0.019
FU #6	-0.090	-0.089 **	-0.097 **	-0.028	-0.043
FU #7	-0.118	-0.116 **	-0.123 **	-0.047	-0.062
SET#4 ADMINISTRATION OF FIRST FOLLOW-UP					
ONE YEAR AFTER HIGH SCHOOL	-0.001	-0.002	-0.001	-0.007	-0.005
TWO YEARS AFTER HIGH SCHOOL	0.002	0.002	0.001	0.007	0.006
SET#5 STUDENT STATUS AT FOLLOW-UP					
FULL-TIME STUDENT	0.012		-0.029		-0.091 **
PART-TIME STUDENT	-0.064		-0.065 *		-0.073 *
NOT A STUDENT	0.004		0.021 *		0.048 **
SET#6 WORK STATUS AT FOLLOW-UP					
FULL-TIME CIVILIAN JOB	0.012		0.018		-0.006
MILITARY SERVICE	0.264		0.227		0.213
PART-TIME JOB	-0.024		-0.029		-0.011
HOMEMAKER	-0.142		-0.121 **		-0.003
NONSTUDENT, NOT EMPLOYED	0.067		0.053		0.056
OTHER	0.028		0.011		0.009
SET#7 LIVING ARRANGEMENT AT FOLLOW-UP					
MARRIED	-0.158			-0.117 **	-0.134 **
PARTNER	0.142			0.141 **	0.136 **
PARENT(S)	0.040			0.031	0.036
DORM	0.062			0.042	0.097 *
LIVE ALONE	0.126			0.089 *	0.081 *
OTHER	0.141			0.086 **	0.096 **
SET#8 ENGAGEMENT STATUS AT FOLLOW-UP					
ENGAGED	-0.007			-0.118 **	-0.123 **
NOT ENGAGED	0.001			0.011 **	0.012 **
SET#9 IS R PREGNANT AT FOLLOW-UP?					
YES	-0.353			-0.267 **	-0.279 **
NO	0.021			0.016 **	0.016 **
SET#10 PARENTHOOD STATUS AT FOLLOW-UP					
MARRIED PARENT	-0.196			-0.079 **	-0.083 **
SINGLE PARENT	0.240			0.152 **	0.133 **
NOT A PARENT	0.035			0.009	0.012
Multiple-R		0.0781	0.0900	0.1442	0.1520
R Sqr.		0.0061 **	0.0081 **	0.0208 **	0.0231 **
R Sqr., adjusted		0.0051	0.0067	0.0192	0.0211

* indicates statistical significance at .05 level. ** indicates statistical significance at .01 level. (Statistical significance is not indicated for bivariate coefficients or constants.)

[a] Means of these interval-scaled variables are necessary to calculate the predicted change in drug use associated with these variables. See Table A.3 for means; see appendix text for instructions.

(Table continued on next page)

| WOMEN (cont.) | | REGRESSION COEFFICIENTS FOR MEN | | | | | | |
| Based on Cases from Follow-Ups 1 and 2 | | Based on Full Set of Cases from Follow-Ups 1-7 | | | | | Based on Cases from Follow-Ups 1 and 2 | |
BIVARIATE COEFF.	ALL SETS	BIVARIATE COEFF.	BKGD.	BKGD.+ STUD./WORK	BKGD.+ LIV. ARR.	ALL SETS	BIVARIATE COEFF.	ALL SETS
0.127	0.127	0.214	0.214	0.214	0.214	0.214	0.191	0.191
SET#1								
0.008	0.004	-0.004	-0.007	-0.006	-0.003	-0.002	0.000	-0.001
0.003	0.002	0.137	0.151 **	0.139 **	0.108 *	0.095 *	0.082	0.060
-0.066	-0.035	-0.069	-0.055	-0.055	-0.055	-0.053	-0.060	-0.039
SET#2								
-0.020	-0.020	-0.029	-0.019	-0.019	-0.021	-0.023	-0.003	0.009
0.038	0.032 *	0.047	0.046 **	0.047 **	0.047 **	0.048 **	0.046	0.045 **
0.008	0.011	-0.013	-0.029	-0.031	-0.024	-0.025	-0.019	-0.030
-0.056	-0.051 **	-0.027	-0.009	-0.008	-0.017	-0.014	-0.046	-0.039
0.006	0.000	-0.010	-0.006	-0.002	-0.004	-0.001	-0.010	0.000
0.026	0.036 **	-0.017	-0.008	0.006	-0.009	0.005	-0.014	0.028 *
-0.021	-0.024 **	-0.022	-0.018	-0.016	-0.020	-0.019	-0.018	-0.012
SET#3								
-0.011	-0.011	-0.063	-0.062 **	-0.035	-0.064 **	-0.047	-0.041	-0.026 **
0.013	0.013	0.026	0.027	0.041	0.012	0.025	0.049	0.031 **
		0.044	0.044	0.036	0.037	0.030		
		0.031	0.030	0.014	0.035	0.023		
		0.027	0.025	0.005	0.037	0.023		
		-0.023	-0.026	-0.046	-0.007	-0.021		
		-0.040	-0.042	-0.066	-0.023	-0.040		
SET#4								
		0.005	0.005	0.007	0.006	0.007		
		-0.006	-0.006	-0.008	-0.007	-0.008		
SET#5								
-0.006	-0.063 **	-0.082		-0.064 *		-0.073 *	-0.069	-0.066 **
-0.015	-0.001	-0.046		-0.047		-0.045	0.007	0.008
0.010	0.076 **	0.043		0.035 **		0.039 **	0.082	0.077 **
SET#6								
0.024	0.009	0.008		-0.012		-0.005	0.041	0.013
0.182	0.121	0.189		0.161 **		0.162 **	0.253	0.160 **
-0.012	-0.004	-0.055		-0.012		-0.017	-0.058	-0.021
-0.140	-0.026	0.037		0.049		0.045	-0.060	-0.055
-0.034	-0.023	0.154		0.110 *		0.085	0.066	0.007
0.004	-0.003	-0.081		-0.028		-0.041	-0.067	-0.035
SET#7								
-0.146	-0.148 **	-0.082			0.136 **	-0.154 **	-0.045	-0.159 **
0.053	0.067 *	0.170			0.143 **	0.141 **	0.190	0.139 **
-0.014	-0.013	-0.014			0.018	0.023	-0.037	-0.029 *
0.029	0.046 *	-0.094			-0.023	0.048	-0.078	0.004
0.098	0.059	0.074			0.067	0.051	0.106	0.049
0.096	0.078 **	0.090			0.100 **	0.098 **	0.092	0.075 **
SET#8								
-0.054	-0.089 **	0.042			-0.055	-0.065	0.074	-0.004
0.007	0.011 **	-0.003			0.004	0.005	-0.006	0.000
SET#9								
-0.344	-0.291 **	-0.030			0.024	0.021	0.022	0.017
0.013	0.011 **	0.001			-0.001	-0.001	0.000	0.000
SET#10								
-0.180	-0.060	-0.043			0.063	0.062	0.010	0.081
0.004	-0.032	0.372			0.258 **	0.250 **	0.256	0.160 *
0.011	0.005	-0.010			-0.025 **	-0.025 **	-0.007	-0.007 *
	0.1162		0.0583	0.0787	0.0980	0.1118		0.1175
	0.0135 **		0.0034 **	0.0062 **	0.0096 **	0.0125 **		0.0138 **
	0.0118		0.0022	0.0043	0.0077	0.0099		0.1118

Notes:
Sets #1 and #2 were measured at Base Year;
Sets #3 and #4 were determined by timing of follow-up;
Sets #5 - #10 were measured at follow-up.
Detailed guidelines for table interpretation are provided in text of the appendix.

209

Regression Analyses Linking Post-High-School Experiences to Changes in 30-Day
AlcoholUse

VARIABLE	REGRESSION COEFFICIENTS FOR WOMEN				
	Based on Full Set of Cases from Follow-Ups 1-7				
	BIVARIATE COEFF.	BKGD.	BKGD.+ STUD./WORK	BKGD.+ LIV. ARR.	ALL SETS
CONSTANT	0.124	0.124	0.124	0.124	0.124
SET#1 RACE					
WHITE	-0.021	-0.026 **	-0.026 **	-0.027 **	-0.027 **
BLACK	0.189	0.250 **	0.245 **	0.235 **	0.232 **
OTHER	-0.007	-0.019	-0.012	0.007	0.008
SET#2 REGION					
NORTHEAST	0.013	0.013	0.006	-0.024	-0.024
NORTH CENTRAL	-0.044	-0.003	-0.007	-0.011	-0.011
SOUTH	-0.015	-0.051 *	-0.048 *	-0.024	-0.025
WEST	0.095	0.083 **	0.092 **	0.099 **	0.101 **
HIGH SCHOOL GRADES[a]	0.105	0.083 **	0.075 **	0.072 **	0.073 **
R WILL ATTEND 4YR COLLEGE[a]	0.197	0.139 **	0.110 **	0.068 **	0.072 **
URBANICITY[a]	0.061	0.028 *	0.024	0.012	0.013
SET#3 FOLLOW-UP NUMBER					
FU #1	0.117	0.097 **	0.034	-0.098 **	-0.088 **
FU #2	0.182	0.173 **	0.140 **	0.067 **	0.075 **
FU #3	0.058	0.057 *	0.073 *	0.059 *	0.057 *
FU #4	-0.069	-0.061	-0.030	0.037	0.030
FU #5	-0.154	-0.141 **	-0.092 *	0.021	0.012
FU #6	-0.292	-0.267 **	-0.211 **	-0.045	-0.055
FU #7	-0.336	-0.309 **	-0.242 **	-0.057	-0.067
SET#4 ADMINISTRATION OF FIRST FOLLOW-UP					
ONE YEAR AFTER HIGH SCHOOL	0.001	-0.001	-0.007	-0.021	-0.020
TWO YEARS AFTER HIGH SCHOOL	-0.002	0.001	0.007	0.023	0.022
SET#5 STUDENT STATUS AT FOLLOW-UP					
FULL-TIME STUDENT	0.329		0.148 **		-0.047
PART-TIME STUDENT	0.033		-0.014		-0.033
NOT A STUDENT	-0.141		-0.059 **		0.024
SET#6 WORK STATUS AT FOLLOW-UP					
FULL-TIME CIVILIAN JOB	-0.006		0.073 **		0.003
MILITARY SERVICE	0.260		0.270		0.200
PART-TIME JOB	0.087		-0.049		0.004
HOMEMAKER	-0.609		-0.426 **		-0.097 *
NONSTUDENT, NOT EMPLOYED	-0.250		-0.099		-0.034
OTHER	0.291		0.050		0.035
SET#7 LIVING ARRANGEMENT AT FOLLOW-UP					
MARRIED	-0.445			-0.266 **	-0.270 **
PARTNER	-0.020			0.029	0.028
PARENT(S)	0.096			0.027	0.029
DORM	0.565			0.353 **	0.369 **
LIVE ALONE	0.426			0.228 **	0.223 **
OTHER	0.413			0.283 **	0.284 **
SET#8 ENGAGEMENT STATUS AT FOLLOW-UP					
ENGAGED	-0.079			-0.237 **	-0.240 **
NOT ENGAGED	0.008			0.023 **	0.023 **
SET#9 IS R PREGNANT AT FOLLOW-UP?					
YES	-1.147			-0.871 **	-0.872 **
NO	0.067			0.051 **	0.051 **
SET#10 PARENTHOOD STATUS AT FOLLOW-UP					
MARRIED PARENT	-0.617			-0.275 **	-0.258 **
SINGLE PARENT	-0.166			-0.269 **	-0.268 **
NOT A PARENT	0.188			0.101 **	0.096 **
Multiple-R		0.2005	0.2214	0.3127	0.3135
R Sqr.		0.0402 **	0.0490 **	0.0978 **	0.0983 **
R Sqr., adjusted		0.0392	0.0476	0.0963	0.0965

* indicates statistical significance at .05 level. ** indicates statistical significance at .01 level. (Statistical significance is not indicated for bivariate coefficients or constants.)

[a] Means of these interval-scaled variables are necessary to calculate the predicted change in drug use associated with these variables. See Table A.3 for means; see appendix text for instructions.

(Table continued on next page)

WOMEN (cont.)		REGRESSION COEFFICIENTS FOR MEN						
Based on Cases from Follow-Ups 1 and 2		Based on Full Set of Cases from Follow-Ups 1-7					Based on Cases from Follow-Ups 1 and 2	
BIVARIATE COEFF.	ALL SETS	BIVARIATE COEFF.	BKGD.	BKGD.+ STUD./WORK	BKGD.+ LIV. ARR.	ALL SETS	BIVARIATE COEFF.	ALL SETS
0.271	0.271	0.370	0.370	0.370	0.370	0.370	0.426	0.426
SET#1								
0.015	-0.003	-0.018	-0.024 **	-0.024 **	-0.025 **	-0.025 **	0.002	-0.013
0.003	0.076 *	0.265	0.375 **	0.374 **	0.367 **	0.364 **	0.080	0.177 **
-0.123	-0.050	-0.036	-0.066	-0.064	-0.044	-0.042	-0.071	-0.021
SET#2								
0.050	0.002	0.068	0.047	0.047	0.026	0.025	0.107	0.069 *
0.024	0.021	0.004	0.043	0.043	0.045	0.046	0.064	0.074 **
-0.060	-0.031	-0.119	-0.133 **	-0.133 **	-0.117 **	-0.119 **	-0.153	-0.134 **
0.001	0.018	0.113	0.093 *	0.093 *	0.090 *	0.092 *	0.018	0.015
0.093	0.045 **	0.117	0.096 **	0.094 **	0.088 **	0.089 **	0.085	0.045 **
0.187	0.061 **	0.183	0.100 **	0.092 **	0.062 **	0.066 **	0.157	0.045 **
0.058	0.022	0.099	0.051 **	0.050 **	0.038 *	0.037 *	0.075	0.025
SET#3								
-0.029	-0.077 **	-0.051	-0.063 *	-0.085 **	-0.175 **	-0.170 **	-0.109	-0.128 **
0.034	0.091 **	0.184	0.178 **	0.164 **	0.096 **	0.101 **	0.129	0.151 **
		0.116	0.114 **	0.120 **	0.102 **	0.100 **		
		-0.001	0.006	0.019	0.056	0.051		
		-0.087	-0.076	-0.059	0.028	0.023		
		-0.214	-0.200 **	-0.180 **	-0.044	-0.048		
		-0.241	-0.224 **	-0.202 **	-0.028	-0.031		
SET#4								
		-0.001	-0.002	-0.004	-0.013	-0.013		
		0.001	0.003	0.004	0.015	0.014		
SET#5								
0.222	-0.010	0.204		0.019		-0.043	0.165	0.025
-0.104	-0.033	0.021		-0.015		-0.007	-0.064	-0.006
-0.246	0.019	-0.094		-0.006		0.020	-0.185	-0.029
SET#6								
-0.135	-0.033	-0.077		-0.019		0.003	0.161	-0.009
0.053	0.061	0.127		0.147 *		0.125	0.108	0.096
0.094	0.019	0.153		0.037		0.031	0.102	0.040
-0.618	-0.079	-0.563		-0.474		-0.391	-0.429	-0.359
-0.349	-0.038	-0.234		-0.145		-0.177 *	-0.312	-0.147 *
0.239	0.041	0.183		0.039		-0.025	0.162	-0.017
SET#7								
-0.586	-0.380 **	-0.355			-0.230 **	-0.246 **	-0.450	-0.352 **
-0.198	-0.065	-0.024			-0.008	-0.006	-0.061	-0.005
-0.081	-0.067 **	-0.048			-0.036	-0.028	-0.168	-0.114 **
0.422	0.274 **	0.362			0.244 **	0.285 **	0.296	0.211 **
0.182	0.114	0.228			0.131 *	0.119 *	0.040	0.021
0.335	0.227 **	0.350			0.238 **	0.236 **	0.288	0.198 **
SET#8								
-0.274	-0.254 **	-0.117			-0.191 **	-0.199 **	-0.303	-0.271 **
0.034	0.032 **	0.009			0.014 **	0.015 **	0.023	0.021 **
SET#9								
-1.121	-0.761 **	-0.386			-0.132	-0.133	-0.307	0.021
0.043	0.029 **	0.017			0.006	0.006	0.006	0.000
SET#10								
-0.788	-0.311 **	-0.492			-0.212 **	-0.210 **	-0.592	-0.227 *
-0.326	-0.237 **	-0.054			-0.078	-0.074	-0.046	0.030
0.063	0.030 **	0.101			0.046 **	0.046 **	0.022	0.007
	0.2769		0.1803	0.1833	0.2191	0.2214		0.2071
	0.0767 **		0.0325 **	0.0336 **	0.0480 **	0.0490 **		0.0429 **
	0.0752		0.0313	0.0318	0.0461	0.0465		0.0409

Notes: Sets #1 and #2 were measured at Base Year;
Sets #3 and #4 were determined by timing of follow-up;
Sets #5 - #10 were measured at follow-up.
Detailed guidelines for table interpretation are provided in text of the appendix.

Regression Analyses Linking Post-High-School Experiences to Changes in 2-Week Heavy Alcohol Use

VARIABLE	BIVARIATE COEFF.	BKGD.	BKGD.+ STUD./WORK	BKGD.+ LIV. ARR.	ALL SETS
	REGRESSION COEFFICIENTS FOR WOMEN				
	Based on Full Set of Cases from Follow-Ups 1-7				
CONSTANT	-0.096	-0.096	-0.096	-0.096	-0.096
SET#1 RACE					
WHITE	-0.016	-0.018 **	-0.018 **	-0.017 **	-0.017 **
BLACK	0.137	0.157 **	0.151 **	0.136 **	0.133 **
OTHER	0.006	0.004	0.007	0.018	0.018
SET#2 REGION					
NORTHEAST	-0.001	0.007	0.003	-0.013	-0.014
NORTH CENTRAL	-0.032	-0.008	-0.009	-0.013	-0.013
SOUTH	0.030	0.001	0.003	0.017	0.017
WEST	0.008	0.002	0.008	0.012	0.013
HIGH SCHOOL GRADES[a]	0.062	0.052 **	0.047 **	0.046 **	0.046 **
R WILL ATTEND 4YR COLLEGE[a]	0.107	0.069 **	0.049 **	0.029 **	0.029 **
URBANICITY[a]	0.017	0.001	-0.001	-0.008	-0.007
SET#3 FOLLOW-UP NUMBER					
FU #1	0.176	0.166 **	0.111 **	0.041 *	0.035
FU #2	0.148	0.143 **	0.118 **	0.086 **	0.084 **
FU #3	-0.008	-0.008	0.010	0.008	0.010
FU #4	-0.109	-0.105 **	-0.074 **	-0.040	-0.037
FU #5	-0.166	-0.159 **	-0.120 **	-0.064 *	-0.061 *
FU #6	-0.230	-0.217 **	-0.175 **	-0.098 **	-0.095 **
FU #7	-0.256	-0.243 **	-0.197 **	-0.109 **	-0.106 **
SET#4 ADMINISTRATION OF FIRST FOLLOW-UP					
ONE YEAR AFTER HIGH SCHOOL	0.004	0.003	-0.002	-0.009	-0.010
TWO YEARS AFTER HIGH SCHOOL	-0.004	-0.004	0.002	0.010	0.011
SET#5 STUDENT STATUS AT FOLLOW-UP					
FULL-TIME STUDENT	0.269		0.097 **		-0.014
PART-TIME STUDENT	-0.030		-0.036		-0.035
NOT A STUDENT	-0.107		-0.035 **		0.011
SET#6 WORK STATUS AT FOLLOW-UP					
FULL-TIME CIVILIAN JOB	-0.056		0.010		-0.015
MILITARY SERVICE	0.133		0.132		0.095
PART-TIME JOB	0.086		-0.018		0.004
HOMEMAKER	-0.308		-0.181 **		-0.037
NONSTUDENT, NOT EMPLOYED	-0.113		-0.029		-0.004
OTHER	0.274		0.089 **		0.064 *
SET#7 LIVING ARRANGEMENT AT FOLLOW-UP					
MARRIED	-0.276			-0.207 **	-0.204 **
PARTNER	-0.105			-0.029	-0.028
PARENT(S)	0.086			0.050 **	0.053 **
DORM	0.483			0.326 **	0.307 **
LIVE ALONE	0.120			0.084 *	0.085 *
OTHER	0.250			0.209 **	0.205 **
SET#8 ENGAGEMENT STATUS AT FOLLOW-UP					
ENGAGED	-0.093			-0.181 **	-0.179 **
NOT ENGAGED	0.009			0.017 **	0.017 **
SET#9 IS R PREGNANT AT FOLLOW-UP?					
YES	-0.417			-0.233 **	-0.234 **
NO	0.025			0.014 **	0.014 **
SET#10 PARENTHOOD STATUS AT FOLLOW-UP					
MARRIED PARENT	-0.334			-0.059 *	-0.060 *
SINGLE PARENT	-0.091			-0.143 **	-0.144 **
NOT A PARENT	0.102			0.029 **	0.029 **
Multiple-R		0.1808	0.1934	0.2392	0.2402
R Sqr.		0.0327 **	0.0374 **	0.0572 **	0.0577 **
R Sqr., adjusted		0.0318	0.0360	0.0557	0.0558

* indicates statistical significance at .05 level. ** indicates statistical significance at .01 level. (Statistical significance is not indicated for bivariate coefficients or constants.)

[a] Means of these interval-scaled variables are necessary to calculate the predicted change in drug use associated with these variables. See Table A.3 for means; see appendix text for instructions.

(Table continued on next page)

WOMEN (cont.)		REGRESSION COEFFICIENTS FOR MEN						
Based on Cases from Follow-Ups 1 and 2		Based on Full Set of Cases from Follow-Ups 1-7					Based on Cases from Follow-Ups 1 and 2	
BIVARIATE COEFF.	ALL SETS	BIVARIATE COEFF.	BKGD.	BKGD.+ STUD./WORK	BKGD.+ LIV. ARR.	ALL SETS	BIVARIATE COEFF.	ALL SETS
0.067	0.067	-0.026	-0.026	-0.026	-0.026	-0.026	0.164	0.164
SET#1								
0.011	0.001	-0.014	-0.013 *	-0.013 *	-0.013 *	-0.013 *	0.014	0.004
-0.005	0.015	0.155	0.180 **	0.178 **	0.159 **	0.157 **	-0.043	-0.001
-0.086	-0.025	0.016	-0.012	-0.012	0.001	0.001	-0.084	-0.030
SET#2								
0.045	0.016	0.037	0.030	0.029	0.007	0.006	0.108	0.074 **
0.007	0.002	-0.021	0.007	0.007	0.010	0.011	0.026	0.026
-0.013	0.005	-0.014	-0.023	-0.021	-0.008	-0.008	-0.072	-0.046 *
-0.048	-0.034	0.013	-0.014	-0.014	-0.017	-0.016	-0.058	-0.061 *
0.061	0.026 **	0.072	0.054 **	0.050 **	0.048 **	0.048 **	0.069	0.026 **
0.122	0.031 **	0.133	0.081 **	0.064 **	0.045 **	0.044 **	0.139	0.043 **
0.026	0.005	0.055	0.023	0.021	0.008	0.008	0.041	-0.004
SET#3								
0.013	-0.020 *	0.157	0.149 **	0.101 **	0.006	-0.004	-0.031	-0.058 **
-0.016	0.023 *	0.226	0.222 **	0.194 **	0.135 **	0.130 **	0.036	0.069 **
		0.054	0.053	0.066 *	0.052	0.055		
		-0.114	-0.109 **	-0.079 *	-0.037	-0.031		
		-0.219	-0.212 **	-0.174 **	-0.087 *	-0.079		
		-0.327	-0.318 **	-0.276 **	-0.148 **	-0.139 **		
		-0.359	-0.348 **	-0.304 **	-0.150 **	-0.140 *		
SET#4								
		0.024	0.026 *	0.022	0.013	0.013		
		-0.027	-0.028 *	-0.025	-0.014	-0.014		
SET#5								
0.167	0.010	0.292		0.058		-0.003	0.168	0.039
-0.103	-0.036	-0.048		-0.052		-0.047	-0.099	-0.034
-0.180	-0.005	-0.123		-0.018		0.008	-0.181	-0.040
SET#6								
-0.118	-0.028	-0.127		-0.036 *		-0.013	-0.169	-0.024
-0.123	-0.118	0.087		0.092		0.097	0.065	0.093
0.047	-0.005	0.205		0.038		0.023	0.067	-0.001
-0.374	-0.076	-0.387		-0.357		-0.287	-0.315	-0.253
-0.228	-0.042	-0.121		-0.054		-0.100	-0.227	-0.076
0.217	0.069 **	0.298		0.093 *		0.031	0.201	0.031
SET#7								
-0.371	-0.284 **	-0.430			-0.329 **	-0.331 **	-0.464	-0.393 **
-0.226	-0.126 **	-0.174			-0.080	-0.076	-0.263	-0.157 *
-0.064	-0.044 **	0.078			0.052 *	0.063 *	-0.113	-0.062 **
0.329	0.210 **	0.484			0.322 **	0.310 **	0.299	0.179 **
0.056	0.053	0.091			0.092 *	0.089	-0.063	-0.052
0.232	0.186 **	0.322			0.251 **	0.241 **	0.237	0.173 **
SET#8								
-0.207	-0.169 **	-0.197			-0.268 **	-0.267 **	-0.375	-0.312 **
0.026	0.021 **	0.015			0.020 **	0.020 **	0.029	0.024 **
SET#9								
-0.537	-0.276 **	-0.430			-0.113	-0.112	-0.382	-0.019
0.021	0.011 **	0.019			0.005	0.005	0.007	0.000
SET#10								
-0.427	-0.067	-0.493			-0.067	-0.068	-0.536	-0.103
-0.191	-0.104 *	-0.055			-0.031	-0.027	-0.136	0.029
0.035	0.009 *	0.101			0.015	0.015	0.022	0.003
	0.2202		0.1769	0.1830	0.2293	0.2307		0.1942
	0.0485 **		0.0313 **	0.0335 **	0.0526 **	0.0532 **		0.0377 **
	0.0469		0.0301	0.0317	0.0507	0.0508		0.0357

Notes: Sets #1 and #2 were measured at Base Year;
Sets #3 and #4 were determined by timing of follow-up;
Sets #5 - #10 were measured at follow-up.
Detailed guidelines for table interpretation are provided in text of the appendix.

213

TABLE A.8

Regression Analyses Linking Post-High-School Experiences to Changes in 30-Day MarijuanaUse

VARIABLE	REGRESSION COEFFICIENTS FOR WOMEN				
	Based on Full Set of Cases from Follow-Ups 1-7				
	BIVARIATE COEFF.	BKGD.	BKGD.+ STUD./WORK	BKGD.+ LIV. ARR.	ALL SETS
CONSTANT	-0.195	-0.195	-0.195	-0.195	-0.195
SET#1 RACE					
WHITE	-0.015	-0.017 **	-0.017 **	-0.019 **	-0.019 **
BLACK	0.125	0.144 **	0.145 **	0.155 **	0.157 **
OTHER	0.005	0.007	0.008	0.014	0.015
SET#2 REGION					
NORTHEAST	-0.128	-0.101 **	-0.102 **	-0.106 **	-0.107 **
NORTH CENTRAL	-0.011	0.008	0.008	0.006	0.006
SOUTH	0.078	0.037 *	0.037 *	0.042 **	0.042 *
WEST	0.058	0.060 *	0.063 **	0.060 *	0.062 **
HIGH SCHOOL GRADES[a]	0.066	0.058 **	0.057 **	0.055 **	0.056 **
R WILL ATTEND 4YR COLLEGE[a]	0.085	0.049 **	0.048 **	0.034 **	0.038 **
URBANICITY[a]	-0.042	-0.045 **	-0.045 **	-0.047 **	-0.046 **
SET#3 FOLLOW-UP NUMBER					
FU #1	0.192	0.185 **	0.182 **	0.158 **	0.166 **
FU #2	0.125	0.123 **	0.121 **	0.104 **	0.108 **
FU #3	0.034	0.034	0.035	0.032	0.029
FU #4	-0.079	-0.076 **	-0.075 **	-0.063 *	-0.068 *
FU #5	-0.184	-0.181 **	-0.179 **	-0.156 **	-0.162 **
FU #6	-0.264	-0.255 **	-0.253 **	-0.218 **	-0.224 **
FU #7	-0.340	-0.332 **	-0.328 **	-0.288 **	-0.294 **
SET#4 ADMINISTRATION OF FIRST FOLLOW-UP					
ONE YEAR AFTER HIGH SCHOOL	0.008	0.008	0.008	0.005	0.006
TWO YEARS AFTER HIGH SCHOOL	-0.009	-0.009	-0.008	-0.006	-0.006
SET#5 STUDENT STATUS AT FOLLOW-UP					
FULL-TIME STUDENT	0.192		0.015		-0.023
PART-TIME STUDENT	-0.066		-0.063		-0.065 *
NOT A STUDENT	-0.070		0.003		0.019
SET#6 WORK STATUS AT FOLLOW-UP					
FULL-TIME CIVILIAN JOB	-0.040		0.015		0.001
MILITARY SERVICE	-0.137		-0.187		-0.215
PART-TIME JOB	0.075		-0.011		0.001
HOMEMAKER	-0.177		-0.061		0.007
NONSTUDENT, NOT EMPLOYED	-0.058		-0.010		0.006
OTHER	0.158		0.004		0.001
SET#7 LIVING ARRANGEMENT AT FOLLOW-UP					
MARRIED	-0.158			-0.046 *	-0.050 *
PARTNER	0.011			0.062	0.060
PARENT(S)	0.045			-0.024	-0.023
DORM	0.283			0.045	0.056
LIVE ALONE	0.036			0.039	0.039
OTHER	0.122			0.077 **	0.083 **
SET#8 ENGAGEMENT STATUS AT FOLLOW-UP					
ENGAGED	0.000			-0.074 *	-0.075 *
NOT ENGAGED	0.000			0.007 *	0.007 *
SET#9 IS R PREGNANT AT FOLLOW-UP?					
YES	-0.213			-0.128 **	-0.133 **
NO	0.013			0.008 **	0.008 **
SET#10 PARENTHOOD STATUS AT FOLLOW-UP					
MARRIED PARENT	-0.232			-0.054	-0.058
SINGLE PARENT	-0.149			-0.120 **	-0.126 **
NOT A PARENT	0.078			0.025 **	0.027 **
Multiple-R		0.1857	0.1873	0.1949	0.1962
R Sqr.		0.0345 **	0.0351 **	0.0380 **	0.0385 **
R Sqr., adjusted		0.0335	0.0337	0.0364	0.0366

* indicates statistical significance at .05 level. ** indicates statistical significance at .01 level. (Statistical significance is not indicated for bivariate coefficients or constants.)

[a] Means of these interval-scaled variables are necessary to calculate the predicted change in drug use associated with these variables. See Table A.3 for means; see appendix text for instructions.

(Table continued on next page)

WOMEN (cont.)		REGRESSION COEFFICIENTS FOR MEN						
Based on Cases from Follow-Ups 1 and 2		Based on Full Set of Cases from Follow-Ups 1-7					Based on Cases from Follow-Ups 1 and 2	
BIVARIATE COEFF.	ALL SETS	BIVARIATE COEFF.	BKGD.	BKGD.+ STUD./WORK	BKGD.+ LIV. ARR.	ALL SETS	BIVARIATE COEFF.	ALL SETS
-0.034	-0.034	-0.175	-0.175	-0.175	-0.175	-0.175	0.040	0.040
SET#1								
-0.002	-0.010 *	-0.011	-0.011	-0.012	-0.012 *	-0.013 *	0.003	-0.004
0.059	0.092 **	0.074	0.088	0.098	0.093	0.105 *	0.038	0.078
-0.041	-0.013	0.048	0.039	0.036	0.045	0.045	-0.053	-0.021
SET#2								
-0.060	-0.059 **	-0.086	-0.063 *	-0.064 *	-0.073 **	-0.072 **	-0.017	-0.025
-0.001	0.001	0.004	0.021	0.020	0.023	0.022	0.028	0.031
0.030	0.024	0.048	0.025	0.026	0.032	0.032	-0.005	0.000
0.028	0.033	0.027	0.002	0.003	0.000	0.000	-0.019	-0.023
0.047	0.033 **	0.077	0.054 **	0.054 **	0.052 **	0.052 **	0.051	0.020 **
0.071	0.033 **	0.135	0.101 **	0.098 **	0.087 **	0.088 **	0.116	0.068 **
-0.009	-0.011	-0.031	-0.059 **	-0.058 **	-0.065 **	-0.063 **	0.004	-0.022
SET#3								
0.031	0.027 **	0.235	0.225 **	0.223 **	0.175 **	0.197 **	0.020	0.011
-0.036	-0.032 **	0.192	0.188 **	0.192 **	0.156 **	0.170 **	-0.023	-0.013
		0.046	0.046	0.048	0.043	0.041		
		-0.098	-0.093 **	-0.092 *	-0.070	-0.082 *		
		-0.239	-0.231 **	-0.232 **	-0.186 **	-0.205 **		
		-0.367	-0.358 **	-0.362 **	-0.294 **	-0.318 **		
		-0.466	-0.454 **	-0.460 **	-0.374 **	-0.402 **		
SET#4								
		0.019	0.019	0.019	0.015	0.016		
		-0.021	-0.021	-0.021	-0.016	-0.018		
SET#5								
0.072	-0.007	0.256		-0.026		-0.048	0.116	0.004
-0.039	-0.011	-0.038		-0.026		-0.022	-0.050	0.005
-0.078	0.011	-0.108		0.015		0.025	-0.128	-0.005
SET#6								
-0.037	0.011	-0.092		0.001		0.009	-0.073	0.019
-0.284	-0.315 **	-0.332		-0.353 **		-0.389 **	-0.406	-0.413 **
0.033	0.006	0.207		0.043		0.042	0.071	0.032
-0.200	-0.042	-0.049		-0.034		0.000	-0.087	-0.070
-0.081	0.016	-0.018		0.027		0.019	-0.089	0.007
0.067	-0.010	0.258		0.061		0.037	0.137	0.032
SET#7								
-0.169	-0.095 **	-0.283			-0.120 **	-0.108 **	-0.293	-0.172 **
0.015	0.073 *	-0.052			0.061	0.050	-0.006	0.051
-0.048	-0.048 **	0.072			0.010	-0.016	-0.061	-0.062 **
0.125	0.063 *	0.381			0.002	0.085	0.195	0.077 *
0.022	0.024	-0.002			0.051	0.061	-0.005	0.055
0.130	0.117 **	0.161			0.077 *	0.104 **	0.084	0.108 **
SET#8								
-0.072	-0.074 **	-0.074			-0.128 *	-0.125 *	-0.141	-0.114 *
0.009	0.009 **	0.005			0.010 *	0.009 *	0.011	0.009 *
SET#9								
-0.311	-0.216 **	-0.228			-0.037	-0.040	-0.159	0.069
0.012	0.008 **	0.010			0.002	0.002	0.003	-0.001
SET#10								
-0.236	-0.076	-0.356			-0.046	-0.045	-0.375	-0.129
-0.119	-0.103 *	-0.226			-0.140	-0.142	-0.128	-0.083
0.020	0.009 *	0.082			0.016	0.016	0.016	0.007
	0.1334		0.1939	0.2007	0.2017	0.2086		0.1421
	0.0178 **		0.0376 **	0.0403 **	0.0407 **	0.0435 **		0.0202 **
	0.0161		0.0364	0.0386	0.0388	0.0411		0.0181

Notes: Sets #1 and #2 were measured at Base Year;
Sets #3 and #4 were determined by timing of follow-up;
Sets #5 - #10 were measured at follow-up.
Detailed guidelines for table interpretation are provided in text of the appendix.

TABLE A.9

Regression Analyses Linking Post-High-School Experiences to Changes in 12-Month Marijuana Use

VARIABLE	REGRESSION COEFFICIENTS FOR WOMEN				
	Based on Full Set of Cases from Follow-Ups 1-7				
	BIVARIATE COEFF.	BKGD.	BKGD.+ STUD./WORK	BKGD.+ LIV. ARR.	ALL SETS
CONSTANT	-0.330	-0.330	-0.330	-0.330	-0.330
SET#1 RACE					
WHITE	-0.030	-0.033 **	-0.033 **	-0.036 **	-0.036 **
BLACK	0.231	0.261 **	0.259 **	0.268 **	0.268 **
OTHER	0.036	0.040	0.042	0.055	0.055
SET#2 REGION					
NORTHEAST	-0.163	-0.119 **	-0.123 **	-0.140 **	-0.141 **
NORTH CENTRAL	-0.011	0.024	0.023	0.020	0.021
SOUTH	0.117	0.049 *	0.050 *	0.066 **	0.065 **
WEST	0.035	0.033	0.038	0.038	0.039
HIGH SCHOOL GRADES[a]	0.105	0.096 **	0.094 **	0.091 **	0.092 **
R WILL ATTEND 4YR COLLEGE[a]	0.130	0.066 **	0.057 **	0.027 *	0.032 *
URBANICITY[a]	-0.053	-0.060 **	-0.061 **	-0.068 **	-0.068 **
SET#3 FOLLOW-UP NUMBER					
FU #1	0.388	0.378 **	0.352 **	0.268 **	0.273 **
FU #2	0.249	0.246 **	0.233 **	0.187 **	0.190 **
FU #3	0.050	0.051	0.059	0.054	0.051
FU #4	-0.170	-0.165 **	-0.151 **	-0.113 **	-0.116 **
FU #5	-0.361	-0.357 **	-0.338 **	-0.267 **	-0.271 **
FU #6	-0.511	-0.500 **	-0.479 **	-0.376 **	-0.378 **
FU #7	-0.654	-0.643 **	-0.620 **	-0.496 **	-0.499 **
SET#4 ADMINISTRATION OF FIRST FOLLOW-UP					
ONE YEAR AFTER HIGH SCHOOL	0.022	0.022	0.020	0.011	0.011
TWO YEARS AFTER HIGH SCHOOL	-0.024	-0.024	-0.022	-0.012	-0.012
SET#5 STUDENT STATUS AT FOLLOW-UP					
FULL-TIME STUDENT	0.382		0.067		-0.033
PART-TIME STUDENT	-0.092		-0.080		-0.085
NOT A STUDENT	-0.144		-0.016		0.026
SET#6 WORK STATUS AT FOLLOW-UP					
FULL-TIME CIVILIAN JOB	-0.090		0.022		-0.014
MILITARY SERVICE	-0.122		-0.198		-0.242
PART-TIME JOB	0.147		-0.025		0.002
HOMEMAKER	-0.367		-0.145 **		0.033
NONSTUDENT, NOT EMPLOYED	-0.035		0.058		0.090
OTHER	0.327		0.021		0.009
SET#7 LIVING ARRANGEMENT AT FOLLOW-UP					
MARRIED	-0.367			-0.185 **	-0.191 **
PARTNER	0.048			0.152 **	0.147 **
PARENT(S)	0.143			0.018	0.019
DORM	0.596			0.206 **	0.218 **
LIVE ALONE	0.047			0.059	0.061
OTHER	0.253			0.192 **	0.200 **
SET#8 ENGAGEMENT STATUS AT FOLLOW-UP					
ENGAGED	0.009			-0.176 **	-0.175 **
NOT ENGAGED	-0.001			0.017 **	0.017 **
SET#9 IS R PREGNANT AT FOLLOW-UP?					
YES	-0.301			-0.084	-0.093
NO	0.018			0.005	0.006
SET#10 PARENTHOOD STATUS AT FOLLOW-UP					
MARRIED PARENT	-0.507			-0.116 **	-0.132 **
SINGLE PARENT	-0.259			-0.277 **	-0.292 **
NOT A PARENT	0.165			0.056 **	0.062 **
Multiple-R		0.2319	0.2345	0.2514	0.2528
R Sqr.		0.0538 **	0.0550 **	0.0632 **	0.0639 **
R Sqr., adjusted		0.0529	0.0536	0.0617	0.0619

* indicates statistical significance at .05 level. ** indicates statistical significance at .01 level. (Statistical significance is not indicated for bivariate coefficients or constants.)

[a] Means of these interval-scaled variables are necessary to calculate the predicted change in drug use associated with these variables. See Table A.3 for means; see appendix text for instructions.

(Table continued on next page)

REGRESSION COEFFICIENTS FOR MEN				
Based on Full Set of Cases from Follow-Ups 1-7				
BIVARIATE COEFF.	BKGD.	BKGD.+ STUD./WORK	BKGD.+ LIV. ARR.	ALL SETS
-0.214	-0.214	-0.214	-0.214	-0.214
SET#1				
-0.018	-0.018 *	-0.019 *	-0.019 *	-0.021 **
0.083	0.110	0.128	0.105	0.128
0.110	0.092	0.087	0.104	0.105
SET#2				
-0.081	-0.046	-0.048	-0.070 *	-0.067 *
0.008	0.033	0.031	0.037	0.034
0.043	0.011	0.015	0.028	0.029
0.020	-0.020	-0.019	-0.025	-0.025
0.103	0.078 **	0.076 **	0.072 **	0.072 **
0.167	0.115 **	0.105 **	0.083 **	0.083 **
-0.043	-0.081 **	-0.081 **	-0.096 **	-0.092 **
SET#3				
0.363	0.353 **	0.333 **	0.225 **	0.261 **
0.324	0.319 **	0.318 **	0.239 **	0.261 **
0.077	0.077	0.084 *	0.071	0.067
-0.148	-0.143 **	-0.131 **	-0.083	-0.101 *
-0.389	-0.381 **	-0.370 **	-0.267 **	-0.297 **
-0.595	-0.585 **	-0.578 **	-0.425 **	-0.464 **
-0.754	-0.740 **	-0.736 **	-0.544 **	-0.591 **
SET#4				
0.037	0.038 *	0.036 *	0.026	0.029
-0.041	-0.042 *	-0.040 *	-0.029	-0.033
SET#5				
0.405		-0.022		-0.074
-0.081		-0.052		-0.045
-0.168		0.017		0.039
SET#6				
-0.147		-0.007		0.012
-0.639		-0.678 **		-0.697 **
0.337		0.093		0.088
-0.119		-0.105		-0.038
0.054		0.103		0.074
0.417		0.125 *		0.071
SET#7				
-0.533			-0.306 **	-0.279 **
-0.010			0.147 *	0.128
0.141			0.045	-0.000
0.630			0.256 **	0.231 **
-0.005			0.072	0.094
0.302			0.188 **	0.237 **
SET#8				
-0.068			-0.205 **	-0.196 **
0.005			0.015 **	0.015 **
SET#9				
-0.397			-0.027	-0.031
0.017			0.001	0.001
SET#10				
-0.645			-0.087	-0.084
-0.272			-0.209 *	-0.214 *
0.142			0.028 *	0.027 *
	0.2216	0.2354	0.2415	0.2536
	0.0491 **	0.0554 **	0.0583 **	0.0643 **
	0.0479	0.0537	0.0565	0.0618

Notes: Sets #1 and #2 were measured at Base Year;
Sets #3 and #4 were determined by timing of follow-up;
Sets #5 - #10 were measured at follow-up.
Detailed guidelines for table interpretation are provided in text of the appendix.

Regression Analyses Linking Post-High-School Experiences to Changes in 30-Day
Cocaine Use

VARIABLE	REGRESSION COEFFICIENTS FOR WOMEN				
	Based on Full Set of Cases from Follow-Ups 1-7				
	BIVARIATE COEFF.	BKGD.	BKGD.+ STUD./WORK	BKGD.+ LIV. ARR.	ALL SETS
CONSTANT	0.009	0.009	0.009	0.009	0.009
SET#1 RACE					
WHITE	-0.001	-0.002	-0.002	-0.002	-0.002
BLACK	0.017	0.020	0.020	0.017	0.017
OTHER	-0.005	-0.002	-0.002	-0.001	-0.001
SET#2 REGION					
NORTHEAST	0.008	0.009	0.009	0.007	0.007
NORTH CENTRAL	0.005	0.006	0.006	0.006	0.006
SOUTH	-0.001	-0.004	-0.004	-0.002	-0.002
WEST	-0.018	-0.017	-0.016	-0.017 *	-0.017 *
HIGH SCHOOL GRADES[a]	0.002	0.003	0.004	0.003	0.004
R WILL ATTEND 4YR COLLEGE[a]	0.001	-0.002	-0.001	-0.005	-0.003
URBANICITY[a]	0.000	0.000	0.000	-0.001	-0.001
SET#3 FOLLOW-UP NUMBER					
FU #1	0.005	0.006	0.009	-0.001	0.004
FU #2	0.013	0.013	0.015	0.008	0.010
FU #3	0.014	0.014	0.013	0.012	0.010
FU #4	-0.001	-0.001	-0.003	0.003	0.000
FU #5	-0.018	-0.019	-0.021 *	-0.012	-0.016
FU #6	-0.023	-0.024 *	-0.026 *	-0.013	-0.016
FU #7	-0.031	-0.032 *	-0.034 *	-0.019	-0.022
SET#4 ADMINISTRATION OF FIRST FOLLOW-UP					
ONE YEAR AFTER HIGH SCHOOL	0.003	0.004	0.004	0.003	0.003
TWO YEARS AFTER HIGH SCHOOL	-0.004	-0.004	-0.004	-0.003	-0.004
SET#5 STUDENT STATUS AT FOLLOW-UP					
FULL-TIME STUDENT	0.004		-0.004		-0.014
PART-TIME STUDENT	-0.012		-0.012		-0.013
NOT A STUDENT	0.000		0.003		0.008
SET#6 WORK STATUS AT FOLLOW-UP					
FULL-TIME CIVILIAN JOB	0.003		0.005		0.000
MILITARY SERVICE	-0.030		-0.034		-0.040
PART-TIME JOB	-0.003		-0.006		-0.003
HOMEMAKER	-0.022		-0.015		0.006
NONSTUDENT, NOT EMPLOYED	0.015		0.014		0.016
OTHER	0.003		-0.003		-0.003
SET#7 LIVING ARRANGEMENT AT FOLLOW-UP					
MARRIED	-0.028			-0.022 **	-0.025 **
PARTNER	0.034			0.044 **	0.043 **
PARENT(S)	0.006			0.001	0.001
DORM	0.007			-0.002	0.008
LIVE ALONE	0.018			0.014	0.013
OTHER	0.027			0.023 *	0.026 **
SET#8 ENGAGEMENT STATUS AT FOLLOW-UP					
ENGAGED	-0.015			-0.040 **	-0.041 **
NOT ENGAGED	0.001			0.004 **	0.004 **
SET#9 IS R PREGNANT AT FOLLOW-UP?					
YES	-0.034			-0.017	-0.019
NO	0.002			0.001	0.001
SET#10 PARENTHOOD STATUS AT FOLLOW-UP					
MARRIED PARENT	-0.037			-0.014	-0.015
SINGLE PARENT	0.009			-0.011	-0.014
NOT A PARENT	0.010			0.005	0.006
Multiple-R		0.0424	0.0469	0.0678	0.0714
R Sqr.		0.0018 *	0.0022	0.0046 **	0.0051 **
R Sqr., adjusted		0.0008	0.0007	0.0030	0.0031

* indicates statistical significance at .05 level. ** indicates statistical significance at .01 level. (Statistical significance is not indicated for bivariate coefficients or constants.)

[a] Means of these interval-scaled variables are necessary to calculate the predicted change in drug use associated with these variables. See Table A.3 for means; see appendix text for instructions.

(Table continued on next page)

| WOMEN (cont.) | | REGRESSION COEFFICIENTS FOR MEN | | | | | | |
| Based on Cases from Follow-Ups 1 and 2 | | Based on Full Set of Cases from Follow-Ups 1-7 | | | | | Based on Cases from Follow-Ups 1 and 2 | |
BIVARIATE COEFF.	ALL SETS	BIVARIATE COEFF.	BKGD.	BKGD.+ STUD./WORK	BKGD.+ LIV. ARR.	ALL SETS	BIVARIATE COEFF.	ALL SETS
0.018	0.018	0.025	0.025	0.025	0.025	0.025	0.030	0.030
SET#1								
0.002	0.001	-0.002	-0.002	-0.002	-0.002	-0.002	0.002	0.001
-0.001	0.005	0.038	0.036	0.037	0.032	0.033	0.000	0.002
-0.017	-0.014	-0.010	-0.009	-0.009	-0.008	-0.007	-0.012	-0.011
SET#2								
0.016	0.014 *	0.014	0.015	0.014	0.012	0.012	0.026	0.025 **
0.001	0.000	-0.007	-0.005	-0.005	-0.005	-0.005	-0.007	-0.009
-0.008	-0.005	0.003	0.000	0.000	0.002	0.002	-0.012	-0.010
-0.010	-0.009	-0.012	-0.010	-0.010	-0.012	-0.011	0.000	0.001
0.001	0.001	0.001	0.000	0.001	0.000	0.000	-0.001	-0.003
0.000	-0.002	0.006	0.005	0.007	0.002	0.004	0.008	0.008
0.003	0.002	0.002	-0.001	-0.001	-0.003	-0.002	0.002	-0.003
SET#3								
-0.004	-0.003	-0.005	-0.006	-0.002	-0.020	-0.012	-0.011	-0.011 *
0.004	0.004	0.018	0.018	0.021 *	0.007	0.012	0.013	0.013 *
		0.016	0.016	0.015	0.014	0.013		
		0.010	0.010	0.008	0.018	0.013		
		-0.014	-0.014	-0.017	0.001	-0.006		
		-0.031	-0.031	-0.035 *	-0.011	-0.019		
		-0.033	-0.032	-0.038	-0.009	-0.018		
SET#4								
		-0.006	-0.006	-0.006	-0.007	0.007		
		0.007	0.007	0.007	0.008	0.007		
SET#5								
0.000	-0.008	0.001		-0.020		-0.027 *	0.002	-0.011
-0.014	-0.011	-0.012		-0.011		-0.010	-0.007	-0.001
0.003	0.012	0.001		0.010		0.013 *	-0.001	0.014
SET#6								
0.002	-0.003	-0.001		-0.003		0.001	-0.003	-0.001
-0.042	-0.057	-0.049		-0.058 *		-0.062 **	-0.038	-0.058 **
-0.001	0.001	0.006		0.010		0.009	0.003	0.007
-0.019	0.008	0.039		0.046		0.054	0.023	0.033
0.004	0.007	0.019		0.009		0.003	0.010	0.004
0.002	0.002	0.010		0.015		0.008	0.007	0.006
SET#7								
-0.028	-0.031 **	-0.044			-0.050 **	-0.050 **	-0.053	-0.058 *
0.013	0.023	0.007			0.017	0.014	0.006	0.010
-0.004	-0.005	0.006			0.010	0.005	0.008	-0.010
-0.002	-0.001	0.009			0.017	0.026	0.004	0.007
0.051	0.048 *	0.015			0.011	0.011	0.015	0.016
0.023	0.023 **	0.043			0.040 **	0.046 **	0.027	0.031 **
SET#8								
-0.025	-0.034 **	-0.027			-0.047 *	-0.048 *	-0.033	-0.039 *
0.003	0.004 **	0.002			0.004 *	0.004 *	0.003	0.003 *
SET#9								
-0.039	-0.026	-0.036			-0.001	-0.002	-0.046	-0.010
0.002	0.001	0.002			0.000	0.000	0.001	0.000
SET#10								
-0.038	-0.021	-0.046			0.000	0.000	-0.052	-0.001
-0.022	-0.033	0.024			0.003	0.002	0.001	0.001
0.003	0.003 *	0.008			0.000	0.000	0.002	0.000
	0.0608		0.0424	0.0500	0.0671	0.0742		0.0624
	0.0037 **		0.0018	0.0025	0.0045 **	0.0055 **		0.0039
	0.0021		0.0005	0.0007	0.0025	0.0029		0.0018

Notes: Sets #1 and #2 were measured at Base Year;
Sets #3 and #4 were determined by timing of follow-up;
Sets #5 - #10 were measured at follow-up.
Detailed guidelines for table interpretation are provided in text of the appendix.

TABLE A.11

Regression Analyses Linking Post-High-School Experiences to Changes in 12-Month Cocaine Use

VARIABLE	BIVARIATE COEFF.	BKGD.	BKGD.+ STUD./WORK	BKGD.+ LIV. ARR.	ALL SETS
	REGRESSION COEFFICIENTS FOR WOMEN				
	Based on Full Set of Cases from Follow-Ups 1-7				
CONSTANT	0.067	0.067	0.067	0.067	0.067
SET#1 RACE					
WHITE	0.002	0.001	0.001	0.001	0.001
BLACK	0.016	0.024	0.024	0.019	0.019
OTHER	-0.039	-0.039	-0.038	-0.035	-0.034
SET#2 REGION					
NORTHEAST	0.034	0.033 *	0.032 *	0.026	0.025
NORTH CENTRAL	0.008	0.009	0.010	0.009	0.009
SOUTH	-0.017	-0.020	-0.020	-0.013	-0.013
WEST	-0.031	-0.028	-0.026	-0.030	-0.029
HIGH SCHOOL GRADES[a]	0.002	0.004	0.004	0.004	0.005
R WILL ATTEND 4YR COLLEGE[a]	0.002	-0.003	0.000	-0.015 *	-0.009
URBANICITY[a]	0.010	0.007	0.008	0.005	0.006
SET#3 FOLLOW-UP NUMBER					
FU #1	-0.002	-0.001	0.010	-0.024	-0.010
FU #2	0.053	0.053 **	0.058 **	0.033 *	0.041 **
FU #3	0.045	0.046 **	0.041 *	0.039 *	0.034 *
FU #4	0.005	0.005	-0.002	0.016	0.006
FU #5	-0.039	-0.040 *	-0.047 *	-0.016	-0.027
FU #6	-0.085	-0.087 **	-0.093 **	-0.049 *	-0.059 *
FU #7	-0.103	-0.106 **	-0.111 **	-0.058 *	-0.069 *
SET#4 ADMINISTRATION OF FIRST FOLLOW-UP					
ONE YEAR AFTER HIGH SCHOOL	-0.002	-0.001	0.000	-0.004	-0.003
TWO YEARS AFTER HIGH SCHOOL	0.002	0.001	0.000	0.004	0.003
SET#5 STUDENT STATUS AT FOLLOW-UP					
FULL-TIME STUDENT	0.006		-0.010		-0.042 *
PART-TIME STUDENT	-0.042		-0.045 *		-0.049 *
NOT A STUDENT	0.004		0.011		0.024 **
SET#6 WORK STATUS AT FOLLOW-UP					
FULL-TIME CIVILIAN JOB	0.015		0.019 *		0.004
MILITARY SERVICE	-0.101		-0.108		-0.130
PART-TIME JOB	-0.015		-0.022		-0.011
HOMEMAKER	-0.084		-0.067 **		0.004
NONSTUDENT, NOT EMPLOYED	0.036		0.031		0.038
OTHER	0.004		-0.007		-0.006
SET#7 LIVING ARRANGEMENT AT FOLLOW-UP					
MARRIED	-0.090			-0.078 **	-0.088 **
PARTNER	0.125			0.151 **	0.147 **
PARENT(S)	0.013			0.002	0.003
DORM	0.008			0.000	0.029
LIVE ALONE	0.069			0.053	0.049
OTHER	0.091			0.080 **	0.088 **
SET#8 ENGAGEMENT STATUS AT FOLLOW-UP					
ENGAGED	-0.025			-0.109 **	-0.111 **
NOT ENGAGED	0.002			0.010 **	0.011 **
SET#9 IS R PREGNANT AT FOLLOW-UP?					
YES	-0.062			-0.005	-0.011
NO	0.004			0.000	0.001
SET#10 PARENTHOOD STATUS AT FOLLOW-UP					
MARRIED PARENT	-0.122			-0.045 *	-0.047 *
SINGLE PARENT	0.010			-0.056	-0.067 *
NOT A PARENT	0.034			0.018 **	0.019 **
Multiple-R		0.0648	0.0742	0.1095	0.1158
R Sqr.		0.0042 **	0.0055 **	0.0120 **	0.0134 **
R Sqr., adjusted		0.0032	0.0041	0.0105	0.0114

* indicates statistical significance at .05 level. ** indicates statistical significance at .01 level. (Statistical significance is not indicated for bivariate coefficients or constants.)

[a] Means of these interval-scaled variables are necessary to calculate the predicted change in drug use associated with these variables. See Table A.3 for means; see appendix text for instructions.

(Table continued on next page)

BIVARIATE COEFF.	BKGD.	BKGD.+ STUD./WORK	BKGD.+ LIV. ARR.	ALL SETS
REGRESSION COEFFICIENTS FOR MEN				
Based on Full Set of Cases from Follow-Ups 1-7				
0.142	0.142	0.142	0.142	0.142
SET#1				
-0.002	-0.002	-0.002	-0.001	-0.002
0.056	0.058	0.058	0.046	0.047
-0.027	-0.027	-0.029	-0.023	-0.022
SET#2				
0.045	0.042 *	0.041 *	0.033	0.033
-0.008	-0.005	-0.005	-0.002	-0.003
-0.013	-0.015	-0.015	-0.007	-0.007
-0.025	-0.022	-0.021	-0.030	-0.028
-0.001	-0.002	0.000	-0.003	-0.001
0.008	0.005	0.011	-0.006	0.002
0.015	0.009	0.011	0.003	0.005
SET#3				
-0.048	-0.048 **	-0.035	-0.088 **	-0.063 **
0.055	0.055 **	0.066 **	0.018	0.035
0.074	0.074 **	0.070 **	0.064 **	0.059 **
0.040	0.040	0.032	0.060 *	0.045
-0.020	-0.019	-0.030	0.025	0.004
-0.083	-0.083 **	-0.096 **	-0.017	-0.042
-0.126	-0.125 **	-0.142 **	-0.044	-0.073
SET#4				
-0.011	-0.010	-0.010	-0.013	-0.012
0.012	0.011	0.011	0.015	0.013
SET#5				
-0.017		-0.060 *		-0.078 **
-0.022		-0.020		-0.020
0.011		0.030 **		0.037 **
SET#6				
0.001		-0.008		0.001
-0.151		-0.178 **		-0.191 **
-0.009		0.014		0.009
-0.053		-0.025		0.002
0.124		0.094 *		0.073
0.017		0.048		0.029
SET#7				
-0.141			-0.156 **	-0.156 **
0.115			0.130 **	0.121 **
0.012			0.022	0.006
-0.027			0.020	0.046
0.045			0.026	0.026
0.140			0.130 **	0.147 **
SET#8				
-0.028			-0.118 **	-0.120 **
0.002			0.009 **	0.009 **
SET#9				
-0.092			0.017	0.013
0.004			-0.001	-0.001
SET#10				
-0.157			-0.022	-0.021
0.073			-0.014	-0.021
0.028			0.005	0.005
	0.0663	0.0819	0.1131	0.1245
	0.0044 **	0.0067 **	0.0128 **	0.0155 **
	0.0031	0.0049	0.0109	0.0130

Notes: Sets #1 and #2 were measured at Base Year;
Sets #3 and #4 were determined by timing of follow-up;
Sets #5 - #10 were measured at follow-up.
Detailed guidelines for table interpretation are provided in text of the appendix.

References

Ajzen, I. (1985). From decisions to actions: A theory of planned behavior. In J. Kuhl & J. Beckmann (Eds.), *Action–control: From cognition to behavior* (pp. 11–39). New York: Springer.

Akers, R. L. (1977). *Deviant behavior: A social learning approach* (2nd ed.). Belmont, CA: Wadsworth.

Andrews, F. M., Morgan, J. N., Sonquist, J. A., & Klem, L. (1973). *Multiple classification analysis: A report on a computer program for multiple regression using categorical predictors* (2nd ed.). Ann Arbor, MI: Institute for Social Research.

Antonucci, T. C., & Mikus, K. (1988). The power of parenthood: Personality and attitudinal changes during the transition to parenthood. In G. Y. Michaels & W. A. Goldberg (Eds.), *The transition to parenthood: Current theory and research* (pp. 62–84). New York: Cambridge University Press.

Armstrong, B. G., McDonald, A. D., & Sloan, M. (1992). Cigarette, alcohol, and coffee consumption and spontaneous abortion. *American Journal of Public Health, 82*, 85–87.

Aseltine, R. H., & Gore, S. (1993). Mental health and social adaptation following the transition from high school. *Journal of Research on Adolescence, 3*(3), 247–270.

Aseltine, R. H., & Kessler, R. C. (1993). Marital disruption and depression in a community sample. *Journal of Health & Social Behavior, 34*(3) 237–251.

Axinn, W. G., & Thornton, A. (1992). The relationship between cohabitation and divorce: Selectivity or causal influence? *Demography, 29*(3), 357–374.

Bachman, J. G. (1987, July). *Changes in deviant behavior during late adolescence and early adulthood*. Paper presented at the ninth biennial Meeting of the International Society for the Study of Behavioral Development, Tokyo, Japan. (ERIC Document ED No. 309 365)

Bachman, J. G., Bare, D. E., & Frankie, E. I. (1986). *Correlates of employment among high school seniors* (Monitoring the Future Occasional Paper No. 20). Ann Arbor, MI: Institute for Social Research.

Bachman, J. G., Johnston, L. D., & O'Malley, P. M. (1981). Smoking, drinking, and drug use among American high school students: Correlates and trends, 1975–1979. *American Journal of Public Health, 71*, 59–69.

Bachman, J. G., Johnston, L. D., & O'Malley, P. M. (1990). Explaining the recent decline in cocaine use among young adults: Further evidence that perceived risks and disapproval lead to reduced drug use. *Journal of Health and Social Behavior, 31*, 173–184.

Bachman, J. G., Johnston, L. D., & O'Malley, P. M. (1991). How changes in drug use are linked to perceived risks and disapproval: Evidence from national studies that youth and young adults respond to information about the consequences of drug use. In R. L. Donohew, H. Sypher, & W. Bukoski (Eds.), *Persuasive communication and drug abuse prevention* (pp. 133–156). Hillsdale, NJ: Lawrence Erlbaum Associates.

Bachman, J. G., Johnston, L. D., & O'Malley, P. M. (1996). *Monitoring the Future project after twenty-two years: Design and procedures* (Monitoring the Future Occasional Paper No. 38). Ann Arbor, MI: Institute for Social Research.

Bachman, J. G., Johnston, L. D., O'Malley, P. M., & Humphrey, R. H. (1988). Explaining the recent decline in marijuana use: Differentiating the effects of perceived risks, disapproval, and general lifestyle factors. *Journal of Health and Social Behavior, 29*, 92–112.

Bachman, J. G., Johnston, L. D., O'Malley, P. M., & Schulenberg, J. E. (1996). Transitions in alcohol and other drug use and abuse during late adolescence and young adulthood. In J. A. Graber, J. Brooks-Gunn, & A. C. Petersen (Eds.), *Transitions through adolescence: Interpersonal domains and contexts.* Hillsdale, NJ: Lawrence Erlbaum Associates.

Bachman, J. G., & O'Malley, P. M. (1989). When four months equal a year: Inconsistencies in students' reports of drug use. In E. Singer & S. Presser (Eds.), *Survey research methods* (pp.173–185). Chicago: University of Chicago Press. (Reprinted from *Public Opinion Quarterly, 45*, 536–548, 1981.)

Bachman, J. G., O'Malley, P. M., & Johnston, J. (1978). *Youth in transition: Vol.6. Adolescence to adulthood: A study of change and stability in the lives of young men.* Ann Arbor, MI: Institute for Social Research.

Bachman, J. G., O'Malley, P. M., & Johnston, L. D. (1981). *Changes in drug use after high school as a function of role status and social environment* (Monitoring the Future Occasional Paper No. 11). Ann Arbor, MI: Institute for Social Research.

Bachman, J. G., O'Malley, P. M., & Johnston, L. D. (1984). Drug use among young adults: The impacts of role status and social environments *Journal of Personality and Social Psychology, 47*, 629–645.

Bachman, J. G., O'Malley, P. M., & Johnston, L. D. (1986). *Change and consistency in the correlates of drug use among high school seniors: 1975–1986* (Monitoring the Future Occasional Paper No. 21). Ann Arbor, MI: Institute for Social Research.

Bachman, J. G., O'Malley, P. M., Johnston, L. D., Rodgers, W. L., & Schulenberg, J. E. (1992). *Changes in drug use during the post-high school years* (Monitoring the Future Occasional Paper No. 35). Ann Arbor, MI: Institute for Social Research.

Bachman, J. G., O'Malley, P. M., Johnston, L. D., Rodgers, W. L., Schulenberg, J. E., Lim, J., & Wadsworth, K. N. (1996). *Changes in drug use during ages 18–32* (Monitoring the Future Occasional Paper No. 39). Ann Arbor, MI: Institute for Social Research.

Bachman, J. G., & Schulenberg, J. E. (1993). How part-time work intensity relates to drug use, problem behavior, time use, and satisfaction among high school seniors: Are these consequences, or merely correlates? *Developmental Psychology, 29*(2), 220–235.

Bachman, J. G., Schulenberg, J. E., O'Malley, P. M., & Johnston, L. D. (1990, March). *Short-term and longer-term effects of educational commitment and success on the use of cigarettes, alcohol, and illicit drugs.* Paper presented at the Third Biennial Meeting of the Society for Research on Adolescence, Atlanta, GA.

Bachman, J. G., Wadsworth, K. N., O'Malley, P. M., Schulenberg, J. E., & Johnston, L. D. (1997). Marriage, divorce, and parenthood during the transition to young adulthood: Impacts on drug use and abuse. In J. E. Schulenberg, J. L. Maggs, & K. Hurrelmann (Eds.), *Health risks and developmental transitions during adolescence.* New York: Cambridge University Press.

Baer, J. S. (1993). Etiology and secondary prevention of alcohol problems with young adults. In J. S. Baer, G. M. Marlatt, & R. J. McMahon (Eds.), *Addictive behaviors across the life span: Prevention, treatment, and policy issues* (pp. 111–137). Newbury Park, CA: Sage.

Bailey, S. L., & Hubbard, R. L. (1990). Developmental variation in the context of marijuana initiation among adolescents. *Journal of Health and Social Behavior, 31*, 58–70.

Baltes, P. B. (1987). Theoretical propositions of life-span developmental psychology: On the dynamics between growth and decline. *Developmental Psychology, 23*, 611–626.

Baltes, P. B., Reese, H. W., & Lipsett, L. P. (1980). Life-span developmental psychology. *Annual Review of Psychology, 31*, 65–110.

Bandura, A. (1982). Self-efficacy mechanisms in human agency. *American Psychologist, 37,* 122–147.

Belsky, J., & Pensky, E. (1988). Marital change across the transition to parenthood. *Marriage and the Family Review, 12,* 133–156.

Booth, E., & Amato, P. (1991). Divorce and psychological stress. *Journal of Health and Social Behavior, 32,* 396–407.

Bray, R. M., Kroutil, L. A., & Marsden, M. E. (1995). Trends in alcohol, illicit drug, and cigarette use among U.S. military personnel: 1980–1992. *Armed Forces & Society, 21,* 211–217.

Bray, R. M., Marsden, M. E., & Peterson, M. R. (1991). Standardized comparisons of the use of alcohol, drugs, and cigarettes among military personnel and civilians. *American Journal of Public Health, 81*(7), 865–869.

Brennan, A. F., Walfish, S., & AuBuchon, P. (1986). Alcohol use and abuse in college students: II. Social/environmental correlates, methodological issues, and implications for intervention. *International Journal of the Addictions, 21*(4–5), 475–493.

Brim, O. G., Jr., & Kagan, J. (1980). Constancy and change: A view of the issues. In O. G. Brim, Jr., & J. Kagan (Eds.), *Constancy and change in human development* (pp. 1–25). Cambridge, MA: Harvard University Press.

Bronfenbrenner, U. (1979). *The ecology of human development.* Cambridge, MA: Harvard University Press.

Brook, J. S., Whiteman, M., Cohen, P., & Shapiro, J. (1995). Longitudinally predicting late adolescent and young adult drug use: Childhood and adolescent precursors. *Journal of the American Academy of Child and Adolescent Psychiatry, 34*(9), 1230–1238.

Brooks-Gunn, J. (1987). Pubertal processes in girls' psychosocial adaptation. In R. Lerner & T. T. Foch (Eds.), *Biological–psychosocial interactions in early adolescence: A life-span perspective* (pp. 123–153). Hillsdale, NJ: Lawrence Erlbaum Associates.

Brooks-Gunn, J., & Chase-Lansdale, P. L. (1995). Adolescent parenthood. In M. Bornstein (Ed.), *Handbook of parenting: Vol. 3. Status and social conditions of parenting* (pp. 113–150). Hillsdale, NJ: Lawrence Erlbaum Associates.

Brown, J. W., Glaser, D., Waxer, E., & Geis, G. (1974). Turning off: Cessation of marijuana use after college. *Social Problems, 21,* 527–538.

Brunswick, A. F., Messeri, P. A., & Titus, S. P. (1992). Predictive factors in adult substance abuse: A prospective study of African American adolescents. In M. Glantz & R. Pickens (Eds.), *Vulnerability to drug abuse* (pp. 419–472). Washington, DC: American Psychological Association.

Burke, K. C., Burke, J., Regier, D., & Rae, D. S. (1990). Age at onset of selected mental disorders in five community populations. *Archives of General Psychiatry, 47,* 511–518.

Burton, R. P. D., Johnson, R. J., Ritter, C., & Clayton, R. R. (1996). The effects of role socialization on the initiation of cocaine use: An event history analysis from adolescence into middle adulthood. *Journal of Health and Social Behavior, 37,* 75–90.

Buss, D. M. (1984). Marital assortment for personality dispositions: Assessment with three different data sources. *Behavior Genetics, 4*(2), 111–123.

Cate, R. M., Huston, T. L., Nesselroade, J. R. (1986). Premarital relationships: Toward the identification of alternative pathways to marriage. *Journal of Social & Clinical Psychology, 4*(1), 3–22.

Chasnoff, I. J. (1991). Cocaine and pregnancy: Clinical and methodologic issues. *Clinical Perinatology, 18,* 113–123.

Chassin, L., Presson, C., Sherman, S. J., & Edwards, D. A. (1992). The natural history of cigarette smoking and young adult social roles. *Journal of Health and Social Behavior, 33,* 328–347.

Chen, K., & Kandel, D. B. (1995). The natural history of drug use from adolescence to the mid-thirties in a general population sample. *American Journal of Public Health, 85*(1), 41–47.

Chilman, C. S. (1980). Social and psychological research concerning adolescent childbearing: 1970–1980. *Journal of Marriage & the Family, 42*(4), 793–805.

Clausen, J. A. (1991). Adolescent competence and the shaping of the life course. *American Journal of Sociology, 96*, 805–842.

Coombs, L. C., & Fernandez, D. (1978). Husband–wife agreement about reproductive goals. *Demography, 15*, 57–73.

Cowan, P. A., & Cowan, C. P. (1988). Changes in marriage during the transition to parenthood: Must we blame the baby? In G. Y. Michaels & W. A. Goldberg (Eds.), *The transition to parenthood: Current theory and research* (pp. 114–156). New York: Cambridge University Press.

Cowan, C. P., Cowan, P. A., Heming, G., & Miller, N. (1991). Becoming a family: Marriage, parenting, and child development. In P. A. Cowan & M. Hetherington (Eds.), *Family transitions* (pp. 79–110). Hillsdale, NJ: Lawrence Erlbaum Associates.

Cronbach, L., & Furby, L. (1969). How to measure change—or should we? *Psychological Bulletin, 74*, 68–80.

DeMaris, A., & MacDonald, W. (1993). Premarital cohabitation and marital instability: A test of the unconventionality hypothesis. *Journal of Marriage and the Family, 55*, 399–407.

DeMaris, A., & Rao, K. V. (1992). Premarital cohabitation and subsequent marital stability in the United States: A reassessment. *Journal of Marriage and the Family, 54*, 178–190.

Dickens, W. J., & Perlman, D. (1981). Friendships over the life-cycle. In S. Duck & R. Gilmour (Eds.), *Personal relationships: Vol. 2. Developing personal relationships* (pp. 91–120). San Francisco: Academic Press.

Dishion, T. J., Patterson, G. R., Stoolmiller, M., & Skinner, M. L. (1991). Family, school, and behavioral antecedents to early adolescent involvement with antisocial peers. *Developmental Psychology, 27*, 172–180.

Donovan, J. E., Jessor, R., & Jessor, L. (1983). Problem drinking in adolescence and young adulthood: A follow-up study. *Journal of Studies on Alcohol, 44*, 109–137.

Duncan, G. J. (1991). The economic environment of childhood. In A. Huston (Ed.), *Children in poverty* (pp. 23–50). New York: Cambridge University Press.

Elliot, D. S., Huizinga, D., & Menard, S. (1989). *Multiple problem youth: Delinquency, substance use, and mental health problems.* New York: Springer-Verlag.

Erikson, E. H. (1968). *Identity, youth, and crisis.* New York: Norton.

Esbensen, F. A., & Elliot, D. S. (1994). Continuity and discontinuity in illicit drug use: Patterns and antecedents. *Special Issue: Drugs and Crime Revisited, Journal of Drug Issues, 24*(1–2), 75–97.

Fawcett, J. T. (1978). The value and the cost of the first child. In W. B. Miller & L. F. Newman (Eds.), *The first child and family formation* (pp. 244–265). Chapel Hill: University of North Carolina, Carolina Population Center.

Featherman, D. L. (1983). Life-span perspectives in social science research. In P. B. Baltes & O. G. Brim, Jr. (Eds.), *Life-span development and behavior* (Vol. 5, pp. 1–59). New York: Academic Press.

Fedele, N. M., Golding, E. R., Grossman, F. K., & Pollack, W. S. (1988). Psychological issues in the adjustment to first parenthood. In G. Y. Michaels & W. A. Goldberg (Eds.), *The transition to parenthood* (pp. 85–113). New York: Cambridge University Press.

Fischer, C. S., & Phillips, S. L. (1982). Who is alone? Social characteristics of people with small networks. In L. A. Peplau & D. Perlman (Eds.), *Loneliness: A sourcebook of current theory, research, and therapy* (pp. 21–39). New York: Wiley Interscience.

Fried, P. A., Barnes, M. V., & Drake, E. R. (1985). Soft drug use after pregnancy compared to use before and during pregnancy. *American Journal of Obstetrics and Gynecology, 151,* 787–792.

Fried, P. A., Watkinson, B., & Willan, A. (1984). Marijuana use during pregnancy and decreased length of gestation. *American Journal of Obstetrics and Gynecology, 150,* 23–27.

Galinsky, E. (1981). *Between generations: The stages of parenthood.* New York: Berkeley.

Gerber, R.W., & Newman, I. M. (1989). Predicting future smoking of adolescent experimental smokers. *Journal of Youth and Adolescence, 18*(2), 191–201.

Gottlieb, B. H., & Pancer, S. M. (1988). Social networks and the transition to parenthood. In G. Y. Michaels & W. A. Goldberg (Eds.), *The transition to parenthood: Current theory and research* (pp. 235–269). New York: Cambridge University Press.

Greenberger, E., & Steinberg, L. D. (1986). *When teenagers work: The psychological and social costs of adolescent employment.* New York: Basic Books.

Gunnarsson, L., & Cochran, M. (1990). The social networks of single parents: Sweden and the United States. In M. Cochran, M. Larger, D. Riley, L. Gunnarsson, & C. Henderson, Jr. (Eds.), *Extending families: The social networks of parents and their children* (pp. 105–116). New York: Cambridge University Press.

Hallberg, H. (1992). Life after divorce: A five-year follow-up study of divorced middle-aged men in Sweden. *Family Practice, 9*(1), 49–56.

Hanna, E., Faden, V., & Harford, T. C. (1993). Marriage: Does it protect young women from alcoholism? *Journal of Substance Abuse, 5*(1), 1–14.

Hatch, E. E., & Bracken, M. B. (1986). Effect of marijuana use in pregnancy on fetal growth. *American Journal of Epidemiology, 124,* 986–993.

Hawkins, J. D., & Weis, J. G. (1985). The social development model: An integrated approach to delinquency prevention. *Journal of Primary Prevention, 6,* 73–97.

Heath, D. H. (1978). What meaning and effects does fatherhood have for the maturing of professional men? *Merrill–Palmer Quarterly, 24*(4), 265–278.

Hirschi, T. (1969). *Causes of delinquency.* Berkeley: University of California Press.

Hoffman, L. W. (1978). Effects of the first child on the woman's role. In W. B. Miller & L. F. Newman (Eds.), *The first child and family formation* (pp. 340–367). Chapel Hill: University of North Carolina, Carolina Population Center.

Hoffman, L. W., & Manis, J. (1978). Influences of children on marital interaction and parental satisfactions and dissatisfactions. In R. M. Lerner & G. W. Spanier (Eds.), *Child influences on marital and family interaction: A life-span perspective* (pp. 165–213). New York: Academic Press.

Horwitz, A. V., & White, H. R. (1991). Becoming married, depression, and alcohol problems among young adults. *Journal of Health and Social Behavior, 32,* 221–237.

Hurrelmann, K. (1990). Health promotion for adolescents: Preventive and corrective strategies against problem behavior. *Journal of Adolescence, 13,* 231–250.

Ihlen, B. M., Amundsen, A., Sande, H. A., & Daae, L. (1990). Changes in the use of intoxicants after onset of pregnancy. *British Journal of Addictions, 85,* 1627–1631.

Jessor, R. (1992). Risk behavior in adolescence: A psychosocial framework for understanding action. *Developmental Review, 12,* 374–390.

Jessor, R., Donovan, J. E., & Costa, F. M. (1991). *Beyond adolescence: Problem behavior and young adult development.* New York: Cambridge University Press.

Johnson, R. J., & Kaplan, H. B. (1991). Developmental processes leading to marijuana use: Comparing civilians and the military. *Youth & Society, 23,* 3–30.

Johnston, L. D. (1973). *Drugs and American youth.* Ann Arbor, MI: Institute for Social Research.

Johnston, L. D. (1982). A review and analysis of recent changes in marijuana use by American young people. In *Marijuana: The national impact on education* (pp. 8–13). New York: American Council on Marijuana.

Johnston, L. D. (1985, March). Should alcohol epidemiology and drug abuse epidemiology be merged? *The Drinking and Drug Practices Surveyor, 20,* 11–14.

Johnston, L. D., Bachman, J. G., & O'Malley, P. M. (1995). *Monitoring the future: Questionnaire responses from the nation's high school seniors, 1993.* Ann Arbor, MI: Institute of Social Research.

Johnston, L. D., & O'Malley, P. M. (1985). Issues of validity and population coverage in student surveys of drug use. In B. A. Rouse, N. J. Kozel, & L. G. Richards (Eds.), *Self-report methods of estimating drug use: Meeting current challenges to validity* (National Institute on Drug Abuse Research Monograph No. 57, [ADM] 85–1402, pp. 31–54). Washington, DC: U.S. Government Printing Office.

Johnston, L. D., & O'Malley, P. M. (1997). The recanting of earlier-reported drug use by young adults. In L. Harrison (Ed.), *Validity of self-reported drug use: Improving the accuracy of survey estimates.* (National Institute on Drug Abuse Research Monograph). Rockville, MD: National Institute on Drug Abuse.

Johnston, L. D., O'Malley, P. M., & Bachman, J. G. (1984). *Drugs and American high school students: 1975–1983* (DHHS [ADM] 85–1374). Washington, DC: U.S. Government Printing Office.

Johnston, L. D., O'Malley, P. M., & Bachman, J. G. (1997). *Drug use among American high school seniors, college students and young adults, 1975–1995, Volume I: Secondary school students* (DHHS Pub. No. [NIH] 97–4139) and *Volume II: College students and young adults* (DHHS Pub. No. [NIH] 97–4140). Rockville, MD: National Institute on Drug Abuse.

Johnston, L. D., O'Malley, P. M., Bachman, J. G., & Schulenberg, J. E. (1992). *The aims and objectives of the Monitoring the Future study* (Monitoring the Future Occasional Paper No. 34). Ann Arbor, MI: Institute for Social Research.

Kandel, D. B. (1980). Drug and drinking behavior among youth. *Annual Review of Sociology, 6,* 235–285.

Kandel, D. B. (1984). Marijuana users in young adulthood. *Archives of General Psychiatry, 41,* 200–209.

Kandel, D. B. (1991). The social demography of drug use. *The Milbank Quarterly, 69*(3), 365–414.

Kandel, D. B. (1995). Ethnic differences in drug use: Patterns and paradoxes. In G. J. Botvin, S. Schinke, & M. A. Orlandi (Eds.), *Drug abuse prevention with multiethnic youth* (pp. 81–104). Newbury Park, CA: Sage.

Kandel, D. B., & Davies, M. (1991). Cocaine use in a national sample of U.S. youth (NLSY): Ethnic patterns, progression, and predictors. In S. Schrober & C. Schade (Eds.), *The epidemiology of cocaine use and abuse* (DHHS Publication No. [ADM] 91–1787, pp. 151–188). Rockville, MD: National Institute on Drug Abuse.

Kandel, D. B., Davies, M., Karus, D., & Yamaguchi, K. (1986). The consequences in young adulthood of adolescent drug involvement. *Archives of General Psychiatry, 43,* 746–754.

Kandel, D. B., & Yamaguchi, K. (1987). Job mobility and drug use: An event history analysis. *American Journal of Sociology, 92*(4), 836–878.

Kandel, D. B., & Yamaguchi, K. (1993). From beer to crack: Developmental patterns of drug involvement. *American Journal of Public Health, 83,* 851–855.

Kandel, D. B., Yamaguchi, K., & Chen, K. (1992). Stages of progression in drug involvement from adolescence to adulthood: Further evidence for the gateway theory. *Journal of Studies on Alcohol, 53,* 447–457.

Kessler, R. C., & Greenberg, D. F. (1981). *Linear panel analysis: Models of quantitative change.* New York: Academic Press.

Kroutil, L. A., Bray, R. M., & Marsden, M. E. (1994). Cigarette smoking in the United States military: Findings from the 1992 worldwide survey. *Preventive Medicine, 23*(4), 521–528.

Kusserow, R. P. (1991). *Youth and alcohol: A national survey—drinking habits, access, attitudes, and knowledge.* Rockville, MD: Department of Health and Human Services.

Labouvie, E. W. (1976). Longitudinal designs. In P. M. Bentler, D. J. Lettieri, & G. A. Austin (Eds.), *Data analysis strategies and designs for substance abuse research* (National Institute on Drug Abuse Research Issues No. 13, pp. 45–60). Rockville, MD: National Institute on Drug Abuse.

Lee, E. S., Forthofer, R. N., & Lorimor, R. J. (1989). *Analyzing complex survey data.* Newbury Park, CA: Sage.

Lerner, R. M. (1984). *On the nature of human plasticity.* New York: Cambridge University Press.

Lerner, R. M. (1986). *Concepts and theories of human development* (2nd ed.). New York: Random House.

Liker, J. K., Augustyniak, S., & Duncan, G. J. (1985). Panel data and models of change: A comparison of first differences and conventional two-wave models. *Social Science Research, 14,* 80–101.

Mare, R. D. (1991). Five decades of educational assortative mating. *American Sociological Review, 56,* 15–32.

McLoyd, V., & Wilson, L. (1991). The strain of living poor: Parenting, social support, and child mental health. In A. Huston (Ed.), *Children in poverty* (pp. 105–135). New York: Cambridge University Press.

Mikus, K. (1981). *Paradoxes of early parenthood.* Ann Arbor, MI: University Microfilms.

Miller-Tutzauer, C., Leonard, K. E., & Windle, M. (1991). Marriage and alcohol use: A longitudinal study of "maturing out." *Journal of Studies on Alcohol, 52,* 434–440.

Newcomb, M. D. (1987). Cohabitation and marriage: A quest for independence and relatedness. *Applied Social Psychology Annual, 7,* 128–156.

Newcomb, M. D., & Bentler, P. M. (1985). The impact of high school substance use on choice of young adult living environment and career direction. *Journal of Drug Education, 15*(3), 253–261.

Newcomb, M. D., & Bentler, P. M. (1986). Drug use, educational aspirations, and work force involvement: The transition from adolescence to young adulthood. *American Journal of Community Psychology, 14,* 303–321.

Newcomb, M. D., & Bentler, P. M. (1987). Changes in drug use from high school to young adulthood: Effects of living arrangement and current life pursuit. *Journal of Applied Developmental Psychology, 8,* 221–246.

Newcomb, M. D., & Bentler, P. M. (1988). *Consequences of adolescent drug use: Impact on the lives of young adults.* Newbury Park, CA: Sage.

Nock, S. (1995). A comparison of marriages and cohabiting relationships. *Journal of Family Issues, 16*(1), 53–76.

O'Donnell, J. A., Voss, H. L., Clayton, R. R., Slatin, G. T., & Room, R. (1976). *Young men and drugs—A nationwide survey* (National Institute on Drug Abuse Monograph No. 5, DHEW Publication No. [ADM] 76–311). Rockville, MD: National Institute on Drug Abuse.

O'Malley, P. M., Bachman, J. G., & Johnston, L. D. (1983). Reliability and consistency of self-reports of drug use. *International Journal of the Addictions, 18,* 805–824.

O'Malley, P. M., Bachman, J. G., & Johnston, L. D. (1984). Period, age, and cohort effects on substance use among American youth. *American Journal of Public Health, 74,* 682–688.

O'Malley, P. M., Bachman, J. G., & Johnston, L. D. (1988a). Period, age, and cohort effects on substance use among young Americans: A decade of change, 1976–1986. *American Journal of Public Health, 78,* 1315–1321.

O'Malley, P. M., Bachman, J. G., & Johnston, L. D. (1988b). *Differentiation of period, age, and cohort effects on drug use 1976–1986* (Monitoring the Future Occasional Paper No. 22). Ann Arbor, MI: Institute for Social Research.

O'Malley, P. M., & Wagenaar, A. C. (1991). Effects of minimum drinking age laws on alcohol use, related behaviors, and traffic crash involvement among American youth: 1976–1987. *Journal Studies on Alcohol, 52,* 478–491.

Osgood, D. W., Johnston, L. D., O'Malley, P. M., & Bachman, J. G. (1988). The generality of deviance in late adolescence and early adulthood. *American Sociological Review, 53,* 81–93.

Pandina, R. J., Labouvie, E. W., & White, H. R. (1984). Potential contributions of the life span developmental approach to the study of adolescent alcohol and drug use. *Journal of Drug Issues, 14,* 253–270.

Petraitis, J., Flay, B. R., & Miller, T. Q. (1995). Reviewing theories of adolescent substance use: Organizing pieces of the puzzle. *Psychological Bulletin, 117*(1), 67–86.

Public Health Service. (1964). *Smoking and health. Report of the advisory committee to the Surgeon General of the Public Health Service* (United States Department of Health, Education, and Welfare, Public Health Services, PHS Publication No. 1103). Washington, DC: Superintendent of Documents, U.S. Government Printing Office.

Robbins, C. A. (1991). Social roles and alcohol abuse among older men and women. *Family and Community Health, 13,* 126–139.

Robins, L. N. (1974). *The Vietnam drug user returns* (Special Action Office Monograph, Series A, No. 2). Washington, DC: Executive Office of the President (Special Action Office for Drug Abuse Prevention).

Rodgers, W. L. (1989, September). *Reliability and validity in measures of subjective well-being.* Paper presented at the International Conference on Social Reporting, Wissenschaftszentrum Berlin fur Sozialforschung.

Rodgers, W. L., & Bachman, J. G. (1988). *The subjective well-being of young adults.* Ann Arbor, MI: Institute for Social Research.

Ruble, D. N., Fleming, A. S., Hackel, L. S., & Stangor, C. (1988). Changes in the marital relationships during the transition to first time motherhood: Effects of violated expectations concerning division of household labor. *Journal of Personality and Social Psychology, 55,* 78–87.

Schaie, K. W. (1965). A general model for the study of developmental problems. *Psychological Bulletin, 64,* 92–107.

Schulenberg, J. E., Bachman, J. G., O'Malley, P. M., & Johnston, L. D. (1994). High school educational success and subsequent substance use: A panel analysis following adolescents into young adulthood. *Journal of Health and Social Behavior, 35*(1), 45–62.

Schulenberg, J. E., & Ebata, A. T. (1994). Adolescence in the United States. In K. Hurrelmann (Ed.), *International handbook of adolescence* (pp. 414–430). Westport, CT: Greenwood.

Schulenberg, J. E., O'Malley, P. M., Bachman, J. G., & Johnston, L. D. (March, 1992). Getting drunk and becoming an adult: Trajectories of binge drinking and competence during the transition to young adulthood. In J. E. Schulenberg & J. Mortimer (Chairs), *Competence during the transition from adolescence to young adulthood.* Symposium conducted at the 1992 Biennial Meetings of the Society for Research on Adolescence, Washington, DC. (abstract published)

Schulenberg, J. E., O'Malley, P. M., Bachman, J. G., Wadsworth, K. N., & Johnston, L. D. (1996). Getting drunk and growing up: Trajectories of frequent binge drinking during the transition to young adulthood. *Journal of Studies on Alcohol, 57,* 289–304.

Schulenberg, J. E., Wadsworth, K. N., O'Malley, P. M., Bachman, J. G.,& Johnston, L. D. (1996). Adolescent risk factors for binge drinking during the transition to young adulthood: Variable- and pattern-centered approaches to change. *Developmental Psychology, 32*(4), 659–674.

Segal, D. R. (1977). Illicit drug use in the U.S. Army. *Sociological Symposium, 18,* 66–83.

Serdula, M., Williamson, D., Kendrick, J., Anda, R., & Byers, T. (1991). Trends in alcohol consumption by pregnant women: 1985 through 1988. *Journal of the American Medical Association, 265*(7), 876–879.

Shoemaker, D. J. (1990). *Theories of delinquency: An examination of explanations of delinquent behavior* (2nd ed.). New York: Oxford University Press.

Shulman, N. (1975). Life-cycle variations in the patterns of close relationships. *Journal of Marriage and the Family, 37,* 813–921.

Simmons, R., Burgeson, R., Carleton-Ford, S., & Blyth, D. (1987). The impact of cumulative change in early adolescence. *Child Development, 58,* 1220–1234.

Steinberg, L. D., & Dornbusch, S. M. (1991). Negative correlates of part-time employment during adolescence: Replication and elaboration. *Developmental Psychology, 27,* 304–313.

Stueve, C. A., & Gerson, K. (1977). Personal relationships across the life-cycle. In C. S. Fischer (Ed.), *Networks and places: Social relations in the urban setting* (pp.79–99). New York: The Free Press.

Surra, A. (1985). Courtship types: Variations in interdependence between partners and social networks. *Journal of Personality and Social Psychology, 49*(2), 357–375.

Thornton, A., Axinn, W. G., & Hill, D. H. (1992). Reciprocal effects of religiosity, cohabitation, and marriage. *American Journal of Sociology, 98*(3), 628–651.

Tschann, J. M., Johnston, J. R., & Wallerstein, J. S. (1989). Resources, stressors, and attachment as predictors of adult adjustment after divorce: A longitudinal study. *Journal of Marriage and the Family, 51,* 1033–1046.

United States Department of Health and Human Services. (1994). *Preventing tobacco use among young people: A report of the Surgeon General.* (U.S. Department of Health and Human Services, Public Health Service, Centers for Disease Control and Prevention, National Center for Chronic Disease Prevention and Health Promotion, Office of Smoking and Health, Publication No. 017–001–00491–0.U.S). Washington, DC: Government Printing Office.

Wallace, J. M., Jr., & Bachman, J. G. (1993). Validity of self-reports in student-based studies on minority populations: Issues and concerns. In M. de LaRosa (Ed.), *Drug abuse among minority youth: Advances in research and methodology* (National Institute on Drug Abuse Research Monograph 130, pp. 167–200). Rockville, MD: National Institute on Drug Abuse.

Wallerstein, J. S. (1994). The early psychological tasks of marriage. *American Journal of Orthopsychiatry, 64*(4), 640–650.

Wechsler, H., Dowdall, G., Davenport, A., & Castillo, S. (1995). Correlates of college students binge drinking. *American Journal of Public Health, 85*(7), 921–926.

Wechsler, H., Dowdall, G., Davenport, A., & Rimm, E. (1995). A gender-specific measure of binge drinking among college students. *American Journal of Public Health, 85,* 982–985.

Wechsler, H., & Isaac, N. (1992). "Binge" drinkers at Massachusetts colleges: Prevalence, drinking style, time trends, and associated problems. *The Journal of the American Medical Association, 267,* 2929–2931.

Weintraub, M., & Gringlas, M. (1995). Single parenthood. In M. Bornstein (Ed.), *Handbook of parenting: Vol. 3. Status and social conditions of parenting* (pp. 65–88). Hillsdale, NJ: Lawrence Erlbaum Associates.

William T. Grant Foundation Commission on Work, Family, and Citizenship. (1988). *The forgotten half: Pathways to success for America's youth and young families.* Washington, DC: William T. Grant Foundation.

Wyngaarden, J. B. (1988). Effects of moderate alcohol use during pregnancy. *Journal of the American Medical Association, 259*(1), 20.

Yamaguchi, K., & Kandel, D. B. (1984). Patterns of drug use from adolescence to young adulthood: Sequences of progression. *American Journal of Public Health, 74,* 668–672.

Yamaguchi, K., & Kandel, D. B. (1985a). Dynamic relationships between premarital cohabitation and illicit drug use: An event-history analyses of role selection and role socialization. *American Sociological Review, 50*(4), 530–546.

Yamaguchi, K., & Kandel, D. B. (1985b). On the resolution of role incompatibility: Life event history analysis of family roles and marijuana use. *American Journal of Sociology, 90,* 1284–1325.

Yamaguchi, K., & Kandel, D. B. (1993). Marital homophily on illicit drug use among young adults: Assortative mating or marital influence? *Social Forces, 72*(2), 505–528.

Zucker, R. A. (1979). Developmental aspects of drinking through the young adult years. In H. T. Blane & M. E. Chafetz (Eds.), *Youth, alcohol, and social policy* (pp. 91–146). New York: Plenum.

Zucker, R. A. (1987). The four alcoholisms: A developmental account of the etiologic process. In P. C. Rivers (Ed.), *Nebraska Symposium on Motivation, 1987: Alcohol and addictive behavior* (pp. 27–83). Lincoln: University of Nebraska Press.

Author Index

233

Subject Index